Children of the Sea

Children of the Sea

The Story of the Eyemouth
Disaster

PETER AITCHISON

TUCKWELL PRESS

First published in Great Britain by
Tuckwell Press
The Mill House
Phantassie
East Linton
East Lothian EH40 3DG
Scotland

ISBN 1 86232 240 6

British Library Cataloguing-in-Publication Data
A catalogue record for this book is available
on request from the British Library

Typeset by Carnegie Publishing Ltd, Lancaster
Printed by Cromwell Press, Trowbridge

Contents

For Peggy Dale and Peter Waddell. They provided the inspiration, the support, the enthusiasm but above all the love.

Acknowledgements

As I write this I have just passed my thirty seventh birthday, yet it is no exaggeration to say that *Children of the Sea* has been twenty-five years or more in the making. The inspiration came from stories told to me as I sat on my granny's knee as a boy – of the great Fishing Disaster and of 'our ain folk' who died, of characters she could remember and others her parents had told her about. Peggy Dale Waddell, and my papa, Peter Waddell fired my imagination.

Like Peter Waddell many of the people who have helped so much are now sadly gone. Christina Maltman (Teeny Matt) who had a marvellous grasp on the oral tradition of the fishing. Robbie Nisbet, a master of photography – his pictures provide a true social history of the Berwickshire coast; Margaret Waddell wrote out the names of the streets as the people knew them and the tee-names the folk used rather than the ones given to them at birth. This proved an invaluable aide to other sources. Campbell Muir, the former burgh clerk and secretary to Eyemouth Harbour Trust unearthed a mass of documents, without which this book would have been much the poorer. Others like Lizbeth and John Windram ever welcomed me into their homes and spoke at length of the old days, sometimes good, often less-so.

John Home-Robertson MSP not only opened his family archives to me but also advised on parts of the script, and Jackie Miller gave both her time and expertise in helping locate appropriate photographs from Paxton House Trust. John Bellany has generously allowed the use of some of his fabulous images of Eyemouth to illustrate the cover, the transparencies of which were kindly supplied by Reg and Patricia Singh of Beaux Arts in London.

Support, advice, information and much more besides has come from Fay and Iain Waddell, Peter Fishbourne, James Evans, Elsie and Douglas Birch and David Clark, the former superintendent of the Fishermen's Mission in Eyemouth. I have enjoyed lecturing to the Eyemouth Literary Society over the past twelve years or so, and would like to pay tribute to the energy and activity of Hector Sutherland and Cath Paxton. The same sense of drive and purpose is evident at the Eyemouth Museum from Simon Furness and Jean Bowie and from the community drama group, which is fortunate to have the enthusiasm of James Barrie, David Wilson, Christine Mutch and many others. I am very grateful to James Tarvitt for allowing me unfettered access to the papers of Lodge St Ebbe Number Seventy, and to David Johnston, the editor of the *Berwickshire News* for giving me free range over the archives contained in his offices. Jean and Alec Gilchrist permitted me to hear tape recordings from the last surviving witness to the fishing disaster. Their son Andrew was my best friend at school. His death at a tragically young age was a bitter blow. Thanks are also due to my colleagues on the Gunsgreen House Trust and in particular to Allan Swan for the provision of photographs and drawings of the secret tobacco or tea chute which has been uncovered inside the building. I am indebted to Ian Eaton and the Eyemouth Port Association who kindly provided a portfolio of photographs of the new berthing basin and the harbour. Trevor Royle gave me timely support and helped shape what had been an academic study into a more accessible manuscript.

Librarians and archivists in Eyemouth, the Queen Mother library in Aberdeen, the Mitchell Library in Glasgow, at Borders Council in Newton St Boswells and Duns, New College Library in Edinburgh, the National Library for Scotland and the National Archives for Scotland have answered my many queries and requests with speed and courtesy. Margaret Sweenie of Lochwinnoch community library managed to order up the most obscure sources in double-quick time. Such facilities should be recognised and protected for the wonderful service they provide not just to authors but to the nation.

There are many in the fishing industry in Berwickshire and elsewhere who have wished me well and made me realise the importance of finishing this book. Men like James 'Pe Dick' Dickson and Billy Grant.

My old history master George Kinghorn gave me more than a bookish education. He urged me to always test accepted wisdom through intellectual debate and enquiry. I was fortunate enough to then go on to Aberdeen University where Donald J Withrington made me appreciate that local history was neither parochial nor unimportant. It is the building block from which all of our experiences stem. It saddens me to think if I was nearing the end of my school career today, I might be persuaded against entering higher education. All tuition should always be free; all students should always have access to some form of grant support.

I have benefited greatly by trying out ideas with people whose opinions I value. In this category I must place my good friends Phil Ramsden and Douglas Macleod. Phil in particular has given tremendous support over a long number of years. The late BBC political correspondent Kenny McIntyre never tired of giving me advice. I promised I would give him an acknowledgement. Thanks Kenny, the world of journalism in Scotland is so much the poorer for your passing.

Thanks are of course due to my family – my parents, Jasmin and Craig, brother Martin and sisters Elaine and Janis. And also to James Aitchison, Myna and Robert Fairley, Dr Cheryl Fairley, Hamish and Elspeth Macrae and Alison and Donald Spence.

My principal debt though is to my wife Gillian and our children David, Jennifer and Jack Hamish Spears Aitchison. They have spent far too many long evenings and weekends in well-practised silence or in making do without a husband or father in the house at all. They have given me the time and the peace to complete this work, and quite simply it could not have been done without them. This book in that sense is as much theirs as it is mine.

A final word ought to go to the ghosts of the past who pulled and tugged at me to get on with the story, because it was a story that needed to be told.

Peter Aitchison

List of illustrations

Foreword

Many people are vaguely aware that there was a fishing disaster on the east coast in 1881, and those closer to the community of Eyemouth know that one hundred and twenty-nine fishermen from the town perished in that autumn's storm. Now, at last, we have a vivid account of the catastrophe and a very readable explanation of its historic cases and consequences in this well-researched book.

Who were the fishermen who put to sea on 14 October 1881? Why did they take that fateful risk in spite of the storm warning? And what about the unique history of the Burgh that bred such fearless seafarers?

Peter Aithison tells the story of Eyemouth with the combined skills of a professional journalist and intrepid historian with all the enthusiasm of a true-born Haimoother.

The geology of south-east Scotland and the history of the border country conspired to create an unusual harbour and a remarkable community of people at the mouth of the Eye Water on the rocky coast of Berwickshire. Centuries of border conflict took their toll; generations of smugglers dodged the excisemen; but a bizarre dispute over the liability of the fishermen of one of Scotland's smallest parishes to pay a 'tithe' to their local Kirk minister became a serious obstruction to the development of a better and safer harbour – with fatal consequences.

Ever since 1597 my own family, the Homes of Wedderburn, influenced events in Eyemouth as the hereditary feudal superiors of the Burgh. They summoned young men to fight and die with them in Scotland's wars; in the early days they administered what passed for justice; the presided over decisions about the town and its harbour and latterly they tried, and conspicuously failed, to influence the votes of their tenants in the town.

Peter Aitchison generously acknowledges the effrts of my great-great-grandfather David Milne-Home, to help to find a solution to the tithe dispute and to promote the development of the harbour. When Peter visited Paxton House to check our archives in 2001, he noted that it was exactly one hundred and twenty-nine years since his forebear, the 'Kingfisher' Willie Spears, had driven the same road to meet the laird to discuss plans for the harbour.

Willie Spears is the hero of this story – the fisherman who led the community onto the streets and through the courts, and who even went to prison to resist the tithe system that was crippling the local fishing industry. This book and the new bronze statue of the Kingfisher in the town centre are fitting tributes to Willie Spears' historic achievements.

I will always be grateful to the voters in the Eyemouth area who helped to send me to Parliament as the new Labour MP for Berwickshire and East Lothian in 1978, an ironic role-reversal for a son of the family who had applied so much futile pressure on the electors of Eyemouth to vote Tory throughout the nineteenth century!

The Official Report at the end of the debate in the Scottish Parliament on the Abolition of Feudal Tenure Bill on 3 May 2000 records my 'heartfelt thanks for the fact that I will be the last ever feudal superior of the barony of Eyemouth. I am not sure whether there will be celebrations in the streets of Eyemouth tonight, but I shall certainly be celerating.' After 403 years of my family's history as feudal superiors of Eyemouth, it was a special pleasure for me to be able to personally endorse the abolition of the feudal system as a Member of the new Scottish Parliment.

The feudal system may have been scrapped at last, but some old habits may persist in Eyemouth – it is said that some fishermen are as reluctant as their forefathers to pay landing due to the Harbour Trust, and that they can be almost as thrawn and ingenious. But that cannot be true ...

Eyemouth is moving into the twenty-first century with a new confidence, not to mention a new deep-water harbour basin; a new fishmarket and a new trust redeveloping Gunsgreen House to interpret the history of the Burgh. Now this excellent book tells the story of Eyemouth as it has never been told before: a fitting tribute to the Kingfisher and to the men who lost their lives in the great disaster of 1881.

John Home Robertson, MSP for East Lothian

Preface

In October 1981 a solemn ceremony was held along the shores of Eyemouth Bay. Wreaths were tossed from the piers into languid waters that lapped gently on the beach and over rocks and into the walls of the harbour. The ministers of the town said prayers and then virtually the entire community of three thousand people sang the sea-hymn 'Eternal Father Strong to Save'. It was an act of remembrance for the one hundred and twenty nine local men who had drowned exactly a century before in the worst fishing disaster ever to strike Scotland. Seventy others from neighbouring villages also perished when a hurricane of unparalleled ferocity ripped along the Berwickshire coast.

As the service ended and the minister raised his hand in benediction, I stood with the rest of the town in solemn silence. I thought of the eight seventeen-year-olds – my own age – who had gone to the deep on Black Friday. Lives wasted before they had even begun. What might have been for the town had the boats not ventured out that afternoon or had the storm dived down elsewhere?

The people who thronged the shore to pay their respects to a lost generation were themselves the descendants of folk who rushed to those self same spots when the heavens opened in a most hellish way on 14 October 1881.

The great East Coast Fishing Disaster should have been the death of Eyemouth. It wasn't. Somehow the community got through the insanity and the poverty and clawed a living once more from the sea. It took until that year of remembrance, that centenary of the horror, for the population to attain the level of 1881. The harbour now, as then, is crowded by creaking, clanking boats of all shapes and sizes. Fishing now, as then, is the primary occupation for almost everyone. It is still now, as it was then, the most dangerous of all professions.

Chapter One

Sparkling Dawn, Damned Night

Carriages without horses shall go
And accidents fill the world with woe ...
The world to an end will come
In eighteen hundred and eighty one
Mother Shipton's prophesy, 1458

In the lee of the old cannon which points seaward from the ruined turf ramparts of Eyemouth Fort is a patch of hallowed ground. For many years folk said it was greener than the rest. It was the covered pit where parts of fishermen's bodies – the parts which could not be identified – were buried in the wake of the terrible storm of 14 October 1881. A day still remembered in the town as 'Black Friday'; 'Disaster Day'. The day when one hundred and twenty-nine of the best men of Eyemouth made their peace with the ocean. Seventy others, from nearby Burnmouth, Coldingham Shore, Cove, Newhaven and Fisherrow also perished. But the Eyemouth total, one in three of the adult male population, was, and is, a staggering statistic.

This communal pit was a secret kept from the womenfolk of the town. It was grotesquely fitting that it was so close to the old cannon – an artillery piece never fired in anger, yet which for a fortnight was trained on Eyemouth bay, where so many of the men had been drowned.

The shot flung in despair churned up the waters, yet only helped in the recovery of thirty-one bodies thought intact enough for burial. A piti-ful amount for the sea to give up, but sufficient to keep the horse-drawn hearses busy for days. 'Here's anither yin,' the young boys or 'callants' cried in their childhood innocence, as the solemn funeral processions clomped over the cobbled streets and on to the graveyard. The watchtower, built from broken headstones to ward off 'resurrectionists' half a century earlier, stood sentry to a more benign ocean in the sorrowful days after the disaster.

It was a game to some of the bairns, running with the death wagon. But it was their fathers; their brothers; their cousins and their future that the overworked and haggard ministers of the town buried.

On the face of it the Eyemouth fleet simply ran into bad luck. Caught in the teeth of the worst gale to hit the Scottish coast for decades the tiny boats were swamped, the men tossed overboard and the hope of a moder-ately successful, if at times wildly optimistic port, forever dashed.

But the obvious fact of the storm and its consequences conceals a more remarkable story. Why, when virtually all other fleets, from Shields to Shetland remained at their moorings, did the Eyemouth men sail? Why did so many prefer to try and ride out the hurricane than chance the harbour? Those who did make for the bay were all too often swamped within yards of safety and within sight and wailing sound of their wives, their mothers and their bairns. The psychological scars on those who survived Black Friday and on those who watched their loved ones drown can be more than just imagined. The event is still close enough for the oral history to be tested; for the consequences of the loss of a third of the men of Eyemouth – the lamented 'pickit men of the toun' – to be quantified.

The last quarter of the nineteenth century was a time of expectation in the fishing industry. Berwickshire had shared in the boom years when haddock and herring almost seemed to leap out of the sea. Gold ran into the pockets of men who had for so long been penurious. The place was at the peak of its population and its prosperity in 1880. Migrants arrived, seemingly with every swelling tide, from the Cornish inlets to the Buchan headlands and all places in between. A curious thing, given the cramped state of the harbour, then as now the kernel of Eyemouth's business.

For decades skippers and ships' captains had railed against the inadequacy of the quays and the low draft of water in the basin. The Harbour Trust, which came into being at the very end of the eighteenth century, had grand ambition but lacked competent direction. While other, perhaps less well placed creeks developed their facilities by tapping into what government cash was available, Eyemouth got nothing. Through mismanagement, a certain degree of bad luck and in spite of an ever-growing number of boats using the port, the Harbour Trust was effectively bankrupt by 1870, just as the good years kicked in. It was the fishermen themselves who had to take on responsibility for raising funds to expand and deepen the basin and to search for collateral for loan applications.

By 1881 the talking had stopped and a grand plan was unveiled which, at a cost of £80,000, would transform Eyemouth into the premier fishing station in Scotland, with the safest and most modern of quayside facilities.

The timing was propitious. At that very moment the government was making sympathetic noises towards an East Coast harbour of refuge. Peterhead seemed to have the strongest case, but the needs of the Berwickshire and southern Fort fleets were also strong. As the harbour proposals sailed ahead, others in the town drew up proposals for a branch line to the main North British railway network. The year 1881 was to be Eyemouth's *annus mirabilis*.

Yet all the heady optimism could not disguise the reality of what remained for most a precarious existence. When times were good, and the shoals regular, as they often were through the 1860s and 1870s, there was plenty to eat, and enough money to ensure that the bars, shebeens and grocery stores supplied liberal quantities to drink. But when fortune and fish deserted the fleet all suffered. While the 'big-men' made loud noises for the future, there was a deathly whisper about the present for many of the poorer folk.

The spring of 1881 brought relentless storms, high tides and low catches. Soup kitchens, unknown in the town for more than a decade, were set up in the Market Place. Children not only went hungry, but many had only thin rags to clothe them in the biting gales that continued into the summer. The ministers of the town noted with some considerable disdain that money was still to be found for strong drink, but they nonetheless dug deep into their collection plates to provide some warm garments for around a hundred of the poorer bairns. Cash was not to be given to the parents. Experience had shown that the temptation to squander it in the Ship Inn was irresistible for some of the more improvident. And as the ministers knew all too well, there were plenty who would rather booze on moonshine than care for their own offspring. Social control of the masses was a perennial issue. There seemed no solution to the vexed question of how to communicate with, educate, moralise and above all, sober up the intemperate poor.

The failure of the winter and spring haddock fishing looked as though it would be followed by an equally disastrous summer herring 'drave'. At the annual burgh picnic the fishery officer, John Doull, tried to talk up the town's prospects. He spoke of the building work that was going on in Eyemouth to accommodate the new families arriving to settle, and of the expected deliverance of a fine new harbour that would bring prosperity to all. It was a fine speech, but the poor fishing clearly had him worried. When the herring crews, scunnered by their lack of success, broke up early, at the very start of September and began to form up again for the winter haddock fishing in their deepsea boats, he wrote in his log book 'Such a lengthened period of bad weather at this time of year has not been known here for a very long series of years past. The fishermen are disheartened at being compelled to remain ashore so long.'

Unless matters improved in the late autumn. Unless the haddock returned. Unless the markets picked up, the fishing families of Eyemouth would be looking for more than clothes for their children. And they would need more charity than the Kirks could offer.

A lot has been made of the much-vaunted self-reliance of the Scots, much of it nonsense. Certainly in Eyemouth handouts had always been readily accepted with no sense of shame; conversely, much sport was had in trying to evade paying the rates, even when the fishing was profitable and money was rolling in like old coin on a poor inn table.

In one very real sense, though, traditional Scots values did persist in the town. Like other fishing communities it was made up of a few large, extended and interconnected families who relied on each other. The Loughs, the Dougals, the Stotts, and the Fairbairns. The Maltmans, the Nisbets, the Scotts, the Purveses, the Windrams, the Dicksons, the Collins and the rest. Those who were not employed catching the fish found work on shore – as line baiters, carters, hawkers, coopers or in the many curing yards that daily threw a funk of odorous smoke over the rooftops. The economy of the town was the economy of these families.

Nor were they tight when they saw the need for giving. As the storms of 1881 continued to lash down, the fleets fishing off Shetland were ravaged in early August. Fifty men were drowned in a single day. Most were on visiting boats from other parts of the country, there for the northern herring season. The Eyemouth folk, even given their own straightened circumstances that summer, offered what they could to the relief fund set up to help the widows and orphans.

On a fishing day, wives and mothers, young and old, roused themselves, their bairns and every other member of the household who could hold a knife, or stir a pot, no later than five a.m. While the men slept on, the factory of the home got to work 'shelling the mussels'.

That was the way it was on Friday 14 October 1881.

Candle flickers silhouetted the dark streets of Eyemouth, and lums began to reek as the sleepy, and often the hungover set to work. Each man was obliged to take with him to the haddock fishing a line of 1,200 hooks, normally baited with mussels. It was the daily duty of the family to slice open the shells and fix the flesh. Little wonder that fishermen tended to marry young, or that they prized the stouter lassies over the graceful ones. Small wonder too, that the old had a place, or that the bairns were required to do their bit from a very tender age. It was gruesomely tiring, but it was work for their own men and not for some anonymous capitalist. The amount of mussels needed for the Eyemouth fleet alone staggers the imagination. With seven men to every boat and more than forty boats in the fleet, 300,000 shellfish were used *every single day of the haddock season*. More than *forty million* a year. The stench of the debris, which was flung out of the windows and piled high in the yards, along the streets and even in the Market Place, must have been overpowering.

Everything deferred to the needs of the fishing, and that included weddings. Marriages were traditionally organised for the end of the herring drave, and were conducted very early in the morning, to allow the bridal party the luxury of a full day's honeymoon jaunt to Edinburgh.

On Friday 14 October 1881 the minister of the Established Kirk had a service to perform. Old Stephen Bell was not a native of the town, though he had by then spent most of his life in Eyemouth. His experiences as parish minister since 1845 had not always been pleasant. There had been legal disputes and fights with the fishermen – quite literally fights with the fishermen. He had been burned in effigy, his wife spat at on the street, his house stoned and its windows put in. That was all an age before, forgotten by some and unknown by many. The rotund little man with a bald pate and a wide gait was now looked up to, even though few came to his Sunday services. Bell no longer let the non-attendance bother him, and he was equally accustomed to some of the demands of those who did use his ministry. Like weddings, and their timing. On that chilly October morning then, Stephen Bell rose shortly before six o'clock and with his overcoat barely covering his nightshirt and slippers, he shuffled to unlock the Manse door. It was the second early morning marriage the minister had performed in less than a week.

The prospective bride and groom – cooper Mathew Crawford and his fiancé Elizabeth Stevenson were already waiting on the step, as were a few members of each family, and the best man James 'Laffy' Lough. With so many surnames and forenames the same, every man had a more popular style, while married women always kept their maiden names. Laffy was a cousin of the groom who, to confuse matters, had been born Matthew Lough. After his father had been lost at sea Matty's mother, Sophia Cribbes, took James Crawford as her second husband.

In contrast to the minister, both Laffy and Matt were resplendent in traditional Eyemouth garb. Each wore black breeks, waistcoats and jerkins. They may even have cleaned their shoes. The bride wasn't exactly blushing. Her dress could hardly disguise the swelling that told of a passionate if, for Eyemouth, all too familiar courtship. Elizabeth Stevenson was heavily pregnant.

The simple ceremony, held in the manse parlour – the Kirk was rarely opened for pre-dawn weddings – was over within minutes. Stephen Bell intoned stern words of advice then made for the stairs to his bedchamber. He didn't wait to see what happened next. The morning had barely started to yawn some light on to the square outside and the gas lamps struggled to do their bit, but there was colour on the street. Weddings, like funerals, were events that required marking.

Along with a throng of women, dressed in their pinstriped shawls and dark skirts, and dozens of expectant, barefooted bairns, a scattering of men had arrived, most drawing on clay pipes, and virtually all already togged-up in their heavy sea clothes. The air may have been chilled, but there was no hint of the squalls that had kept the fleet away from the ocean for the whole of the past week. They would sail and fish that day. They would be working.

The little party strode across the market place, down Chapel Street and then left into St Ella's Square, towards the home of the bride where more folk were waiting, including the town carter Peter Mack, his carriage ready, the horses champing at the bit.

Neighbours of the Stevensons were prominent, either standing in their own doorways, hanging out of windows, or idling at the head of the vennels which led off St Ella's. Men like Henry Angus, skipper of the *Harmony*, William Young of the *Blossom*, his son James from *Fiery Cross* and James Broomfield, a lad who looked much younger than his twenty-eight years, and who sailed on the *Beautiful Star*. That was the family boat of the Scotts and was crewed by three brothers, John, George and William and their father George.

The lanes running out from St Ella's were also taken up with interest in the wedding. Down Commerce Street old James Purves from the *Myrtle* and his wife Jane Mack watched on. It had been almost twenty years since they had tied the knot, and they already had three bairns before Janey persuaded Pur'es to do the right thing by her. Even then it wasn't in the Kirk, or before a minister. A lay priest at Lamberton Toll had married them yards from the English border. The folk didn't much care for the Church in those days. It was the time of the Tithe Row with the minister, a time of riot and unrest.

When the wedding party emerged into the square, a wiry, bearded man, who had the look of Abraham Lincoln and the same charismatic influence, moved forward, a glinting knife in his hand. William Nisbet, skipper of *Forget-Me-Not* flicked it over in theatrical fashion, pressed the handle towards Elizabeth Stevenson and made an ostentatious bow before retreating to the shore end of St Ella's. As the crowds cheered, 'Nibby' hooked his arm under the slumping figure of a drunken old man. He certainly appeared the worse for something. Nibby helped seventy-year-old Willie Spears to his feet. Spears had lost a lot of his reason and at times just shuffled aimlessly about the streets. Plenty in the town, including Janey Mack and fishermen like James Paterson of the *Industry* looked out for the old man, who was still called by many 'the Kingfisher'. Those who did not know Eyemouth might have thought the nickname a cruel joke. But Spears had indeed once been the leader of the people, a mantle now taken on by Nisbet. The old man, almost unnoticed, slipped away and shuffled down towards the broken stones at the beach. Some did hear him pass. They later remembered that

Spears had babbled throughout the day, 'an earthquake's coming . . . there's going to be an earthquake'.

Few focused on the shore end of the square. Attention instead was fixed on the bride and groom. Helped by Laffy, Matthew Crawford hitched up on to his shoulders a wicker basket filled with stones, mussel shells and rotting fish. As he shammed to run at less than full pelt, Elizabeth rushed after him, Nibby's gutting knife in her hand. Barely had the groom reached the edge of the square, back towards Chapel Street and the Market than his new wife, to loud cheers from the women, grabbed hold of the creel and sawed through the ties. The basket crashed to the ground, spewing its rancid contents on to the cobbles. As tradition demanded, Crawford handed over a silver coin for the 'creeling' and Elizabeth then picked it up, proving she was now willing to shoulder part of her man's burdens. Though nobody said so, the silent vows of the Creeling meant much more than the declarations made to a man of the cloth. He had never sailed the Berwick bank in a force nine at midnight, nor spent fourteen hours in a freezing rock pool searching for limpet bait, nor hawked smoked haddies by foot as far as Dumfries nor felt the pain of a child lost to hunger.

The little bridal party then mounted on to the carriage for the three-mile drive to Burnmouth station, where they were to catch a train for a day trip to Edinburgh. Laffy hesitated, and held back from the horse-drawn trap. Like the other men, he hadn't sailed all week and was more anxious to get to sea and put bread on the table, than gallivant. Being Friday if he didn't work that day, he wouldn't work for a further two. Besides, he hadn't arranged for a replacement to take his berth on the *Lily of the Valley*. But to hisses from the crowd, including some from the crew of his own boat, exhortations from the bride and her maid, and, more than anything, the embarrassed silence of his newly wed cousin, Laffy accepted his boots wouldn't see brine that day. His father and skipper of the boat was also James Lough. Standing by old Jimmy was his cousin, and another crewman, Robert Lough, along with his own heavily pregnant wife, Agnes Cribbes. They whooped with the rest of the throng as the little trap thudded out past them, into the market and up Church Street towards the Toll Bridge and out to Burnmouth.

A more sombre occasion was being prepared in the tiny home of Alexander 'Niz' Craig. Niz's infant daughter Elizabeth had died earlier in the week and was to be buried that day. He would not be sailing, and out of respect some of his close family and friends had also arranged substitutes in their boats.

One of these was Paul Paterson. He had only just returned to the sea, having been laid low with rheumatism for many months. Until the spring of 1880 Paterson had skippered the *Star of Hope*. But fishing and fishermen were fickle and sometimes well matched. When his bad back meant he could not work Paterson had nothing put by to sustain his share in the boat – little enough to keep his wife and bairns. Since August others had hired him for a few brief trips. Nothing regular though. Just the odd chance like that now offered on the *Florida*. Ellen Young, Paterson's long-suffering wife, had struggled over the previous year. There were four young children in their home in the Long Entry, and what little money the family managed to scrape together, either from their own labours or parish relief, went on food, whisky and tobacco – and generally not in that order. Sometimes the bairns managed a day or two at school. But it was not a habit either parent encouraged.

Ellen and Paul's close neighbours were the Johnstons. Robert skippered the *Wave* and his seventeen-year-old son Davie had only just been taken on as a crewman. Janet, wife and mother as she was, was noticed that morning on the stairs of their two-roomed dwelling tending to some of the seven other children. Her face, let alone her tortured and wearied body, bore the scars of a lifetime of work, childbirth and a fond affection for the neck of a bottle.

Those who had been at the wedding – unlike Ellen or Janet – were now well behind in their baitin', and returned to the lines, pulling their children along with them. Some of the men went back indoors, but others like David Stevenson, the father of the bride, sauntered down to the elbow at the head of the harbour and the barometer that had guided the town's fishing for more than three decades.

At the pier head, as was usual at this time, a scattering of old men idled their time away with gossip, and tales of their own days at sea. Spears was amongst them, his glazed eyes fixed on the bobbing boats. He was almost the oldest of the throng, but not quite. That honour went to William Pitt McIntosh, named after a heroic prime minister, at a time when Eyemouth thrilled to the news of British victories in the long French Wars.

In spite of the increasingly fine dawn, which had by now started to pierce through the skies and cast light on the crushed tenements, Stevenson noted that the glass had ratcheted down almost an inch overnight. The gales of that October week were only resting. They would be back that day, and with a vengeance. Nothing was surer.

Would they sail? The younger men in particular were anxious to be off. Friday 14 October was the first clear day in seven. Not only did the prospect of a hungry, and for not a few, a thirsty weekend, weigh heavily; they were also acutely aware that if they could get out, make a reasonable catch and get back home again, they would gain handsome prices in an under supplied market. That was the Eyemouth way. That was one of the keys to the port's success, the fishermen's renown and the merchants' speculation. Stevenson shrugged his shoulders and threw down some gear on to his boat the *Blossom*.

A tradition that had been the making of Eyemouth, but would that awful October day be its nemesis, is another indication of the importance of community. If just one boat sailed, all were obliged by honour to follow. The fleet was a family. The boats were bonded siblings. While most others from places as close as Berwick just seven miles to the south, and Shetland, four hundred miles to the north stayed at their moorings, the men of Eyemouth took a chance.

There were plenty who counselled against putting off, including the dominant figure of William Nisbet. Nisbet's best friend, Andrew Cowe told him as they prepared to sail 'What we'll have tae dae this day, we'll need to dae quickly'. But even as the coastguard Mr Ellis raised the warning cone at the entrance to the harbour, there were many more who cried down these fears – 'What's to do? We'll be oot and in afore the wind blaws.'

Nibby, resigned to going to sea, dawdled back to his wife Euphie in Home Street, near to the old graveyard. He quickly fed his pet parrot, a great favourite with the bairns. Strangely the bird, a grand talker, was silent as Willie left. Nibby kissed his wife, and turned for the door, leaving his purse and his gold pocket watch behind. Something he had never done before. William Nisbet then made his way to join the rest of the men at the pier, his heavy seaboots slung across his shoulders. By the time he arrived at the crimson painted hull of *Forget-me-Not*, the Salt Greens quay was alive with activity.

Unusually as the men loaded stores, and set out their small baskets or 'skulls' with the haddock lines coiled and ready, few words were spoken, and there was little tomfoolery.

The curious thing is that the men of Eyemouth had so very often diced with the elements and won home with great catches and even better quayside auction prices. Why did folk feel so odd that particular day? The women, as they always did, crowded the harbour to see the boats off, but their cheering was muted and the waving perhaps a little more heartfelt.

They knew a storm was coming. Did they have an inkling that the luck of the town might have run out? After the Disaster there were many reports that claimed some did. 'For more than a few days before Black Friday' wrote a correspodent to the Kirk's *Life and Work* magazine 'the town was full of feelings of apprehension. Many said they felt strange. As if there was something evil in the air ... some of the most sensible and temperate of the people said they could feel within themselves the ringing of church bells ... one old sailor said over and over again that there was going to be an earthquake'.

That old sailor was William Spears. As the men trooped to the pier he stood upright at the barometer like one of the Crimean volunteers *he* had helped recruit for the nation. Another of the veteran skippers, Alexander Maltman, jumped on board the *Economy*, and taking the tiller shouted to nobody in particular but with his gaze fixed on the Kingfisher, 'There'll be many a tear shed for the Eyemouth fishermen going to sea this day, and the glass so low'.

It was the younger men who had forced the issue that morning, and it was the younger men who were to lead the way. The *Press Home*, newly delivered that very week from the riverside yard of James Weatherhead was first out. The most modern and certainly the most expensive boat ever built in the town, its crew, including the three brothers Stott had an average age of just twenty-six. Leonard Dougal, another cousin of both Mathew Crawford and Laffy was, at eighteen, the bairn of the boat.

The virginal sails of *Press Home* invited the others to follow its wake as the Kirk clock rang out eight times. One by one the forty other boats cast rope, and were teased and coaxed out past the elbow. Strong arms pulled on leaden oars in the almost windless conditions. Bringing up the rear was *Lass O' Gowrie*, skippered by the oldest man sailing that day – sixty year old George 'Seabreeze' Windram. With him went his sons David and William and his nephew James Windram. Making up the six-man crew were Charles Burgon and Robert Kearney – whose heavily pregnant wife, along with the rest of the women, waved the men 'good-luck.'

The sun threw down a thin warmth, as three hundred men from a town of less than three thousand put their faith in their craft and edged past the Hurkur rocks which guard and protect Eyemouth bay; rocks that within a few short hours would cruelly defect to the ocean, inviting the boats homeward only to split their timbers and devour their crew.

As the boats nudged past the roadsteads, a telegram from Yarmouth arrived at the Market Place post office. A warning from the fifty-six Eyemouth men who were at the late Norfolk herring fishing, 'Blowing Gale. Reply Paid.' But the postmaster, John Campbell Macrae, would not have caught the boats even if he had rushed to the pierhead. Which he did not. The warning was too late. The 'reply paid' was equally useless, since the telegraph poles would not survive the wind that was even then heading towards the Berwickshire coast.

For the moment all was still; worryingly tranquil during the long haul to the haddock grounds a dozen miles off shore. Backbreaking work in conditions where sail was of little use. And all the while there was virtual silence in the boats. A fleet in motion, the men becalmed in thought. George Collin, 'Little Dod', skipper of the *White Star* later recounted that the boats reached the main banks at about noon. Things were not right. The air was hanging heavy. It almost crackled.

Lines were swiftly played out from the skulls, with no snagging or catching of hooks. Some of the little fleet had only just caught up with the leading boats and had not even begun to fish when the light wind dropped to a dead calm. George Dougal of the *Onward* told of how 'All in a moment it became as dark as darkness.'

Like the shot of a gun, the storm broke with amazing speed, sweeping all before it.

The light north-westerly breeze shifted to a north-north-easterly gale that hammered down with tremendous, deafening ferocity. The wind whipped the seas to a boiling, foaming, never-ending series of mountains and tumbling, cavernous glens. The rain lashed vertically, and the spray blinded the men, restricting vision to no more than a few hundred yards. This 'scud' which many survivors later told of 'flying before the wind' added confusion to the terror.

At first the crews tried to haul in their expensive lines, but it was obvious within a few minutes that the day would not be about lost lines, but lost lives. The boats, which had been close together, were scattered. Some had sails up which were torn apart, others had only bare poles and were at the mercy of the current; still others were swiftly overturned as the ballast in the holds shifted and flung them beam up. There was no obvious way to deal with the hurricane. Should they make for home, which would mean sailing into the storm, or try and ride it out on the sea?

On the *White Star*, Little Dod hurled orders at his panic stricken crew to secure the ballast and bring in sheets of sail. All the while he sang out his Christian faith. A convert, along with many others, including Willie Nisbet, in one of the many religious revivals, Dod was an accomplished lay preacher. His belief kept him sane in those terrible hours and minutes on Black Friday.

> Jesus, Lover of my soul,
> Let me to Thy bosom Fly,
> While the nearer waters roll,
> While the tempest still is high;
>
> Hide me, O my saviour, hide,
> Till the storm of life is past,
> Safe into the haven guide;
> O receive my soul at last!

The *Onward* was side on to the *White Star*. George Dougal could barely keep command. 'Some of the men said one thing, some said another, but they were at their wits ends, they did not know what to do.' There were calls to lift sail and head for home, or turn about to the depths of the ocean, but the cries were barely audible for the crashing of the waves against the timbers. Dougal for a time was as stunned as the rest of the men, until one massive lump of water smashed across the side and swept away his own twenty-one-year-old son, Alexander. The first known fatality of the day. Alec surfaced only once, yelled out something which the wind carried away, then was pulled down by the current and his own weighty seaboots. Perversely this death shook some sense back into George Dougal, and he ordered the bow of the *Onward* to be hauled towards land. Dougal later said that all he could think was that he had to tell his wife of the death of their eldest boy. He did not consider that in the process he risked consigning her to widowhood as well.

As the *Onward* was turned about, the *White Star* drifted alongside the *Myrtle*. Both crews held fast for about twenty minutes in an attempt to work out their exact position when another tide lunged over both boats. The *White Star* took the blow side on, and as the ballast shifted, the seven crewmen were thrown across the deck. When they staggered back up, desperately pulling on any ropes that came to hand and chucking water out of the boat with every available container, Dod saw that the *Myrtle* had completely tipped over. Two more shots of sea brought the brittle craft upwards, but on the third wave it was gone. The seven men were never sighted. Two fathers and their eldest sons, a pair of brothers and old James Purves were drowned.

Little Dod opted to take the opposite course from the *Onward*. He barked to the men to turn the head of the boat out to sea. The crew jabbered dissent but did as they were ordered when a mighty swell flung the *White Star* over a wave and almost on top of another upturned vessel. Its masts were split, and timber and rigging swirled and danced a macabre shanty in the mocking seas. Which boat was it? The *White Star* thundered past the wreckage so quickly that neither Dod nor his crew had time to be certain. It looked like it could be the *Industry*. There were no men to be seen. All had to be presumed lost. Was that to be the fate of the *White Star*? How long would the sea play with them?

Dod would later tell stories of that awful day. Of the horrors of the galloping breakers, the physical pain and mental exhaustion of the men he led. Of the emotions they all felt when they passed broken boards, or saw blinking lights in the distance that suddenly blinked no more. They shook hands with death that afternoon. God protected the *White Star*.

I remember in the midst of the storm seeing fourteen men, who were in two boats, drowned right in sight of us. I had then no hope of getting home to haven, for I knew that God held the great sea in the hollow of His hand and that He held the winds in His fist. Sometimes when I heard the seas roarin', I thought that the next wave would finish us. It was dark, and we could hear the waves comin' before we saw them, but our little boat rose to meet them, and aye managed to get ower. We could only go on deck one at a time, so fierce was the storm, and I remember after I had been up, one man saying to me 'is't ony better?' I replied, 'Its nae waur onywey; I think the boat's riding better, and she's no shippin' sae much sea'. He said despondingly, 'We shall ne'er see land again', and I said that I believed we would see the light of day and get to land.

The winds finally dropped, and the crew of the *White Star*, now alone in a boundless ocean, in Little Dod's words, 'made a friend of the sea for the night'. When dawn came up on Saturday Dod pulled the prow round and headed for shore. They sailed into Tynemouth late that afternoon, thirty-three hours after leaving home.

One of the boats that the White Star passed as it headed out past the scattering fleet was the *Ariel Gazelle*, a decrepit, battered and leaky vessel even in the calm of harbour. The instinct to make for home was strong in the minds of its crew. But as they tried to hoist sail lumps of water hit the old *Ariel*. The prow was swamped, the sides pummelled, all lines, gear and stores swept away. Somehow the boat stayed upright, throwing the men around like pebbles in a jar. The churning waves pitched them into tumbling company with five other boats. Some may have been hoping for home, others seeking safety by sailing away from the winds. One by one they were overturned in seas which smothered in a single wave. Thirty or more men were dragged to their deaths.

Which boats were these? *Beautiful Star*, with the three Scott brothers and their father George? *Sunshine* with his other son Robert? *Lass O Gowrie* with old Seabreeze Windram, his two sons and his seventeen-year-old nephew James? *Six Brothers* with its two pairs of father and sons as well as the Windram boys, more close cousins of *Seabreeze*? Did they see the last moments of the *Industry*, the *Margaret and Mary*, *Guiding Star*, *Margaret and Catherine* or *Florida* ... with Paul Paterson, who had got a chance, a 'lucky berth' that morning? Or were these unfortunates in some of the other boats that were sunk that dreadful afternoon?

Realising that they were now alone, that the fleet was no more, and that they had witnessed the deaths of so many of their friends and family, the men of the *Ariel Gazelle* belatedly swung around again. One of them, George Craig, said that they felt it was 'plain suicide' to try for home in such conditions. Unlike the *Onward*, the *Ariel Gazelle* was to stay far out on the ocean for not one, but two nights.

While men vainly battled on the seas, and gambled with a dash for port, or a longer war with the deep, while the *Ariel Gazelle, White Star* and others were heading even further out, the scenes on shore were of utter panic, confusion and fear. Above all else, fear.

The very epicentre of the hurricane hovered over Eyemouth. Within minutes of the first thumping crash of the gale the whole town was roused to the beach and the cliffs. They ran with anxious eyes and heavy hearts, but they also rushed a well-worn path. The people had always moved to the shoreline when the fleet was caught in the teeth of a storm.

There were plenty of examples. In February 1844 tar barrels burned all night on the headland as hundreds watched and waited. The boats were all open then, and two were forced to stay on the seas for almost thirty hours. The survivors, who included Laffy's grandfather, Robert Lough, and Robert Angus, the uncle of Henry Angus of the *Harmony*, could hardly move when they eventually got home. In December 1852 the fleet was again caught in a ferocious gale. All just made it safely back, but with considerable damage to boats and gear. Six years later, and despite clear warnings from the pier head barometer, the men again took a chance. Once more no lives were taken, but £300 was lost in torn sails, ruptured timbers and discarded lines. The 'glass' was again ignored and the Eyemouth boats sailed virtually alone in March 1865, January 1866, February 1868, December 1870, October 1875, and Christmas Eve 1880. On that day, as with most of the others, the tide was running with the fleet when the boats raced the gales for home. On 14 October 1881, the sea was already beginning to ebb when the hurricane came down.

It struck the town with as much force as it did the fleet. The public school on the Yard Heads road was pummelled by the winds. The pupils like ten-year-old William 'Nirley' Nisbet were petrified. Years later he told his story. ' I was in the school – we were getting dictation – when it got fair dark, an' a feafu' squall struck the school. Every wundy was blawn oot and the roof o' the school was lifted clean off.' The headmaster, James Cox, could not keep order and ran with the terrified children towards the beach to await the return of the men.

One group of callants took shelter from the storm in the partly upturned hull of a cobble and was showered with cakes and buns when a bakery cart was completely blown over into the River Eye. The terrified horse was almost strangled by the halter before the stunned driver managed to free the beast. The boys cheered their good fortune and tucked into what was probably the only meal enjoyed in the town that afternoon. Nearby, at the head of one of the vennels near the pier head, the red pantiles of a curing shed's roof were sent somersaulting along the lanes, splintering as they hit earth.

Down the coast at Burnmouth, a similar thin line stood against the challenging seas, peering from land to ocean. Amongst their number was Agnes Aitchison. She knew the pain of bereavement. Two of her brothers had drowned off Shields. James was taken in the spring of 1869, and John went down at almost exactly the same spot and on almost precisely the same day, three years later. Her man, William Aitchison – who had lost his own father to the sea when the *Lively* sank in 1853 – and two of their lads were out with the rest of the Burnmouth crews. They would make it home safe, but Aggie would not have the comfort of that certainty for many hours. She stood, with the other women and bairns, soaked from the spray and the rain, sheltering her youngest, four-year-old Jimmie, with a blanket. Eleven-year-old Mary, her eldest girl, idled with some of the others a few feet away, close to a short, low-lying dry stane wall. All of a sudden the dyke collapsed in the wind, tumbling bricks along the pier and showering the crowd with debris. Little Mary was badly cut. Others were bruised and one woman briefly knocked unconscious when she was caught a glancing blow by a lump of brick. When she came round she fought against those who tried to carry her indoors, and insisted on going back to the shore. Her man would expect her to be there when his boat roared past the cliffs and bore down into the little inlet.

Further inland the devastation was manifest. Entire forests, which had stood for centuries, were flattened. On a single estate near Duns Castle more than fifty thousand trees were uprooted. It would take four years to clear the damage.

The howling winds also chased up the Lothian coast and caused destruction even as far as Fife. In Edinburgh, the bridal party rushed back to Waverley station. But it would be some time before their journey home could start. Rail services were badly disrupted by the hurricane.

By one p.m., the massive seas that were pounding Eyemouth Bay began to ebb. Within a few hours the tidal harbour would be completely inaccessible. The crews, battling through the elements would, ironically, run out of water at the very entrance to the port.

But at that early point in the afternoon hope was still the order of the day. The boats *would* return safely. They always had! Effie Scott, whose husband and boys were out on the *Beautiful Star*, rallied those with fainter hearts. Flinging her arms around and cheerily smiling at the other wives and mothers she walked up and down crying, 'They'll turn up! They'll turn up'! But the fears she held inside were as real as those expressed more

publicly and voluminously by others. Effie's man and Effie's sons would
not turn up. As she marched like a soldier down the quay they had already
lost their battle with the elements.

The mood on shore was lifted though when the first vessels came into
view through the blinding spray and surf. Using all their skills and experience
the men of *Father and Sons* negotiated the eastern approaches before the
boat was flung by an almighty wave across the bar and on up the River
Eye. The apprehension of the crowd was lifted again when a few minutes
later, the *Alabahama*, closely followed by the *Onward* and then the *Brittania*
also navigated past the roadsteads.

Some of the fishermen were so exhausted they had to be helped ashore.
Watty Dougal, skipper of the *Alabahama* blacked out as soon as the boat
had been tied up. He was carried home, alive but scarred forever by what
he had come through.

As the *Onward* made fast at the pailings, some of the womenfolk, almost
blown into the harbour by the skirling gales, shouted down to the crew
for reports of their men and the boats which were still at sea. One of the
oldest of the gaggle, Jane Mack, her scarf drawn tightly against her brow
and her skirts sodden from the rain, grabbed George Dougal by the arm
as he wearily climbed up the wooden ladders.

'Did ye see the *Myrtle* Doddy? Hae ye ony news o' ma Jim?' 'No be
worrying Janey', came the reply, 'There's many that'll be flung oot their
bots afore the end o' the day ... Ah' ken. Ma ain son's deed. But big Jim
Pur'es i'll be a'right. Ah saw him strapped tae' the tiller o' the bot.'

But he was wrong. The *Myrtle* was already lost. Purves, bound to the
timbers, was dead. That news, though, would not be confirmed for many
hours.

Later in the afternoon Janey grieved with the rest of the women as reports
came in of boats sunk and men lost. Her boys were away at the Yarmouth
herring and Auld Pur'es was securely strapped, as George Dougal had said,
to the heavy tiller of the *Myrtle*. Janey may have felt she was weeping by
proxy for the dead of others. But in the pallor of the evening, with no sight
of her man, she left her tiny one roomed garret in Commerce Street and
went back to the pier. The *Myrtle* had still not come home. The old woman
would sit at the harbour all night. She did not sleep, she had no peace.

As the women were crowding the *Onward* two small open cobbles peeped
round the headland of Fort Point. As though linked by an undersea chain
they thumped up and over and into smothering surf. For a second the boats
disappeared, then lunged through the racing white horses, both missing the
entrance to the harbour and crashing almost into one another on the shingle.
The men on shore rushed to secure the vessels and drag the eight fishermen

to safety. They had narrowly escaped death, but any thought that the omens were on the side of man that day were soon dispelled.

Within moments a sail, battered and almost shredded from the masts, came up from the horizon and the boat, again at an astonishing pace, bore down for the piers. At the last moment, the *Harmony* was lifted by a massive sea and thrown on to the Hurkurs, a mere two hundred yards from the straining crowds. A shriek went up from the women, while the men, almost by instinct turned away, unable to look on the scene that followed.

When the boat struck the rocks the mast sheered off and came crashing down on a crewman, pinning him to a deck that was already breaking up and sinking. The crowds could hear the sickening splitting of the beams and the death cries of the other five men as they were dragged underwater. Among them was Henry Angus, who only a few hours before had helped celebrate a wedding outside his own door. Slipping to their deaths with him were his nephews, William and Peter Angus. Wull's widow, and she knew it for sure, was Mary Craig. They had six young children, and she had only just found out another was on the way. It isn't clear whether her man even knew. Mary clawed at her hair, her face, her clothes. The pain was just beginning. Agnes Bird saw her husband George Cribbes sink, his arms and hands flaying furiously as he went down. Before the day was out Agnes would be told that two of her sons, James on the *Good Intent* and Alexander on *Forget-Me-Not* had also been taken.

The *Harmony* was the first complete loss of the day. The first total wreck from the town for nine years. And it all happened in front of the helpless, hopeless people of Eyemouth: women, children, the elderly and those who were, for whatever reason, not at sea. From the *Harmony* alone five women were widowed and eleven children rendered fatherless.

Before the shock of this had fully penetrated the numbed onlookers, another boat, the *Radiant*, was swamped as it too approached the piers. The three brothers Fairbairn were in the seven-man crew. All but one of the men disappeared swiftly beneath the waves. Only fifty-seven-year-old John Windram managed to scramble on to the Hurkurs. Even in the crashing thunder of the storm he was close enough to the Gunsgreen shore to hear the urgent cries for him to jump and swim the hundred yards or so to safety. Windram shouted something back and then struck out from the rocks as half-a-dozen of the onlooking crowd linked arms and waded out to grab him. Just as his fingers seemed within touching distance of the link, a mast from the boat, which had also sheered off when it hit the rocks, came lunging forward in a rushing tidal wave and thumped into the swimmer's head. He sank immediately. John Windram's body never reappeared. It was never found. He left a widow, Alison Renton, and three young children. All seven men were lost from the *Radiant*. Four more widows created; another thirteen fatherless young children.

The *Radiant* was thought to be one of the safest boats in the fleet. Watching from the shore, from close to her home in the New Row, was the mother of the three Fairbairn boys, Agnes Burgon. Linking her arms and with terror etched on her face was John Fairbairn's wife – now widow – Mary Crombie.

It was all too much for many of the onlookers. One wrote 'The terrible sight created a profound impression on shore, where now women and children realising the perilous position of husbands and sons and brothers still at sea, were running about weeping in wild distraction.'

Some fell to their knees in prayer and others began to sing hymns and psalms, though little could be heard above the howling of the hurricane and crashing of the waves. Effie Scott tore at her clothes and shouted over and again 'Ma bairns! Ma bairns! Ma bairns' before losing consciousness. She was carried the few yards to her simple home. The *Beautiful Star* and with it her husband and three sons did not return. None of the surviving crews reported even seeing the boat after the storm broke and no bodies were ever recovered.

Time seemed to have no meaning on that bleak October afternoon. Was it but a few seconds or was it many minutes before the next boat, easily identified by its white sails, bounded across the heads of the waves before seeming to brake to a halt at the Hurkurs? The fate of the *Press Home* would surely define the rest of the day. Like the others before it, the newest craft in the fleet was within yards of safety when a huge wave struck, flipping the vessel on to its side and crushing it against the jagged outcrop. For a few moments some of the crew were seen clinging to the hull and one managed to scurry on to the rocks. Sea after sea washed over him as he held on grimly with one hand, while waving the other for assistance. A simple rocket device for shooting rope was all that the people on shore had – but it was of no help to the men of the *Press Home*. One by one their strength left them and they slid down to their deaths. The man on the Hurkurs was the last to fail. A correspondent for the local newspaper watched it all happen.

> How these men must have felt after surviving such terrible suffering that they were for hours subjected to far out on the raging billows, that it was a cruel aggravation of the severity of their fate to be thus brought to perish within reach of the harbour and within sight of the crowds of grief stricken friends whose hearts yearned for them but whom, alas! The enraged elements prevented making the slightest effort for their safety.

Of the six crewmen of the *Press Home* another trio of brothers, Robert, John and James Stott were taken. Their sister Elizabeth not only wept for them, but also for her own husband, another crewman, Andrew Collin. His brother Joseph would be reported as one of the missing from the *Fiery Cross*. The parents of eighteen-year-old Leonard Dougal would also hear news before the day was out of the death of his brother James in the *Lily of the Valley*. And though another member of the *Press Home*, George Windram, had no wife or children, his loss was compounded by that of his brothers John and James from *Six Brothers*. Their Uncle John had only minutes before, and at the very same spot, been swamped to his death. The young crew of the *Press Home* left only two widows. But one of these, Ann Ready, the wife of Robert Stott, was another woman heavy with child.

The best efforts of those on land were restricted to wading out to try and reach those men stuck on rocks, or clinging to wreckage, or in trying to shoot rope from the rocket. George Nisbet tried to get as far out as he could before firing the device, and was swept away to his own death. An outstanding hero, his wife and children were treated dreadfully by the Disaster Relief Committee which refused to give them any allowance from the fund on the basis that Nisbet was not at sea as a fisherman when he perished.

Mixed in with the reality of death that day, were tales of remarkable courage. George Paterson from the *Enterprise* had a miraculous escape, but was forever traumatised by his experience.'When we were about six miles out I was washed overboard.' he said on his return. ' I was clean gone, but had the presence of mind to grip the mizzen sheet when the boat dipped and was, with great difficulty, hauled on board by comrades. About ten minutes afterwards James Windram was washed overboard ... We saw Windram swimming bravely in the wake of the boat, but in the course of two or three minutes he became exhausted, hung his head and sank.'

Windram had two young children, and his widow, Margaret Wilks, was pregnant with their third. Jamesina Windram was born on 1 April 1882.

The family connections ensured a myriad of suffering. James Windram's sister Helen was married to Robert Collin, skipper of the *Fiery Cross*. He drowned along with his brother William, their cousin Joseph, and three other men when the boat was dragged to the deep. They left six widows, half of whom were pregnant, and twenty-two children, the heaviest loss of any boat. Joseph Collin's widow, Elizabeth Cormack, had nine young bairns to care for. In all thirteen, carrying the name Collin were drowned on Disaster Day, the most from any of the families of the town.

Very few men survived when the ocean smashed in their boat or pulled the fragile timbers to the bottom. Hardly any could swim, and their heavy working clothes pulled those who had learned down. Some of the bodies, which were later recovered, showed evidence of penknife marks on the boots, as frantic attempts were made to cut them off. At least one man appeared to have even tried to amputate his own leg.

A handful did manage, somehow, to strike out to safety from their sinking boats and dying colleagues. One was David Stevenson, skipper of the *Blossom* and father of the happy bride in the dawn ceremony, which was an age and a world apart from the rest of that never-to-be-forgotten day. Stevenson was the only survivor from the seven men of the *Blossom* which broke up at Goswick on the north Northumberland coast. He did not speak much in later years of either their loss or his own salvation.

The lifeboat could not be launched on 14 October 1881. Those who would have made up the numbers were all at sea. The coxswain, an honoured position in the town was, of course, Willie Nisbet. Unhappy about sailing, but resigned to the majority decision, he was lost along with all of his crew when the *Forget-Me-Not* overturned off Berwick. More than any other, the death of Nibby was a shattering blow to the community. His was one of the few corpses to be recovered.

Five widows and nine fatherless children were left from the loss of the *Forget-Me-Not*. One of these was born eight months after the Disaster to Isabella Cowe, widow of 28-year-old William Scott. In remembrance of both her husband and the great Nibby the child was christened William Nisbet Scott. The boy died before reaching his second birthday.

Harrowing scenes were also evident at Burnmouth. The agonies of men sucked down in the swell within full sight, sound and almost arm's reach of the people who lined the shore. The *Lily of the Valley* foundered with all hands just south of the main village, at the hamlet of Ross. Other boats made fast to the piers, but with grim news. The *Invincible* reported the loss of John Dougal. He left a widow and three young children. His brother Thomas drowned when the *Florida* went down. Another seven dead, another six widows, another ten fatherless children.

A little before four o'clock, a train pulled into Burnmouth station, which was built on a clifftop redoubt. Matthew Crawford, his bride Elizabeth Stevenson, her sister Rebecca and James 'Laffy' Lough got out. As they turned out of the station Laffy was grabbed from behind. He spun round, to see a tearful youth who stammered. 'Where hae ye come frae'. The lad had known only that Laffy was a crewman on the *Lily of the Valley*, not that he had been on shore all day. Lough first stared at the callant, then followed his gaze down the hill. The youth pointed down to the harbour and said 'Jimmy, they're all lying down there'.

Six men were drowned in the Lough's family boat, including Laffy's own dad. All left widows; three of them pregnant. When these children arrived it brought the total without fathers to sixteen.

As the afternoon wore on many clung to the hope that the unaccounted for boats had made for more accessible harbours, or were trying to sail out the storm. Precedents for this were good, but increasingly, even for those who cherished the firmest conviction, the question was no longer whether there had been a tragedy, it was how deep, how painful, and how massive that tragedy would prove to be.

With the light fading, and the tide deceptively low, despite the still roaring seas, the last boat to chance Eyemouth Bay came thundering past Fort Point. *Pilgrim* was driven hard on to rocks just below the headland, and all hope seemed at an end for the seven-man crew. Desperate efforts were made to reach them as the boat broke up in a whirling swell near the outcrop known as Black Carr. The Rev Stephen Bell could bear the scene no longer and left the shore to break the terrible news to the wife of one of the men, who was at home and in very poor health. No sooner was he gone than ropes were made secure on the broken hull and all of the crew saved from what had seemed certain death. A runner was dispatched and minutes after the minister had broken the news of the poor woman's new found widowhood, the lad burst in to say all of the men of the *Pilgrim* were saved!

But the fortunate were few.

As night fell and the winds dropped to a deceptive, almost benign breeze, reports continued to trickle in of unparalleled losses. Yet still women refused to leave their deathwatches. What must have been going through the minds of those who lined that dark precarious shore? They shivered through a long night of silence, a silence broken only by the screams of the widowed and the tears of the orphans.

Some chose not to sit by the piers. They had families to watch over, things to keep their minds and bodies occupied. Janet Johnston retreated to her flat in the Long Entry and her seven perished, petrified bairns. It would be the following day before the loss of the *Wave* and the death of her husband Robert and son Davie would be confirmed.

Rumours persisted that boats had been sighted heading for the relative shelter of the Isle of May in the Firth of Forth. It was said that some were making for Shields or even Norway. Others had been wrecked on deserted beaches. Their men *were* yet making for home. They *had* to be. For the most part these were hopeful stories, either spun to comfort or imagined in despair.

Eyemouth's fishery officer, John Doull, had stood with the crowds all through the afternoon. Late in the afternoon he returned to his office, tossed his cap into the wide armchair at the side of the reeking fire and with what must have been a heavy and sorrowful heart, wrote a note to his opposite number in Yarmouth. The Eyemouth men there should come home. But by the time Doull's telegram reached Norfolk the five crews who had been there were already on their way back – by rail rather than sea.

The railway companies gave reduced fares to some of these, and a group of more than fifty arrived at Burnmouth Station in the early hours of Saturday morning. The Eyemouth men then tramped the three miles down to home. A strange and silent home. Despite their own fatigue, they joined the others in the continuing search of the beaches and coves above and below the bay. Better to be doing something; better not to be brooding in the house, with the women, and the bairns, and the weeping. Many, of course, had their own bereavements. One fisherman rushed to his elderly father's home in George Street. He found James Dougal bedridden and in a state of shock. One son might have returned from Yarmouth, but another, Andrew James Harrower Dougal would never cross the step again. He had been swept overboard from the *James and Robert*, the only man lost from that boat. Andrew's brother was due to return to the Norfolk fishing on the Monday after the Disaster. But when he went to bid his father goodbye, he found James Dougal had taken a shock and was dead.

Andrew Dougal had married Euphie Lough six days before Black Friday. Not only was she a widow within a week of her wedding, she too was carrying a child who would never know his father. Andrew Harrower Dougal was born on 31 January 1882.

By Saturday morning, Eyemouth was a town of the dead. The known fatalities were bad enough, but the lack of certain information about the large number of men and boats as yet unaccounted for, was just plain torture. John Doull trudged to the telegraph office with a note to be sent to the Hon B F Primrose, head of the Fishery Board in Edinburgh: 'Exceedingly sorry to say that about sixty Eyemouth, three Coldingham and some Burnmouth fishermen lost in yesterday's fearful hurricane. Upwards of twenty boats still missing. Will write further particulars today.'

Later that day at last some good news did come through. The Eyemouth boats *Enterprise*, *Success* and *White Star* had made a safe landing on Tyneside, while the men of the *Iona* from Burnmouth telegraphed home their arrival with 'all hands secured' at Shields.

But for every family that rejoiced at the safe return of loved ones so many others clung to the thinnest of hopes.

All that day Doull walked up and down the beach, now strewn with disjointed planks and the debris from broken boats. Some children played amongst the flotsam, dragging an empty seaboot up and down the shoreline.

Who had it belonged to? Doull walked slowly to the heights of the Fort where men had been at their watch all night, hoping for returning boats, but resigned, at best, to recovering bodies.

From the vantage there almost everything seemed normal in the crushed little town below. But when Doull swung his gaze to the bay, there was unnatural activity. Three of the smaller boats were net dragging from the roadsteads to the harbour entrance. They were low in the water from the large number of men perched along the sides, their eyes fixed on the now becalmed seas. Further out, other boats meandered the Berwickshire waters. Some pulled beyond Dunbar, others swung south to Holy Island. The morbid trawl went on and on.

Doull watched for a while. He had few words to exchange with the men on the point. What could be said to comfort? He then made his way up to the cliffs, past the devil's howf, where a persecuted old wife was thought to have hanged herself more than two centuries before. Out towards the Witches Hole, where the ashes of dozens of Satanists who were burned at the stake were said to have been scattered. Back then to the beach, and the bairns who were still playing, their families probably too preoccupied with the business of death to worry about what the living were doing. Doull went around by the smokeless yards, the quiet sheds and deserted vennels, along to his office. He rested himself in his grand captain's chair and did his duty, writing, as he had promised, reports for the Fishery Board. What had happened, how the boats were lost, the men killed and the town deprived of so much:

> Eyemouth cannot recover from the effects of this sad disaster for many years
> to come and it will seriously cripple the important haddock fishing carried
> on from the place ... none of the Berwick or Spittal boats fortunately went
> to sea that morning as the barometer showed great indications of stormy
> weather which unfortunately was unheeded by the Eyemouth or Burnmouth
> fishermen.

The silence of the afternoon was punctuated by the clanking bells of the remnants of the fleet rolling at the moorings; the hourly chiming of the Kirk clock; the intermittent thumps of the Fort cannon, each salvo lobbing more sorrow into the torn heart of the town. As the light faded, Doull put down his pen. He had a meeting to go to.

The Salt Greens quay was normally buzzing on a Saturday night with men flush from the week's fishing, carousing the Ship Inn, the Royal Hotel, the Cross Keys. But like the rest of the town the bars were quiet. Shuttered. Closed.

John Doull made his way back up along the pier, cutting through George

Street and into St Ella's Wynd, past the Methodist Church and on to Chapel Street and the Market Place. The gas lamps were burning in the gloaming of the evening. There was some business being done that night. Men, silently and with hunched shoulders, were making for the Town Hall. Word had been passed about. 'What can we do?' A meeting was needed to decide how the town could overcome the calamity. Mr Bell had made sure that all who needed to know would be there.

It was not a representative gathering. No fishermen attended – most who had survived had neither the time nor the energy to care about what was being said or done on their behalf. Their priority was with their own folk. Sitting, comforting, occasionally weeping, and certainly drinking. Funerals needed to be settled, and families sorted out. Some bairns would need to be fostered within the town. Some women could not manage on their own.

These were also the thoughts uppermost at the meeting in the Town Hall. When the fishery officer arrived it was just getting underway, with the Chief Magistrate, the taciturn Robert Allan, in the chair. Beside him was John Donaldson, a kindly man who, like his father before him, was the Inspector of the Poor. There too were all of the ministers of the town, most of them already dog-tired. James Gibson, laird of Gunsgreen, on the southern shore of the River Eye, sat by the town's two bank managers. Very few of the boats had been properly insured, but the secretary of the East of Fife Boat Club had come down for the meeting. He was alongside James Weatherhead, the owner of the yard where so many of the sunken vessels had been built, and the merchant-curer James Crawford. A very different James Crawford from the one who had celebrated his son's wedding not thirty-six hours before.

Public meetings in the wake of fishing losses were common in Eyemouth, as they were across Scotland. The community always rallied round those whom fate had blighted, and local subscriptions usually raised enough to maintain the families of those lost for at least a short time. Few ever chose to leave. Where would they go? Who else would provide? There was always some work in a fishing village, even if it was just baiting lines or picking whelks.

But nothing, nothing had ever occurred on this scale. The gathering did not last long. After a short prayer, delivered by Stephen Bell, Robert Allan spoke of the loss to the Town and of the money that was already starting to pour in. Every newspaper in the land was carrying the story of the Disaster. Fundraising events were already being planned, and these were welcomed. But there was little more that could be discussed or decided that night. Allan said simply that Eyemouth could not cope on its own. He called on all present to return on Monday when a full public meeting would take place – and in the meantime said he would get in touch with the Superior of the Burgh, the local MP, the Lord Lieutenant of Berwickshire, the Earl of Home and as many other 'influential gentlemen' as possible. Prayers were again then heard, and the good and the great of the town walked home – through the quietest streets an Eyemouth Saturday night had ever experienced.

As dawn was barely breaking on Sunday morning, the lookouts that had been posted on the Fort were roused by a faint outline, which slowly grew on the horizon. Hours passed before a battered, leaking and sail-less structure limped, with bare poles, into the roadsteads, past the Hurkur skerries. The *Ariel Gazelle*, back from the dead and carrying the living proof of hope, forty-five hours after the hurricane had subsided. Once again, the whole population of the town made for the piers as the tiny craft inched its way over the bar and up the harbour. This time the crowd was silent. Which of the unaccounted boats, which of the Eyemouth men still missing had providence returned? The crew of the *Ariel Gazelle* could hardly stand; the skipper Alex Burgon had to have his hands prised from the tiller. As the men slowly climbed over the edge of the ladders and on to dry land the crowds surged forward. The seven men of the *Ariel Gazelle* were taken into the Ship Inn. Numb with emotion George Craig was in tears. 'It made me ashamed to be safe and sound' he later recounted 'passing amongst those women, who had hoped that our boat would prove to be their husband's or their son's boat.'

But the seven men were not immune from loss. The day after being lifted only semiconscious from his boat, Alex Burgon was chief mourner at the funeral of his son John, who had gone down on the *Harmony*. Others from the *Ariel* were told of the death of brothers, uncles, cousins and friends.

There would be no more returning from the storm of 14 October 1881. Seventy-three certain widows and two hundred and sixty-three fatherless children were left in Eyemouth alone. Two dozen of these were born in the days, weeks and months after the Disaster. The weeping would go on, the sorrows not abate within the living memory of those who witnessed the horrors of that day. The stories have been handed down so that the living yet remember the dead.

The decision of the *Ariel Gazelle*, to ride out the storm and eschew Eyemouth harbour, saved the crew and the battered boat. Would others have survived if they had not tried for home? Or did many opt for that course because of the inadequate state of their own haven only to be swamped and sunk at sea? For a full two weeks after Black Friday, Royal Navy gunships scoured from the Tyne to Montrose and out halfway to Denmark but no more boats were sighted. The remaining fishermen of the

Berwickshire ports were left with the necessary but ghoulish task of trawling the inshore waters for the bodies of their drowned colleagues. The few corpses that were recovered were almost always stripped naked by the tides. They were swiftly swaddled and coffined to spare relatives the further agony of missing arms or legs, of gaping, gnawed wounds.

Bits of men. Limbs, lumps of flesh, perhaps even pulped heads, were dragged up or washed ashore. They were taken, with reverence, to the Fort that overlooks the bay, and buried in the shallow pit there. Away from the knowledge of the women. It was a silent place where men could cry with no shame as they shovelled earth on the 'pickit' men of the town. On the hope and heart of the community.

> There was weeping on every side,
> There was na a hame unbereft;
> Fathers and brothers and lovers -
> There was hardly a man of them left!

But eventually, the sea had to be faced again. Two weeks and three days after Black Friday the Eyemouth fleet, nineteen boats and one hundred and twenty-nine men short, and led by the *Ariel Gazelle*, dropped ropes, hoisted sail and made to the deep once more.

Chapter Two

'She is Called not Lucky'

I stood upon the Eyemouth Fort
And guess ye what I saw?
Fairnieside and Flemington
Newhouses and Cocklaw.
The Fairy folk o' Fosterland
The witches o' Edincraw,
The rye rigs o' Reston
And Duns ding a'

Almost three-and-a-half centuries before the Disaster, a roving party gal-
loped into Eyemouth. The common folk were used to raiders. The place
had been at the vortex of conflict between Scotland and England from the
very start of the Wars of Independence. But the man who rode at the head
of the troop as it threaded down the lanes and on to the foreshore had
unusually high rank and position. The Duke of Somerset also had a keen
military brain. He had arrived at the border, in the summer of 1547, as Lord
Protector of the child King of England, Edward VI, and commander of a
force of more than 15,000 men. Two years earlier as the then Earl of
Hertford he had, on the orders of the failing Henry VIII, wasted large tracts
of the south and east in part one of a 'rough wooing' – an attempt to force
the marriage of Prince Edward with the infant Mary, Queen of Scots. Now
he was back and intent on finishing the job.

The key difference this time was that Somerset had a well considered
plan. Though he wished to draw the Scots to battle, the Duke now believed
that the only way to permanently subdue the northern Kingdom was by
occupation. He would establish a necklace of forts along the lowlands,
establishing an English Pale that would be the springboard for total
conquest. The first and most important of these would be built at Eyemouth.

When he ventured into the village in September 1547 Somerset might
have wondered why the Scots had been so dilatory in ignoring what nature
had provided. Perhaps the Duke spent time trotting back and forth along
the beach, gazing at the arched bay and at the topography of the cliffs
which lazed like a sphinx along the northeastern approaches. It was the

existence of this promontory that provided the shelter that made Eyemouth the only safe haven on the Berwickshire coast. The harbour had been noted as useful and capacious as far back as the reign of William the Lion in the late twelfth century. Had it not been for the turmoil of the long wars with England the place would have dined well on the crumbs left over from the trade of Scotland's most prosperous port of Berwick a few miles to the south. But Berwick had been lost to England in 1482; a fact which enhanced Eyemouth's strategic importance.

The commander called up his military architect Robert Lee and work was immediately ordered on the first *Trace Italienne* structure ever seen in Britain. As the name implies it was a continental innovation that allowed defenders to pour fire on an attacking force from three sides. The effects could be devastating.

The policy of fortification was only part of Somerset's strategy. A week after his visit to Eyemouth he defeated a massive Scottish army under the Earl of Arran at Pinkie near Dunbar.

Unlike Flodden, Pinkie is no metaphor for national catastrophe. Yet it was arguably even bloodier. Perhaps as many as ten thousand Scots were slain and more than fifteen hundred captured. The lists of the nobles who fell have, of course, survived. They included George, fifth lord of Wedderburn, the most powerful family in Berwickshire. His brother David succeeded to the title and to the family estates, including the vast lands and riches of Coldingham Priory, which in name only belonged to the Roman Church. The identity of the ordinary men who went willingly or otherwise when Wedderburn called up his levies and who also died at Pinkie are not recorded. Their pain and loss were just as real even though history has not accorded them a voice.

But neither the military upset of Pinkie, nor Somerset's policy of fortification brought rapprochement, still less capitulation. The Scots did the predictable thing. They turned to France for support. Their auld ally and England's inveterate enemy was only too willing to provide men, munitions and money. England continued to be bogged down on the Scottish border, a valuable and draining distraction from the battlefields of France. Scotland was drawn ever further into the French sphere of influence. The most glaring example of this came with the removal of Mary, Queen of Scots to France where she was betrothed to the Dauphin.

Their eventual marriage was the exact opposite of all that Somerset had been striving for. In part at least, his policy of fortification, begun at Eyemouth in 1547, was the catalyst for the dynastic union not of England and Scotland but of Scotland and France. It was a diplomatic disaster.

The Duke was proved correct in one respect. His assessment of the strategic importance of Berwickshire was not now lost on the Scots. They first achieved the destruction of Eyemouth Fort under the terms of the 1550 treaty of Boulogne, and then six years later, surreptitiously built it up again. This time it was the Queen Regent of Scotland, Mary of Guise, who directed matters. She sent a French general and a company of 500 soldiers to the coast to occupy the village and draw the English into conflict. Mary's strategy was designed to convince her own nobles of the danger that still existed on the border. It was a policy that might have been made at Versailles.

For several weeks English dragoons stationed at Berwick sortied across the moors to harry the reconstruction of Eyemouth Fort. These skirmishes culminated in a surprise early morning assault dubbed the Battle of the Barefoots since the Scots had no time to get properly dressed before rushing to the fray. As a confrontation it was a pretty inconclusive affair, but it did achieve Mary of Guise's primary purpose. It persuaded many of the sceptics on her council that they ought to support the Regent in raising an army against the English, who did indeed seem bent once again on invasion.

Eyemouth fort, which was originally a garrison for an English occupation force, now became a storage dump for Scottish munitions and arms, a compound from which it would be possible to launch a lightning attack on Northumberland without dragging supplies the fifty miles or so over treacherous tracks from Edinburgh.

Though it was never actually used for this, the danger the base posed was real enough. It was sufficient to convince Elizabeth that Berwick was under threat. To lose that northern town so soon after England had been ejected from Calais might have imperilled the newly crowned Queen's tenuous grip on power. In 1559 she ordered the immediate refashioning of Berwick's defences. The cost was immense, but Elizabeth considered it money well spent. At the same time she insisted that the thinner lines of Eyemouth Fort be torn down under the terms of the treaty of Câteau-Cambrésis. As the Queen's influential secretary Cecil was quick to point out, it had been rebuilt in the past and this time had to be totally levelled. A close watch was therefore kept on the demolition. In July 1560, General D'Oysel, commander of the Scottish forces on the border wrote to Elizabeth with the news that the process was all but complete. 'We are making and will make all care to ruin and throw down the Fort of Eyemouth ... A loaded cart could go back and forth over the lines of the walls'.

The stones were strewn about the nearby fields, only to be collected for house building in the village, and for the construction two centuries later of a sturdy harbour. Only the earthworks remain as a reminder of the powerful military base that for thirteen years was centred on Eyemouth.

The influence of the hundreds of first English and then French soldiers who lived there, and probably married and certainly procreated with the local girls, would endure for much longer.

Câteau-Cambrésis put a temporary end to some of the bloody conflict on the continent, but could not stem the tide of religious and political revolution destined to burst over Scotland in 1560. The Scottish Reformation, unlike the one engineered by Henry VIII in England, did not hasten an abrupt confiscation of Kirk lands. That process had been going on for decades. Much of the assets of the Catholic Church were already secularised, the livings appropriated, monastic appointments effectively reserved to the Crown or the great families. What did change as a result of the events of 1560 was the growth of the 'lesser lairds' who now also helped themselves to what was left of the assets of the old Church. James VI fostered their development as a bulwark to the magnates as well as for the economic wellbeing of Scotland.

The King presided over the creation of more than a hundred new burghs of barony, most of which were parcelled out to his lairdly supporters. Eyemouth was one of the first and was placed under the feudal superiority of George Home of Wedderburn, whose uncle had fallen at Pinkie. The King looked to families like the Homes for support, loyalty and, in the case of the Wedderburns, money. James knighted George Home and appointed him as Comptroller of the Royal Household. He then proceeded to milk him dry. Massive loans that were advanced by Home to the court were never to be redeemed. In very large measure the Wedderburn finances were ruined by the service George Home gave to the Stewarts. The monarch was far from grateful, and having got what he needed James acquiesced in court intrigue to sack Wedderburn. The laird returned to his power base in Berwickshire, much the poorer for the experience.

Though George Home might have been distracted by his time at court, he did actively encourage the development of his estates, including the burgh of Eyemouth. Perhaps his parlous financial position as a result of royal service also served to motivate commercial instincts.

Baronial burghs did not share the advantages of Royal Burghs, but they were a halfway house to open trade. Each had a common mill and brewery, a mechanism for fixing food prices, a procedure for managing arable and pastoral land, and a code for the defence of commercial rights. The coming of peace with England was a boost to all. For those who lived on the border, it was particularly beneficial. That is not to say that Berwickshire folk were unused to dealing with the English. Through the turmoil of the Middle Ages they had survived, and not a few prospered, by trading with friend and foe alike. They became known as the 'victualing Scots', who literally supplied all comers. It was not a business restricted to the common folk. Self-evidently it required organisation and the patronage of local barons. The Homes were certainly involved and paid only lip service to an Act passed by the Scots Parliament in 1535, which aimed to quash the trade. Forty years later and the problem was still real enough for the Regent Morton to appoint a 'customer and searcher' for the border shires, but this initiative also failed, as did similar moves by the pro-French Scottish Administration in 1559.

By then Eyemouth's trading credentials had become well established. So much so that another Regent, the Earl of Mar, was obliged to slap down Alexander Home of Wedderburn, for trying to charge additional customs duties at the harbour – taxes which the family pocketed. A dozen years after this, in 1584, a petition in the name of the whole population of the village was delivered to the Convention of Royal Burghs alleging that Alexander was again up to his old tricks and had been using force to compel payment. The Homes evidently took more than they gave in return and it fell to the Convention to vote funds for the upkeep of Eyemouth harbour. This was done in 1585, again in 1612–13, and once more in 1619. By then Eyemouth was not only a burgh of barony, but also a parish in its own right.

Ministers mattered in the aftermath of the revolution of 1560. As well as delivering a weekly sermon, they organised poor relief and education, often dispensed basic justice and were the cornerstone of authority. It is somewhat surprising then that Eyemouth was not elevated into a separate parish until well into the seventeenth century. When this eventually did happen, on 27 January 1618 the parochial boundaries were amongst the smallest in Scotland. The tiny extent of the lands, which were no more than a mile square, would later create profound difficulties, especially in the raising of local funds. To offset the shortfall from a tithe on the land, the Wedderburns surrendered to the minister the rights to a tithe on fish landed in the village – rights the Homes had acquired at the time of the Reformation.

The stipend was ratified nine years later when the Rev John Home, a kinsman of the laird, was awarded additional lands to his glebe 'together with teinds and the fishings in the sea and water of the river Eye.' Not only that, but the fish teind was commuted into a cash payment. Each boat based in the village was henceforth obliged to deliver to the Manse a yearly sum in lieu of teind of £20 Scots, or £1 13s. 3d. sterling. With five open cobbles on the beach this amounted to £100 Scots, or about £7 10s. 0d. sterling. At a time when silver was scarce it seemed a generous settlement. The fact that it was a fixed payment, which could never be altered, was not an issue at the time. Yet, as the decades rolled on the real value of the impost declined, squeezing the standard of living of the incumbent. The solution of 1627 stored up a lot of future trouble in the parish. It would be a defining element in the history of Eyemouth. As much as the hurricane, which broke over Eyemouth in October 1881, it was this settlement that would bring death and disaster to the town and its people.

Though the presentation of the parish minister was nominally in the hands of the Crown, the right was almost always exercised by the Wedderburns who, as was the case with John Home, often imposed members of their own clan on congregations. The family also demonstrated their power in the baronial courts and through the slow and halting development of effective local government. Sometimes this was fair and necessary; sometimes it was cruel and perverse, such as in the hounding of alleged witches.

Witchcraft first appeared on the statute book in 1563 and was rooted in a determination to rid Scotland of all of the relics of Roman Catholicism. A comprehensive study of Scottish witch-hunts has shown that most were not spontaneous attacks on frail old women, though spinsters did make up the majority of those seized and executed. The bulk were organised affairs, usually directed by the gentry, and often at the instigation of ministers who sometimes had family connections with the local lords. Significantly many of the witch scares took place in the Lowlands, the Borders and in Fife. The rule of law, long absent in much of Scotland, was fast becoming the norm in these parts. Allegations of sorcery were particularly rampant in the Merse, and especially along the Berwickshire coast. Upwards of thirty women and several men were throttled or burned on the foreshore. Others took their own life before the mob approached.

It was once accepted that as many as 3,000–4,000 'witches' were executed in seventeenth-century Scotland. Now the true figure is thought to be closer to 1,000, yet this was still double that of England. There were several waves of persecution, most of which coincided with particular events or calamities, or when attempts were made to crack down on lawlessness.

Fishing villages were particularly susceptible to these scares. Connections between the devil, ill luck and disasters at sea were obvious. Suspicions of Satanic influence were further invigorated by lurid stories from foreign sailors of persecutions going on in mainland Europe.

The first recorded incident in Berwickshire came in 1594, and followed on from the celebrated North Berwick trial, which had implicated the Earl of Bothwell. A rash of arrests took place across the east of the county in the summer of that year. 'Many there were burnt' say the official records, 'namely one at Roughead, and Cuthbert Hume's mother at Dunse, the parson of Dunse's wife; and sundry of Eyemouth and Coldingham; near a dozen or more and many fugitives.'

These unfortunates were stripped and attacked and throttled, or 'worriet', until they were dead, or at least appeared to be dead. Their corpses were trussed to pyres and burnt in front of the entire community. A conveyer belt of ministers preached continuous sermons, intoning the wrath of God on the frightened and traumatised people.

The uncovering of a witch says much about the developing due process of law. Where in the past anyone suspected of wrongdoing or malice might have been simply seized and killed, the more enlightened government of Scotland now demanded evidence. The accused was required to appear either at the Court of Justiciary in Edinburgh, or before commissions of local gentry and their representatives, themselves appointed by the Privy Council. The acquittal rate for the former, at about fifty per cent, was considered high. That for local trials, which most suspects could expect to face, was substantially lower.

The commissions questioned witnesses, examined any written evidence, took into account the opinion of the minister and often used the services of a witch-pricker. It was widely believed that pacts with the Devil were consummated with the individual being nipped. This area of skin was rendered insensitive to pain and would not bleed even when lanced. It was all nonsense of course, but it fostered a whole new profession of charlatans. Witch-prickers who, like modern day acupuncturists, had learned where to stab their pins without drawing blood or causing pain, travelled Scotland offering their services at trial. Sometimes the accused, confident of their innocence, demanded to be pricked.

Of course, existence of a 'mark' was only one element of evidence. Confessions were also required, and these might involve prolonged tortures. Sleep deprivation over many days and even weeks was the most popular method, but inquisitors were just as ready to try extreme physical abuse involving thumbscrews, the rack and the boot.

The Berwickshire trials of 1594 foreshadowed a century of dread. Burnings moreover did not stop the accusations. If anything they encouraged them. In 1606 a married Eyemouth woman called Issobel Falcouner petitioned the Privy Council to halt proceedings against her on the grounds that the Sheriff-Depute of Berwickshire and others appointed to the case were 'not fit persons for the trial of so high a crime.' When the indictment was ruled in order, Issobel claimed that she was pregnant, and that as the child should not perish for the alleged sins of the mother, no action could be taken until the baby was born. The authorities waited a long time for the delivery. Luckily for Issobel, who was obviously not with child, other matters had diverted attention: whispers of treason and the trial of a traitor.

George Sprott was a notable figure in the village. He was the parish schoolmaster and also worked as a lawyer for Logan of Restalrig, whose estates included Gunsgreen on the southern shore of the River Eye. In 1600 the ambitious Logan was caught up with the Earl of Gowrie in an audacious bid to capture and possibly even murder James VI. The attempt, which involved the luring of the King to Gowrie's home on the pretext of meeting a mysterious stranger who had a horde of gold, failed. Gowrie and his co-conspirators were executed and their lands and titles declared forfeit. Logan, who had remained throughout at his stronghold of Fastcastle, was fortunately never uncovered as one of the plotters. But George Sprott knew of his involvement. In the year before the attempted coup the lawyer over-heard details of the conspiracy. Logan's servant Bour, who could not read, also showed Sprott a file of incriminating letters and even allowed the Eyemouth man to take them away. If it was money Sprott was after he settled readily and at a cheap price. In the aftermath of the plot he confronted Logan and agreed to keep silent for a single payment of just £12 Scots. But Sprott did not hand over the letters and neither did he destroy them. Perhaps they made him feel important, and perhaps he sometimes brought them out to show his associates in their drunken cups.

The laird of Fastcastle and Gunsgreen died from natural causes in 1606 and the truth of the Gowrie Conspiracy ought to have been buried with him. But Sprott liked to act the big man and brag of his own importance. Two years after Logan had been laid to rest this blethering went too far. The Earl of Dunbar became aware of Sprott's stories and ordered his arrest and imprisonment. The petrified lawyer subsequently faced torture by the 'boot'. His feet were tied down in two tight wooden shoes and as the questions were fired at him so pegs were hammered down mangling Sprott's muscle and bone into a bloody pulp. It was not long before he squealed a confession. On the strength of this the body of the long dead Logan was exhumed and tried for high treason. The laird's decomposed corpse obviously had nothing to say, and the Logan lands and estates, including Gunsgreen, were forfeited to the Crown. The sad little man who had been the catalyst for all of this once more expressed contrition as he was brought to the gallows. On the scaffold, and in keeping with the spirit of the times, Sprott ascribed the whole conspiracy to the work of Satan and said he would give a signal of his penitence before he died. To the astonishment of the crowd he clapped his hands three times after his neck was stretched when the trapdoor opened.

Witches had been executed, a traitor hanged, the atmosphere in Eye-mouth was clammy with intrigue. The only surprise is that it took fifteen years before another trial was convened. In the intervening period the people knuckled down to work and to trade, though thoughts of satanism were never far away, especially when misfortune struck. When a boat sank, a barn burned down, a child died in infancy or even a horse went lame, events like these would later be recalled with impossible accuracy to damn those singled out as bad luck. Friendless. Bewitched.

Issobel Falcouner's time eventually came. In 1624 Issobel and her spouse Patrick Sinclair along with Barbara Flint and her husband Archibald Liddell, 'long suspect of being witcheis and sorcerans' were thrown into the common pit, which was all Eyemouth had for miscreants. There they waited until a local commission appointed by the Privy Council arrived. The evidence against Issobel in particular was powerful.

> She most subbtilie and fasllie alledget and confidantle and impudently affirmed that sho wes with chyld, and upon the false informatioun procured ane warrant from our Councaill for continency of hir tryall till she wer delyverit of her birthe; quhille as yitt now after money yearies is not done and meanwhile she continewis in heir devilishe practices

Liddell and Flint were spared, but their 'guilt by association' ensured that the next commission would come hunting for them. There was no escape this time for Issobel Falcouner, or indeed for her husband Patrick Sinclair. They were taken from the pit to the place of their trial, and thence to the beach where the pyres awaited and the people stood, there to be throttled at the stake, their lifeless bodies burned with the aid of boat-pitch. Or perhaps the executioners botched the job. Did Issobel and Patrick revive when the flames began to lap at their legs, melting the flesh from their bone and popping their eyes from their sockets? For the peasants forced to watch, it was a horrible spectacle. The burning human tissue gave a stench, which hung low and heavy in the air. A smell to remind the people of the devil, and of their obligations to the laird, the King and the Godly Reformation. When the fire died, the ashes of the devil worshippers were scattered into the pool that dragged the waters from the edge of Fort Point deep into the black North Sea.

The 1624 executions foreshadowed a prolonged period of madness with the Merse central to some of the worst excesses of witchhunt seen in Scotland. Significantly the bulk of the Eyemouth arrests took place after John Home, a relative of the laird, was installed as Eyemouth minister in 1627. Home the cleric supplied the evidence that Home the Lord acted upon.

Throughout late 1628 and early 1629 suspects from Eyemouth, Ayton and Coldingham were dragged to the pit to await the arrival of a commission. This took some time to organise, as permission had first to be sought from the Privy Council in Edinburgh. Eventually, on 20 January 1629 Sir Patrick

Home of Ayton, John Home of Rentoun and Alexander Lauder of Guns-green were given authorisation to preside over the trial. Yet even before this Commission had arrived at the coast; even before it had been legally assigned, the fervour of the hunt had gripped Eyemouth. If a fate worse than being torched can be imagined, it was visited on one unfortunate woman.

Marion Hardie, was, like Issobel Falconer and Barbara Flint, a married woman. In late 1628 she was denounced to the minister as a witch and duly thrown into the pit. But charges were flying thick and fast in Eyemouth, and there was a deep fear that Marion Hardie would blurt out names of her accomplices to the commission when it eventually arrived. A crowd, including James Wilson, perhaps a relative of the two Wilson sisters who had been much whispered against, moved angrily along the street towards the pit, the day *before* the Privy Council was due to meet. Their torches shone over the dark hole, where Marion cowered. The guard could not prevent what happened next, and, for fear of his own life, Duncan Kendla joined in the savagery. The prisoner was dragged up, screaming and howling for mercy, and literally torn limb from limb. Her son, John Trinche, later petitioned the Privy Council to take action against those who had murdered his mother. His description of the events of 19 January 1629 is chilling. The crowd

> Went to the Pitt and aganis the compleanor putt violent hands on her
> person, band her armes with towes, and so threw the same about that they
> disjoynted and mutilat her armes, and made the sinews to loyp assunder,
> and therefarter with their haill force drew ane great tow about her waist,
> kuist her on her backe, and with their knees they birsed, bruised and punsed
> her so that she was not able to stirre, strake the heid of ane speir threw her
> left foote, to the effusion of her blood in great quantitie and perill of her
> lyffe, wherethrow she lay bedfast in great pain and dolour a long time
> thereafter.

This barbarism is hard to understand without an appreciation of the clawing fear that everyone felt. In the presence of their Lords, Marion might accuse others. She had to be silenced. Perhaps the mob simply intended to warn her, to convince her to keep silent; perhaps the woman said something that indicated she might start blabbing. Whatever the reason, the perpetrators of her murder received no punishment. That in itself suggested they had done good and godly work. But the lynching wasn't the end of the matter. The commission was riding to the village, with a train of armed soldiers. The trials had not yet begun. Scenes that would become sickeningly familiar were played out in the Street and on the beach. Exhaustive testimony over a period of days damned the suspects to hell-fire. Throughout it all a gaggle of ministers, spearheaded by the black-cloaked figure of John Home, reminded the people of their sins and of the presence of Satan.

There was unfinished business in the first session, which convened in March 1629. Barbara Flint and Archibald Liddell who had been released three years earlier were arrested once again. Others who were equally easy targets were bound along with them. Christian Wilsoune, Jennet Williamson and Margaret Andersoun, known as 'deif Meg', whose only crime may have been her disability. Further accusations, denunciations and confessions followed, encouraged no doubt by the preaching of Home. The Commission stayed put and continued to take evidence through the spring and into the summer. In July Margaret Loche was damned; in August it was the turn of Helen Hudie, a spinster from Coldingham; in September justice was meted out to David Nisbet from Coldingham, Maraget Belleny from Ayton, and Agnes Falconer and Janet Liddle of Eyemouth (surely relatives of Issobel Falcouner and Archibald Liddell). At some point during the year Alison and Agnes Wilson were also burned to death on the beach. These poor individuals had nobody to speak up for them. They were the vulnerable, the friendless, and the poor, the expendable detritus.

The Berwickshire coast was now a place of dread, with the ministers both feared for their power and looked to for protection against the devil and against those who would make false accusations. If witches had been found in numbers in 1629 it was logical to assume that others walked amongst them still. Like the sand which built up at the harbour bar, deceptively innocuous, yet ultimately disastrous to ships, so the gossip which took place in the village added layer upon layer to the tales of evil within their midst. The bad harvests and famines that characterise this period also had an effect. The depression, the want and hunger, the misery of the age was the Devil's doing.

The Commission returned to Berwickshire in 1630 and again in 1631. There was at least one burning and probably many more. John Neil was found guilty of murdering Sir George Home of Manderston by placing an enchanted dead foal in his stables, which brought a fatal disease upon the laird. One of the apparently relevant details in the subsequent trial was Neil's nationality. Who would defend an Englishman, especially one accused of killing a powerful member of the Home clan? Neil was convicted of the killing, and of consulting warlocks on Coldingham Law. The records of the time are almost nonchalant. 'The jury found the usual verdict and the usual sentence was pronounced by the Court.' John Neil was executed at Lamberton, a stone's throw from England.

There was little respite from the witch-hunt in the early 1630s. Accusations against those who had been acquitted in previous trials continued to be levelled, and fresh charges were made against two women in particular – Issobel Sinclair and Elizabeth Bathgate. The latter was married to Alexander Pae, a prosperous maltman who sometimes loaned money to his fellow villagers. Elizabeth Bathgate, perhaps from a haughty sense of her own importance or perhaps to protect the family from her husband's profligacy, regularly intervened to prevent the transactions. In another age Pae would have been mocked as a henpecked weakling, his wife as an overpowering snob. In a time of witch scares, when money was scarce, Elizabeth Bathgate was an all too easy target for the poor and the slighted. The rationale behind the whisperings against Isobel Sinclair is unclear. There probably wasn't one.

Both women were arrested and imprisoned pending the arrival of another Commission. At least now there was a jail rather than a pit in the village, and that's where Issobel Sinclair would spend her final days. Elizabeth Bathgate was removed to the tollbooth at Duns and then on to Edinburgh, possibly through fear of another lynching had she remained in Eyemouth. Alexander Pae complained bitterly that there was no case to answer and that the costs of keeping his wife in prison – which he had to bear – were beyond even his means. But being in Edinburgh saved Elizabeth's life. As she sat in a dungeon in the capital her fellow suspect was brought to trial, adjudged guilty and swiftly dispatched in the usual, monstrous way. Issobel Sinclair was burned in March 1634.

Delirium spread and the minister was avalanched with yet more denunciations. Elizabeth Bathgate was summoned back to Eyemouth and a further four women and two men were arrested on the strength of village gossip. The horror of Issobel Sinclair's fate was too much for William Mearns. After delivering a forced confession, Mearns managed to slip away from his captors. He made his way up to Fort Point and out towards the inlet of Killiedraughts where he wrapped a length of rope across the bough of a tree, strung a noose around his neck and cheated the Commission of at least one burning. The memory of Mearns' suicide, though neither his name nor sex, was handed down through the generations. The men who looked out forlornly from the cliffs in the sorrow of October 1881 worried that they too would be touched by the uncleansed evil of a hanged witch.

Mearns' action sealed the fate of the others. He had 'put hands on himself at the devil's instigation'. The subsequent trial was organised with some speed. Elizabeth Bathgate was still the prime suspect when she appeared in front of the Commission in June 1634. Now, though, she was flanked by four co-accused – Jannet Williamson, Alison Wilson and Patrick Smith from

Eyemouth and Margaret Belleny from Ayton. Belleny was another who had escaped a previous encounter with the Commission, having been acquitted in 1629.

The eighteen counts levelled against Elizabeth Bathgate show how the stories of her accusers overlapped and led to their own incrimination. William Mearns had been insistent in the evidence he gave before his suicide that 'the pannel [accused] was not sonsie [wholesome] in regard she had great sorcery with Patrick Smith a notorious warlock'. Bathgate had been seen by two men late at night, 'standing bare legged in her sark-vallie-coat [petticoat], conferring with the Devil'. Mearns said that one of the men took fright and said 'let her alone, she is called not lucky'. Margaret Belleny's evidence was even more sensational. She told the commission that, 'the pannel was a sicker [certain] witch' and added, under item fifteen that Bathgate

Had a horseshoe in a secret part of her door, which she received from the Devil to make all her affairs within her house to prosper, and that the pannel and other witches held a meeting with the Devil; and also the pannel confessed several times that it was a world's wonder if Jennet Williamson were a witch, that the pannel herself was not a witch also seeing they had much private dealing together which few knew but her self. And so it is that the said Jennet Williamson confessed herself to be a witch, and therefore the pannel must be conscious to herself that she is also a witch.

Wild statements poured out creating a web that could not be untangled. They were all caught, all guilty by their own utterances. They had 'met upon the shore of Eyemouth under night and cruelly murdered David Hynd, who was watching the boats under night during the herring drove, for fear he should have uncovered their unlawful meeting'. They then conspired to bring forth spirits to sink George Huldie's ship.

While the other suspects foundered at their trial under the weight of their own words, Elizabeth Bathgate, perhaps because her relative wealth ensured that she had legal representation, was somewhat remarkably found not guilty. As she walked away with her acquittal, those who were guilty were pinioned, worriet and then bound to a series of stakes which were flamed.

There would be no further trials on the coast until the late 1640s. The minds of the gentry who sat in judgement were on other matters. Scotland was drifting towards war with the King.

The blunt, if not totally blundering policies of Charles I pushed men in power, in both Scotland and England to a point of exasperation. The King's actions, especially the 1625 Act of Revocation sounded warning bells amongst the noblemen. Though these grants were all restored, the impression of a drive towards absolute monarchy was indelibly stamped. Nor was the Kirk immune. Charles pushed through reform that suggested a union of the churches in all of his kingdoms, again threatening the hegemony of the established order. Finally and perhaps paradoxically, given the anger expressed at his meddling, the nobles sulked that the King of Scots was now distant and inaccessible. The result was that by 1637 there was something approaching a nationalist revolt in Scotland that spoke under the camouflage of religion and which found expression in the National Covenant.

Sir David Home of Wedderburn, Superior of Eyemouth on the death of his father, represented Berwickshire in the Scots Parliament at various points between 1621 and 1650, but was more of a soldier than a politician. He served with the army in France in 1627 and took a stand when opposition to Charles I spilled over on to the field of battle. Home took up arms for the Covenant and in 1639 raised a regiment from his native Merse. Four years later he was sent to Ireland where he spent £1,200 of his own money on supplies and equipment for the army. This was repaid three times over by Parliament in 1649, and Home was also rewarded with a commission as a colonel in the Regiment of Foot. In spite of this the Wedderburn treasury, drained in the service of James VI, and disrupted by the Wars of the Covenant, was threadbare and vulnerable.

By the late 1640s the war had gone through many guises, and Charles had lost the crown. Regardless of the late intervention of a Scottish army on his behalf he would also lose his head. The King promised to introduce Presbyterianism into England as the price of an 'engagement' treaty with the Scots. It was a vacuous pledge that was never tested. In 1648 a combined Royalist and Scottish force was routed at Preston and Charles finally taken into custody by the Roundheads.

The defeat of the Army of the Covenant propelled Scotland towards a second Reformation. A coup placed government in the hands of the extremist Kirk party, which tasked itself with cleansing society of all of its ills, including the sins of the nobles. It was one of the few periods in history when lords were called to public account for crimes like adultery. And while the Church of Scotland was renewed, the civil authorities likewise made a dash for the moral high ground by issuing several hundred local commissions, mostly in Lothian and the Merse, to root out witchcraft 'which daily increaseth in this land'.

Instability, war, civil unrest and lords who had momentarily lost control; conditions were once more ripe for the witch-hunt, and in Eyemouth another six women were pulled to account. As in 1629 and 1634, a mania of naming others developed. Central in the evidence which was gathered is this account given by Helen Tailyear to the Rev Samuel Douglas.

She confessed these particulars, viz First at Candlemass bygan two years shee cam into Isobell Broun's hous quher the devil was sitting in the liknes of a gentillman at the tabill drinking with Isobell Broun who took hir in [his] airmes ... and layd his hand upon hir head and said 'yea sall be ane of myn so long as yea live' ... She [also] declaris that shee was at ane meeting with Issobel Broun, Alison Cairns, Margarit Dobson and Beatrix Young, and that thai all went along to William Burnitt's hous, he lying seik, and that coming to the hous, Margaret Dobson was in the likeness of ane black hen and went in at the chimley heid, and Beatrix Young in the likeness of ane little foal, and that hir selff was in the liknes of ane little quhelp; Isobell Brounn was in her own likeness with a long taild courtshchew upon her heid, and Alisson Cairns was in her owen likeness.

All of the women, including Helen Tailyear were brought to trial. It was rare for local commissions to send word of the fate of the accused to the authorities in Edinburgh. What was the point and who would pay the cost of a rider? In this instance, though, there is a separate source that confirms the six were indeed executed. It adds weight to the view that unless an acquittal is recorded, those charged with witchcraft were all almost always killed.

The Eyemouth burnings took place in the high summer of 1649, five months after the King's beheading by the English Parliamentarians. This regicide caused deep shock and outrage in Scotland, and Charles's son was swiftly proclaimed Charles II of Scots. Cromwell was outraged. Like a gallery of English generals before him, the Lord Protector readied an invasion force to bring the Scots to heel in a manner not achieved since the days of Edward I. This would be no plundering raid, or dash to battle. Cromwell intended complete occupation and forced union. His tactics were different from those of Somerset in the 1540s. They were also more successful.

In August 1650, just before the final march to meet the Army of the Covenant, Cromwell and a small company of cavalry raided across the Berwickshire headlands. They fed along the cliffs and made their way down to the shore at Eyemouth. The village was deserted. Few strayed from their houses; most were probably convinced they were to be slaughtered and their homes torched. How many of the men had already been seized to serve in the Scots army is unclear, but some would certainly have been forced into Home's regiment. Cromwell guided his men down on the beach and, like Somerset, immediately appreciated the military significance of the bay. There was no time to consider rebuilding the demolished ramparts on the point, but two tower houses were thrown up and garrisoned on the southern shore of Gunsgreen, one overlooking the harbour, the other with guns trained seaward.

The English host then pushed up towards Dunbar, where the Ayatollahs had been purging the ungodly from their army. Unfortunately for the Scots, those who were considered most tainted were the experienced soldiers who at some point in the preceding years had fought on the wrong side. Given the confusion of the Civil War that charge could be levelled at just about anybody.

Regardless of Cromwell's strategic brilliance, the victory he gained on 3 September 1650 was handed to him by military incompetence, abetted by interference from Kirk zealots. The Godly host, which rallied to the call of the Covenant, was starved in advance of the battle, and led to disaster when the force abandoned its tactically secure upland position. Amongst the 3,000 slain were Sir David of Wedderburn, his eldest son George, and many of their clan. It was a curious thing, but at Flodden, 137 years before, the Laird and his eldest son had also fallen, and they too were called David and George. More than 10,000 were taken prisoner after the battle. These were from the feudal levies; ordinary men from towns and villages across the nation, including Home's regiment from the Merse. The fate of these captives would be dire. They were marched south to Berwick, and then on to Newcastle or Chester and Liverpool. Of those who survived the journey, some were pressed into service in the army and the rest transported into slavery in the colonies. In common slang, they were 'Barbadoed'. Perhaps more than a fifth died before they reached the embarkation points.

After Dunbar, the Lordship of Wedderburn passed to the 8th Laird's grandson George, a nine-year-old child. Family affairs for the duration of the minority were vested in the hands of his mother, and more particularly of his uncle, John of Rentoune.

Sir David had been a reasonably tolerant overlord, though he lacked the nurturing benevolence of his own father. John of Rentoune was a throwback to the rapacious Alexander Home of the 1570s and 1580s. In truth Rentoune was merely acting in the best interests of the family in trying to extract all that he could from the estates. That was not how the tenants viewed matters. In 1655 those in Eyemouth staged a minor revolt, and refused to pay certain dues that had been demanded. Rentoune was uncompromising in his response, dispatching his son Harrie Home 'and a party of men to break up John Currie his seller to take syze violentlie and contrary to the peace'.

That raid coincided with an attempt by the new Cromwellian regime to make Scotland pay for the cost of occupation. From March 1654 the Scots were incorporated into 'ane Commonwealth with England', with all policy obviously dictated by Westminster. Traditional trading links with the Continent were effectively closed, at least in law, and Cromwell dispatched one of his most experienced customs commissioners north of the border. Thomas Tucker was shocked by what he uncovered. There seemed to be no effective system in operation at all, so he quickly moved to create one. Eight centres were established around the coast, with the lynchpin at Leith. Smaller havens were also provided with their own officials who were given substantial powers, which even eclipsed those of the feudal superiors.

Tucker found affairs in Eyemouth more wretched and venal than almost anywhere else. Smuggling, which is normally associated with the eighteenth century, had been part of the stock-in-trade of the borders from at least the time of the victualling Scots. There might be Union with England, but the border was still used as an administrative demarcation point, to the great advantage of Eyemouth. 'The distance of it from the first head-port of Scotland [Leith]' wrote Tucker, ' and the vicinity of it to the last of England, whose officers had noe power there, gave an occasion of much deceipt.'

Tucker's men may have caused annoyance, but trade at the port evidently boomed during the Interregnum. The little harbour and bay could scarcely cope with the traffic, and in times of storm, when wind-blown vessels came past the Hurkurs, the lack of adequate accommodation was plain to see. In 1660, after the fall of the Cromwellian regime, the tradesmen of Eyemouth addressed their grievances to the Scottish Admiralty. 'It is knoune to many both strangers and others within the land hou useful this port hathe been for saftie of ships and barges from stormes of weather and from men of ware'.

One reason for this direct approach to the Admiralty rather than to the laird or the superior was confusion over who actually owned the estate of Eyemouth. The Homes were rewarded for their adherence to the Stewarts when Charles II returned to the throne in 1660. John of Rentoune was knighted and was made Lord Justice Clerk while others had their lands and titles restored. George Home of Wedderburn, no longer a minor, consolidated the family holdings, but this did not include the lands of Eyemouth. These had been lost when the debts incurred by his grandfather when Comptroller of the Royal Household were at last called in.

Creditors of the family debt had been kept at bay for more than fifty years. Merchants often found as much profit could be made from money-lending to the landed classes as trade itself. But if the time of James VI had been characterised by a credit boom, that of the Protectorate and the Restoration became the age of the debt collector. Lending money was a business fraught with risks, especially in the second half of the seventeenth century, and, with the new laird of Wedderburn a young boy, the vultures circled. The family owed the remarkable sum of £127,000 sterling, most of which had been incurred on behalf of the Royal Household. A Republican

Protectorate was of course unlikely to stand credit for the extravagancies of the Stewarts and those who were owed most by the Homes foreclosed. The largest creditor, an Edinburgh merchant and innkeeper called Ninian Lewis, was due around 50,000 merks.* The only way in which to pay him was by liquidating or assigning some of the clan assets. The family estate on the Berwickshire coast was subsequently handed over, though Lewis quickly sold on the village, along with 'the lands, tiends, fishings and others' to Robert Dundas. He, likewise, only held it for a short time before, in turn, disposing of the place to Sir Lawrence Scott. For two decades after the Battle of Dunbar ownership of Eyemouth was in limbo. But this did not prevent the last and most dramatic outbreak of witch-hunt in the village.

Lairds and Lords found their powers restored when Charles II returned to pick up the tarnished crown of the Stewarts. Many were anxious to flex their muscles in the localities and show the people that the legitimate elite had returned. What better way to instill discipline and fear than through the witch-hunt? Between 1660–1662 more than six hunded commissions were authorised in Scotland and at least three hundred people were executed, often in bonfires that sparked side by side.

There were two main trials in Berwickshire, one in November 1661 and the other early in the following year. The same local commission presided over both, and the gap can probably be explained by a need to gather more statements. Colonel John Home of Prenderguist took the lead, but for the first time the commission also included merchants and traders. Men like John Curry who had been mentioned in the syze dues revolt of 1655, and the Robison or Robertson brothers, whose family would come to own large chunks of the southern shore of the River Eye. In the first trial evidence was entered against 'Barbara Hood and Helen Belshes who have confessed the horrid crime of withcraft in entering into paction with the Devil, renouncing their baptism and other wayes'. That was enough to consign them to the fires. But these executions once again only served to prompt further stories and recriminations. The commission's work was not done. It stayed put.

In early 1662 ten Berwickshire women, all of them single, came to trial. All were damned by the words of others or even by their own confessions. 'They have confest themselves to be guilty of witchcraft by entering into paction with the Devil'. Named from Eyemouth were Margaret Johnson, Elspeth Bell, Mareon Burnett, Margaret Robison and Helen Wight. A trio

---

* A merk was worth two-thirds of a Scots pound. In turn twelve Scots pounds was the equivalent of one pound sterling. This debt, therefore, was worth about £2,750 sterling, a substantial amount for the period.

from Ayton – Isobell Lawson, Janet Lawson and Elspeth Hay, joined them. To these were added Bessie Profit and Elspeth Blyth from Coldingham and Margaret Edington, from the inland parish of Foulden.

Were they all declared guilty one after another and then immediately throttled and taken to be burned at the stake? Or was the agony played out, with each condemned, but made to wait until the destiny of the entire group was announced, then herded like stricken beasts to the place of execution? To the spot where the crowds were waiting, where torches already smoked in the gloom? How did these women die?

The 1662 hunt was the last major trial in Berwickshire, though a handful of burnings would take place at the very end of the century and one in the early 1700s. Even the upheavals occasioned by the Glorious Revolution of 1688–89 brought few demands for witch trials. That part of Scotland's inglorious past was all but over.

A new start for Eyemouth was promised when Sir Laurence Scott bought the estate on 17 November 1670. Though Scott had still to defer to the Wedderburns, since under Scots Law they retained the feudal superiority, he showed a genuine regard for the village and a determination to make things happen. This was a refreshing change from the uncertainties of the immediate past, and the hard hand of John of Rentoune.

The new laird's arrival also coincided with an important piece of legislation. In 1672 the Scots Parliament acknowledged the right of all communities, and not just the Royal Burghs, to trade legally with the Continent. It was an acceptance of practices which in Eyemouth and elsewhere had been going on for many years, and is evidence of the growing influence of the mercantile class.

The Act was a considerable encouragement to small settlements like Eyemouth and provided a spur to further investment. But major schemes were often beyond the means of small burghs. In 1675, drawing on already well established arguments, Sir Laurence forwarded a petition to the Privy Council requesting help in improving harbour facilities for the benefit of the whole of the east coast. Authority was duly given for a collection to be taken at Kirk doors across the land with the money raised sent to a local merchant called William Nisbet. Further contributions were authorised in the early 1700s, and as late as 1753 the General Assembly of the Church of Scotland directed that a nationwide collection should be made for the harbour at Eyemouth.

The seventeenth century had started with great hope. There was peace with England and a settled religious structure. Life was never easy, but with an end to the perpetual war footing some prosperity began to trickle down to all levels of society.

But it was all an illusion. The seventeenth century in reality brought death to the innocent and horror to all. It was an age of witch-hunt, of religious persecution, of war for the King, for the Kirk, for the King and the Kirk, for the Kirk against the King, the Kirk against the ungodly, the Kirk against the English. It didn't matter too much to the common folk, who were the fodder brought out for battlefield slaughter, or the convenient victims thrown onto the witch-fires.

Nor did things seem any better as the century neared its end, though at least the Merse escaped the religious wars which characterised the age as 'The Killing Times'. Charles II gave little thought to his Northern Kingdom. It was a convenient place to send his haughty Roman Catholic brother, James, Duke of York. York came north in 1679 and again in 1680–82, when he established the first Royal Court in Edinburgh for eighty years. London's relief was Scotland's burden. Though many of his policies were undoubtedly well intentioned, their presentation and his own religious proclivities were a disaster.

York had also brought with him his own favourites, including a young courtier whose sister was the King's mistress. John Churchill was already an able soldier and would in time become one of the most famous commanders Europe has ever seen. Stunning victories followed his progress across the Continent, culminating in the strategic mastery of Blenheim in 1704, by which time Churchill had amassed a number of titles and was known to all as the Duke of Marlborough. However, his very first step towards the peerage came in Scotland. For his service during their time there, James of York invested Churchill as Baron of Eyemouth.

Chapter Three

Jacobites and Brethren

Frauds are being committed in Scotland ... particularly at Eyemouth ...
Make a strict rummage of all the cellars, warehouses and milns within your
district, particularly at Eyemouth

Letter from Commissioners of Excise, Edinburgh
to Dunbar Customs officer, 4 March 1755

The Duke of York, and with him the Baron of Eyemouth, returned to
London in 1682. Three years later on the death of his brother, York ascended
the throne as James VII and II. The reign did not last long. Within a further
three years came the nadir in the unhappy annals of the House of Stewart
when an angry London mob forced the King to flee the capital for exile in
France. Had James faced down the rabble, the crisis, on that occasion at
least, might well have been overcome.

The sudden and dramatic events of 1688–90 were bewildering to the Scots
who had taken no part in the effective deposition of the King. His successors,
William and Mary, were accepted by a Convention in Edinburgh, but like
all monarchs since 1603 they continued to live hundreds of miles away in
England. Jacobite agitators played the nationalist card, promoting the
credentials of the 'King over the Water' and parodying the famine-ridden
1690s as 'King William's lean years'.

At least the troubles of the age did not bring a return to wholesale
witch-hunts. The last documented persecution in Berwickshire was a relatively small affair, involving a trial in Coldingham in 1698. This was
prompted not through fear that Satan stalked the land, but because the
landed class was once more desperate to re-impose its will on the common
folk. Sir Alexander Home of Rentoune pressed for authority to lead a
Commission, lamenting the passing of the great days when his own father
'at one time burnt seven or eight witches.' Home got his wish and arrested
three spinsters. One of them, Jean Hart, managed to escape and was never
again seen or heard in Berwickshire. Under Rentoune's authority, the other
two were put to death.

Imposing harsh laws was one way of commanding respect and retaining
the established order of things. Another was to use the propaganda of the
pulpit. Eastern Berwickshire was an Episcopalian stronghold, and had been
ever since the Reformation. It was a place of dread for Presbyterians. As

far back as 1584 the Kirk divine Andrew Melville sweated as he passed St
Abb's Head and the lands of Alexander Home. 'We were in great feir, but
our Gude God gardit us, making a swek thick mist till arise' allowing the
vessel he sailed in to slip safely into Berwick.

The settlement of 1690 might have restored Presbyterianism in the
Church of Scotland, but Episcopalianism retained strong support across the
social spectrum, especially amongst the elite. With the backing, perhaps
urging, of Wedderburn, the Eyemouth minister had refused to pray, as all
were ordered to do, for William and Mary. David Stirling ought to have
been deprived of the living, but a *via media* was agreed whereby a more
compliant man was drafted in though Stirling was allowed to stay and share
the living. James Ramsay, the new appointee of the crown, was made all
too aware of the feelings of his flock from the chilly induction service he
went through. This was held not in the Kirk but in the kirkyard, the Homes,
for effect, having ordered the church doors to be barred against him. Similar
scenes were common in other parts of the Merse. Only two of the fourteen
ministers in the Presbytery of Chirnside were left untouched by the Glorious
Revolution.

James Ramsay had obvious trouble in corralling his congregation. He
also had money problems. The stipend he was obliged to share with David
Stirling until the latter's death in 1699 was barely enough for one man.
Apart from a small increase granted in 1676, it was really no greater than
that attained by John Home in the 1620s. As the number of boats had
remained at five, the tithe of fish, first mentioned for the reformed Kirk in
1628, was also stuck at £100 Scots. For all his problems though, life for
Ramsay was surely not as bad as that endured by the minister imposed on
nearby Coldingham. Such was the outrage felt by parishioners that for
many years he was obliged to take a pair of loaded pistols into the pulpit
with him, which he placed menacingly on either side of his open bible, in
full view of the recalcitrant flock.

Episcopal meetings continued to be held, even in open-air conventicles.
These were not just an expression of religious defiance. They amounted to
a reservoir of political discontent which Jacobite agitators readily exploited.
Away with the Hanoverian German 'lairdie', away with the disgrace of
incorporated union, away with the forced implementation of Presbyterianism in the Kirk. The image of Jacobitism as a movement of wild Highlanders
in tartan sweeping through the country with claymore and targe, however
distorted, might be applied to the Rising of 1745. That of 1715 was more
national and more nationalistic.

The Homes, though increasingly more interested in the profit their lands
could generate than the fighting men it might sustain, remained a major

martial clan. Like other nobles they fretted on what to do should the Pretender ever return to British shores. Past experience of support for the Stewarts was not encouraging. They had lost heavily at Flodden; been amongst the slaughter at Pinkie; they had backed the loser at Langside; had nearly been destroyed at Dunbar and, of course, the family finances had been all but ruined in the service of James VI and I. But the Wedderburn Homes still felt a loyalty, a fealty to the ancient royal house.

Nostalgic yearnings of this kind were given a practical edge when the promised economic benefits of union failed to materialise. Taxes were increased and foreign trade with Scotland's traditional partners virtually banned. Even peripheral industries like fishing, marginal at the best of times, had to bear the cost of a hike in salt duties. The conditions were ripe for revolt and in 1715 the Homes responded to the raising of the Earl of Mar's standard. This would be the final rallying call of the Merse mosstroopers. George of Wedderburn took with him many of his extended circle including James Home of Ayton Castle and John Winram, Master of Eyemouth.

His father, George Winram had been a Lieutenant Colonel in the Regiment of Foot Guards, established by the then Duke of York in 1681. He might well have rubbed shoulders with James and his favourites, including John Churchill. In 1688 Winram married the daughter of the laird of Eyemouth, Sir Laurence Scott. Within a few months of the wedding, the knight was dead and Colonel George the new laird in right of his wife. It is a curious thing but under Scots law there is no need for a connection between ownership of the land, allocation of title or exercise of feudal superiority. In Eyemouth the Homes of Wedderburn were the overlords, Churchill had the right to the title, but the laird of the estate was Winram.

When news of the Jacobite rising reached the coast Colonel George prudently stayed at home. His eldest son, though, spurred his horse to the gallop, and with a little band of men, raced to join up with the Homes. The border army wandered into northern England where they expected substantial support from English Jacobites. Like the followers of the Bonnie Prince thirty years later all they found was hostility and opposing troops. Home and the Borderers engaged a government force at Preston in November 1715. In some hard street fighting the Scots initially appeared to have the upper hand, but on the second day of the battle they lost heart and fragmented. Hundreds were taken prisoner. John Winram was captured and marched south to a London jail along with George Home, his brother Francis and his son George.

Whatever fate was to be meted out to the rest of the rebels, Wedderburn clearly expected better treatment. He was astonished when at his trail in

London he was declared a traitor and along with his brother Francis and John Winram of Eyemouth, was condemned to hang. After a time in jail, these sentences were lifted. But relief at having their necks saved was transitory. They were to be sold into slavery and transported, like the Covenanters of 1650, to the American colonies. Wedderburn managed to obtain a pardon and Winram was also spared exile and slavery, though at a considerable financial cost. As his father, the laird, had not been 'out' the estate was not forfeited, but dalliance with the rebels would eventually ruin the Winrams.

Nothing could be done for George Home's brother, at least initially. Francis Home was marched to Liverpool and shipped off to Virginia. Unlike the common soldiers, however, he had a guardian angel in the shape of his distant cousin the Rev Ninian Home of Sproutston, an episcopal priest and avowed Jacobite. The Wedderburns had helped finance Ninian's university education and he had long cherished a desire to fuse the two branches of the family together. In the aftermath of Preston he repaid the kindness of his kin. Ninian helped save the Wedderburn lands by buying up all the family debts. When matters settled down the minister of Sproutston handed everything under entail back to George Home, though under certain financial obligations.

Francis had no inkling of what was going on, and it must have been a considerable relief, after a choppy crossing to the Chesapeake on the hulk _Elizabeth and Anne_, to be told that his freedom had already been purchased by Ninian in far off Berwickshire. Now unburdened from the dread prospect of slavery, Francis looked around and liked what he saw. He opted to stay and settle, and even encouraged others to emigrate – voluntarily in their cases.

It was a close-run thing for the Wedderburns, who would not rise again when Charles Edward Stewart called the clans to arms thirty years later. That was a relief for the common folk of Berwickshire who were spared forced service in the army and none of whom volunteered. How many had been forced out in 1715 never to return is impossible to gauge. When John Winram and his little band of followers heeded the call, others in Eyemouth took the opportunity to vent their anger at the established Church. The pulpit was vacant at the time, and the Kirk session books have not survived to tell us exactly what happened. They were, perhaps significantly, 'carried away by the violence of the times.' Those who did not fall at Preston either died on the forced march to the embarkation ports or were slammed into the slave ships.

The fishing trade, which had waxed and waned through the ages, began to show some signs of its future promise just as news of the failure of the

'15 filtered through. The government's action in imposing a salt tax in 1712 had depressed the industry. Six years later the state intervened in a much more positive fashion with the introduction of a bounty scheme on herring. Fishermen and traders would be paid a set amount to catch and cure fish. More importantly than this welcome action was the sudden appearance of millions of herring in the southern approaches to the Firth of Forth. Crews from as far away as Fife trailed the fish to Berwickshire for a short summer season. It lasted no more than two weeks in July and depended on the shoals surging towards rectangular nets, which were erected in the shallows of the bay. For six or seven years, though, this 'ground drave' put a little money into the pockets of the fisherfolk.

The industry impressed the writer and English government spy, Daniel Defoe, who arrived in the village in 1724 as part of his *Tour of the Whole Island of Great Britain*. Like Somerset and Cromwell before him, Defoe admired the fine, sweeping bay, and deepwater anchorages. He noted Eyemouth's Churchillian connections, though doubted if the great general had ever done anything to advance the place. 'For the town is at present, just what it always was, a good fishing town, and some fishing vessels belong to it; for such it is a good harbour, and little else.'

The prosperity of that time may have been transient, but in the year that Defoe strode the shore, the Eyemouth congregation was able to give generously to a relief fund set up to help the poor of a struggling colonial outpost called New York. A new minister, the Rev William Allan, who was also pleased at the additional fish teind coming his way, gathered in the money. The increase was not so much from the home fleet, stubbornly stuck at five boats, but from the dozens of visiting boats that came for the drave. From these he could take half teind, though he never managed to get anything close to that. The boats were supposed to give the other half to their home Kirk. But fish tithe was increasingly a rarity along the coast. If they did not pay at home, why should visiting fishermen give money to the Kirk at Eyemouth? This defiance stoked up the resentment of the local crews. The occupant of the Manse was no longer all-powerful, especially after the failure of the Jacobite rising. The old days when the minister's word was thought synonymous with that of God himself were past; fear of the witch-hunt a folk memory. The fishermen began to withhold their tithe money.

In a different part of the country they might have got away with it. Once fairly common in pre-Reformation Scotland, by the second quarter of the eighteenth century fish teind was exceptional. In those coastal parishes where it persisted, it was also changing in form. In Kilrenny on the Fife coast it had been commuted to a small fixed payment which for many years

had been leased out to a tacksman. The same was true in Leith and
Newhaven. Over on the west, at Ayr, fish teind had become the property
of the Society of Writers and was no longer an element of the parish living.
In other ports, such as Dunbar, it was subsumed into a harbour rate. Even
closer to home, three miles south at Burnmouth, the minister simply
stopped asking for payment from the solitary crew based in the hamlet. It
was not worth the trouble. To the north, the minister of Coldingham was
likewise entitled to a tithe from the village boats that beached at St Abbs,
but he had no real need of the additional income. Everywhere the story
was the same. Fish teind was dying out.

But not at Eyemouth. Even if the minister had wanted to get rid of it
he couldn't. The parish, artificially created in 1618, was compact with little
arable land to tithe. Taking into account all elements of the benefice, even
as late as 1764 the manse only drew in around £70 sterling a year, lower
than any other Berwickshire parish. In Ayton, to the south and west, the
stipend was about £115, whilst in Coldingham, to the immediate north, it
was more than £500.

William Allan could not stand back and allow the tithe strike to carry
on. But in resorting to law he estranged himself from his flock even further.
The support of the courts for the religious establishment was not surprising.
But scenes of poinding and the public auction of the chattels of fishermen
were not a great advert for the Christian goodness of the Church. Respect
for authority both civil and ecclesiastical hit a new low. Diddling the
minister out of his just dues became a way of life, as moral a crime as
could be found anywhere in Scotland.

In any case the fishing boom, and with it the migrant fleets, did not last
long. The herring stopped driving into the ground drave nets in 1725, and
would not return in massive numbers until the 1770s. Stranger boats sailed
elsewhere and the local crews were again forced to supplement their catches
by tilling the 'Fisher Lands' – runrigs on the margins of the beach. The
business of the sea became subsistence once more.

William Allan's son James, who succeeded to the Eyemouth charge in
1737, rarely exercised his right of tithing twenty pounds Scots or £1 13s. 4d.
sterling from each of the five fishing boats. To take that amount would
often, quite literally, have been to steal the milk from the bowls of the
bairns. For the whole thirty years he ministered in the village, James Allan
always disregarded at least a quarter of what he was due and for several
years took a good deal less.

James had been only two years old when his father had moved to
Eyemouth. He lived all his days there and knew nothing else. His only
sibling, Grace, married James Edgar, an Eyemouth merchant. In every sense

therefore the Allans had become an Eyemouth family, and the minister was patently aware of the problems the fish tithe brought. Yet even James Allan could not entirely give it up. When questioned by the Presbytery in 1756 he said that he 'Always teinded something under the stock to make the payment light; sometimes considerably lower, still to make it easier.' However, he was no soft touch. If the fishing folk abused the latitude Allan was prepared to give he hit them hard. 'Whenever controversy arose, and a poinding or process followed, he never abated of his highest demands.' Fish tithe, even in the worst season, when Allan was most lenient in his demands, was still worthwhile. It brought in about the same as the annual wages of a labourer; twice as much as that paid to a housemaid.

Allan's inconsistency, of sometimes demanding little, and other times rouping the very beds they slept in when the men refused his demands and burnt the bills, bred resentment, especially amongst the very poor. When they were starving James Allan still took something from their plates; when they had a little bit of good fortune, there was the 'black craw' pacing the pier, demanding his share. The spectre of the minister and his tallyman, peering seawards from the shore, noting in their little books who was landing and how well they were doing, entered folklore.

Rather sadly this good man could neither win the respect of the fishermen nor that of his fellow ministers in the Kirk. To the people he was a leech who cared more about teind money than soul saving; to the Church his lax approach to the benefice set a worrying precedent. But during Allan's time as minister there was more to Eyemouth than fishing – much more. The main business of the village was in trade, sometimes legal, sometimes not.

From at least the mid seventeenth century Lowland proprietors had been experimenting with their lands. The process gained momentum in the years after the Act of Union, with the open lands of the Tweed valley rapaciously eaten away by enclosure. New strains of seed and livestock were introduced, and sheep were turned out on to lands that used to support people. An exodus similar to that which would occur in the Highlands a century later took place. No widespread unrest pricked the conscience of the erstwhile clan chiefs, but the lives of hundreds if not thousands were just as radically turned upside down. These lowland clearances have been called a silent revolution – not because the tenants found the change easy, but because they had options.

The 'Age of Improvement' certainly paid dividends for the elite that now became gentlemen farmers. The annual rental value of land soared and commentators thrilled at the fortunes being made, especially in Berwick-shire. In five years the rental income from one estate rose from £500 to £1,200 while in another it went up from £500 to £1,500. Who could afford such vast increases? Certainly not the ordinary cottars. While they struggled on, or gave up and hiked to the towns, the lairds discussed how to improve their yields and how to get the produce to market.

In the 1740s a scheme to build a major commercial canal linking Kelso to Eyemouth was proposed by a company of Dutch engineers. As well as conveying corn to the coast, it would have allowed the movement of Tweed salmon and the wider inland distribution of Eyemouth haddock and herring. Serious discussions were held, with the engineers prepared to undertake the work in return for ten years' dues. The plan eventually foundered but it nonetheless put the imperative of better transport links firmly into the minds of the farmers. There were few roads in Scotland, and at least until the 1770s most were in a very poor state of repair. Seaports were generally the best, sometimes only, means of conveyance – and Berwickshire, where the heart of Scottish agricultural change beat fastest, at that time had but one accessible harbour. It was a rudimentary and ancient haven, too often crowded and dangerous. For the success of the corn trade, for the continued prosperity of the farming gentry in Berwickshire, Eyemouth harbour would have to be rebuilt. And there were plenty willing to contribute to the cost.

William Crowe, laird of Netherbyres, on the western approaches to the village, gave a lead. Described by contemporaries as 'a melancholy bachelor' he drew up a plan to construct a stone bullwark to protect the inner basin as a more practical alternative to the canal. As in the seventeenth century, help was sought from the Convention of Royal Burghs, which gave the application a sympathetic hearing when it met at Haddington in July 1750. However the farmers of Berwickshire met the bulk of the cost, which ran to more than two thousand pounds. A very large sum at the time. The work took three years to complete, with labourers carting stones that had once made up the old Fort down the brae to the quayside. Melancholy William Crowe died mid way through the construction, but a standing committee of 'resident Berwickshire gentlemen' continued the project. This body was also supposed to ensure that repairs and improvements were carried out as and when necessary.

The new port facilities were built for trade rather than the comfort of the fishermen, but the pier had obvious advantages to the fleet. James Allan encouraged the local men to be more adventurous and industrious. When the open lands of Eyemouth were enclosed in the 1760s he urged the now landless peasants to the sea. There, he said, was a new field to plough. No landlord to pay rent to and only a moderate teind to be given to their pastor – which had never been demanded in full. As with the Highland Clearances, work at the margins of the coast was seen as the salvation of a whole class of people. Allan felt he was living in a watershed. 'Fishing in

Scotland' he wrote 'is a child that needs nursing and discipline. The first to promote the thriving among other more propitious and spreading plants, the last to check a wildness that seems natural to it and without which the protection and encouragement of the public cannot be expected; yet from the low state of this still hopeful child, our bias ought to be the benign extreme'.

Evidence of a move towards that 'benign extreme' came in the halting actions of the Westminster government. After the final defeat of the Jacobites at Culloden Moor, and a general peace in Europe signalled by the 1748 Treaty of Aix-la-Chapelle, Britain moved to rebuild its navy. The Admiralty looked to the seaports and fishing towns for sailors, either as volunteers or as forced recruits. Dutch weakness at this time also provided an opportunity for the underdeveloped domestic fisheries to at last exploit the teeming North Sea shoals. A new government bounty was unveiled in 1750, with the aim of emulating the system of Dutch herring 'busses'. This subsidy would operate, in one guise or another, for the next eighty years. For the incentive to work, fairly obviously, the fish had to be plentiful and close enough to the shore. In the waters off Berwickshire, that was not the case. At least not until the late 1770s.

James Allan might have been a bit confused as to why his stipend seemed to be worth less as the years rolled on. Other ministers also felt the cold blast of rapidly rising prices and the matter was brought for consideration to the General Assembly of the Kirk. A whole series of Kirk acts from 1750 to the mid 1760s emphasised the need to protect and defend the way the national church was financed, especially the contributions, given willingly or otherwise, from ordinary folk. Allan was caught up in the argument. In 1756 an action reached the Court of Session in Edinburgh over an element in the Eyemouth living. It was a row not over fish tithe, but the victual stipend he was entitled to. A lengthy legal dispute established that because the minister of Eyemouth had taken a chalder of corn which had originally been part of another parish's living for more than forty years, it was his to possess for good.

The case may have been one element in the actions of the General Assembly which passed Acts in 1759, 1760 and 1762 forbidding any further reductions by ministers of their stipends without the express authority of local presbyteries. The main reason though was galloping inflation – that and the impact of changes taking place in some parts of the Lowlands. The enclosure movement led to a reappraisal of what ministers were paid, what ground they should hold and what teinds they were entitled to. By the time a start was made to this process in Eyemouth James Allan was already an old man.

The reason why Eyemouth was thirty years behind other parts of Berwickshire lay in the lack, once more, of a settled incumbent laird. The Winrams never recovered from their dalliance with Jacobitism and for years the estate was mired in debt. Eventually Henry Trotter of Mortonhall took it over and the Winrams, like Hardy's D'Urbervilles tumbled out of the lairdly class. Trotter began the late enclosure of the Eyemouth lands and Mr Allan was allotted a new glebe and had his stipend codified. Along with the victual and cash elements, it stipulated that 'The minister of Eyemouth is by decreet entitled to the vicarage teind and teinds of fish within the parish by old decreet, estimated at £100 Scots annually.'

James Allan went along with the process, and was probably content to see his rights put into black and white. It did not change his outlook. Exhortations from the General Assembly couldn't alter the poor state of fishing in the village. The minister did not pursue with due vigour every last ha'penny which he was due in fish teind. He even disputed the estimated annual amount that could be raised, saying that as he had always disregarded the first quarter, it was only £75 Scots, about six pounds ten shillings. In any case, Allan was too old for the battles, too wearied for the trouble and too settled to be bothered with the little additional silver that might come his way.

But it was commercial trade, not fishing, that was the making of Eyemouth. The stout little pier was completed at a vital time. Eyemouth offered a cheaper and often more accessible base for the export of vast quantities of corn now being produced in the enclosed lands of the Merse than Berwick-upon-Tweed. The village became *the* boomtown in Berwickshire. A digest of the county, written at the close of the eighteenth century, said that in some years more than 40,000 bolls of corn and meal passed through the place.

When it is considered that it took on average two days to carry four bolls of wheat from the West End of the county to the coast, at times the quayside at Eyemouth must have fairly hummed to the tune of commerce. It also sang a different song with a lilting free-trade air. It is in the 1750s, significantly after the completion of the harbour, that Eyemouth becomes an important, and for the authorities, brazenly open centre for smuggling:

4 March 1755. The Commissioners at London having transmitted to us an information of frauds being committed in Scotland and particularly about Eyemouth and the neighbourhood thereof by smuggling of tobacco and conveying of the same into England by the artful management of certificates from the port of importation. We direct you to take from your books an account of each merchant's credit for tobacco, tobacco snuff and tobacco

stalks and with the utmost diligence to make a strict rummage in all of the cellars, warehouses and milns within your district, particularly at Eyemouth.

Smuggling has been called the great growth industry in Scotland in the decades after 1707 and at times it would have seemed that there was almost as much liquid stored away in the cellars and stairwells, the ox bladders and water barrels, as washed through Eyemouth harbour. Duties, which had been relatively low, quadrupled in the reign of William and Mary, and continued to rise steeply after 1707. Malt was heavily taxed to bring Scotland into line with England, and the national drink of French claret was made prohibitively expensive.

Had the law been taken at its word small communities like Eyemouth might well have collapsed. Business therefore continued as it had done before the Union; the difference was that post 1707 it was often illegal. The other obvious change was its greater profitability. Smuggling in the post Union era did not come about because of a few wide-boy profiteers. It was conceived through necessity, nurtured by the loose policing of the coast and brought to precocious maturity by success. By the time concerted attempts were made to strike smuggling down, it had became core to many in the mercantile classes, and had all but taken over some of the nation's coastal creeks.

William Crowe's stone breakwater ushered in a golden age for the village. Money was made from the burgeoning corn trade, but much more came from the profits of more nefarious activities. For at least three decades the primary occupation of virtually every member of the community was the illicit importation and re-export of contraband tobacco, brandy, gin, wine, rum, coffee and tea. Eyemouth acquired the sobriquet, 'London Docks of the Borders'. It was a den for criminals and cut-throats.

As Thomas Tucker had observed to his great frustration in the 1650s, union of the two kingdoms did not mean uniformity of law. Eyemouth was supposed to be watched by the customs centre at Dunbar, but that was twenty miles away, across the vast expanse of Coldingham moor on dirt tracks that were treacherous even in good weather. The officers stationed at Berwick just seven miles away might as well have been in Berkshire. They were on the other side of the border and were powerless to intervene.

The Berwickshire revenue men therefore had considerable autonomy. Some were conscientious, others much less so. The temptation to turn a blind eye, or worse to become actively involved with the smugglers was overwhelming. Most of them went native in one sense. Alcohol abuse was endemic amongst the customs men in Berwickshire.

Like the prohibition years almost two centuries later in the United States, smuggling was hardly viewed as serious crime. The clergy would preach against the evils of drink or tobacco, the gentry occasionally try to enforce the harsh excise laws. But everyone knew that they both retired of an evening to their fine parlours with generous glasses of claret and cognac, hawked to their elegant villas by ragamuffins from the coast. And more than that, for the business to happen in the first place, it needed complex planning and it needed capital. In short, smuggling was organised by the gentry.

Other similarities can be drawn with the Chicago of Al Capone. The merchants who brokered the deals were well known, but nearly always managed to keep their hands clean. The Eyemouth Cosa Nostra involved the Robertsons, the Graemes, the Grieves, the Pattersons and, above all, the Nisbets. That family had been small-scale coastal traders for many decades, but after the completion of the pier they moved on to a grander stage altogether. By the late 1750s the three brothers, John, David and Patrick Nisbet, had amassed so much capital that they were able to commission one of Britain's most renowned architects to build an Edinburgh town house on the southern shore of Eyemouth harbour. It didn't matter where their wealth had come from; they wanted to show the world what kind of people they had become. They acted the part of gentlemen.

Gunsgreen House would not have looked out of place in Edinburgh's New Town. It was the neighbour of many fine residences in the capital, but as a folly in Eyemouth it appeared like a stern old uncle, in starched collar and fine britches, curtly nodding over the water to the ragged rows of houses, granaries and curing sheds. It did differ in one crucial respect from other Adam mansions. As well as being a symbol of wealth, the house was a repository for contraband. Recent investigations have found what local people have long said was there – hollow walls and secret repositories. As much as a thousand pounds in weight of tea or tobacco could have been concealed at any one time within the house. The cellars offered other possibilities for storing alcohol or other luxury goods until the time was right to shift the stuff to grateful customers.

The authorities were not blind to the activities of the Nisbets, but to their great frustration, and in spite of the seizure of numerous cargoes in and around Eyemouth, sometimes with direct connections to the family, there was never enough evidence for a prosecution. One ruse when smuggling tobacco was to pay duty on a single load and retain the certificate from the original port of entry. This paper could be used over and over again if over-vigilant officers ever intercepted any load. The stamped certificate was only ever surrendered when the cutters intervened. In that event a further 'legal' load was ordered and another precious certificate duly procured.

As the walls of Gunsgreen House started to fill in (and, as we know, some were deliberately left with useful cavities!) David Nisbet even made a public declaration of the family probity. He appeared in person in front of the customs officers in Dunbar in 1754 to protest against the annoyance caused by the constant pestering of the excisemen. Regardless of this piece of pantomime a close watch was kept on the Nisbets over the next two decades. Several loads of tobacco were confiscated, including one weighing more than five thousand pounds. The brothers were up to the task and always managed to get their cargoes returned. By the 1760s they had diversified into other areas of business, including wine, brandy and tea. But still they could not be caught. Almost in exasperation, this missive of May 1763 was sent from Edinburgh to the local customs man in Eyemouth:

> We direct you to transmit to us a state of the credit of John Nesbitt, merchant Eyemouth for wine, distinguishing whether French or other wine, and how arising ... whether by wine imported, brought coastwise, or condemned in the Court of Exchequer [this was sale by public auction of seized contraband] and this to be done with secrecy.

Ships from Eyemouth sailed across the North Sea as far as Bergen in Norway and down to Guernsey in the Channel Islands. More important was the big business carried out with the Dutch and the French at Rotterdam, Camp Vere and Boulogne. Just occasionally vessels sailed into the bay direct from America or the Caribbean. Trade continued during the Seven Years War with France, prompting concerns that Berwickshire corn was being sent to the enemy, particularly when prices fell at home.

Most of the so-called smugglers in the village were passive rather than active. They worked as pilots for the luggers, labourers to offload the contraband or carters to take it to clients. Some of the crews ditched fishing altogether, leading Adam Smith, the Commissioner of Customs for Scotland, to recommend that any boats caught ferrying contraband should be seized and burned and their crews pressganged.

There was also employment and profit from what, for a time, was Scotland's most southerly whisky still. Brownsbank distillery on the banks of the River Eye was operating at full pelt by the third quarter of the eighteenth century, at times producing 20,000 gallons of spirit a year, valued at almost £5,000 – and that was only the amount which was officially declared and registered. Much more would have been diverted away, duty not paid, tax not surrendered, to an army of grateful customers.

Across the harbour from Gunsgreen the homes of the ordinary folk changed shape and changed character to accommodate the smugglers. Like a Chinese puzzle, Eyemouth snaked outwards, coiled back to the beach and stretched along the riverbank. The single lane, which linked the community, became a maze within the space of a few years. Subterranean tunnels linked the house and the wynds. To the few who visited, Eyemouth seemed haphazard and ugly. If it served its purpose by both providing areas to stash booze and a confusion of roads to confound the excise, then local people thought their village beautiful indeed. A few of these twisting lanes and vennels still exist, but most of the darker, more close set parts of the town were demolished in a rush of ill conceived modernity in the 1960s. Two centuries or so before those hapless planners vandalised the character of the place, virtually every building was constructed with smuggling in mind.

As if dealing with the smugglers was not a task enough, the customs men regularly quarrelled amongst themselves, usually over what share each was entitled to of the value of confiscated goods. This compromised the effectiveness of what was in any case a fairly amateur service. In May 1759 Daniel Dow, commander of the King's boat in Eyemouth, reported that three of his men, Alexander Mair, Alexander Geddes and Andrew Stevenson watched as 'a number of horses laden with goods made off from them and dispersed through the fields.' And that on another occasion 'they saw a sloop come into the Bay in the evening, which they believed to be the vessel that had smuggled there the night before' yet did nothing to intervene. In all probability these three men had been got at, and were in the pay of the smugglers.

So much material was coming through Eyemouth that even the limp efforts of the excise saw a dramatic increase in the amount that was impounded and by the summer of 1759 a new warehouse was required. It was an opportunity that some enterprising 'Haimoothers' could not ignore. They tunnelled into the storehouse and grabbed back what they could. When the discovery was made Dow had to pen a rather embarrassed report to his superiors. 'David Deans, cooper, young Black, a servant to Mr Martin, and Thomas Bertram a lad and servant to Mr Robertson, who by means of a pass entered the King's warehouse and stole from thence forty gallons of spirits and about eight pounds of coffee.'

Dow went after the three lads, but Bertram made good his escape through the rather drastic measure of enlisting in the navy. Deans and Black had hot footed it out of Eyemouth and were heard of no more. Further episodes of incompetence, and sometimes high drama, followed. In September 1765 as Dow and his colleagues inspected a load at the harbour, their stables were broken into and the horses stolen. But was Dow as assiduous as he could have been? His seizures were never great, and after his death in 1769, the smugglers suddenly become more militant. Perhaps they had lost an ally. Perhaps Daniel Dow, like others in the trade, was sympathetic to the merchants who involved themselves in free trade, and was rewarded with more than a wink and a smile.

George Henderson, who moved down from Fife, succeeded Dow as commander of the King's boat in Eyemouth. Henderson was a cautious man, and with good reason. When he was eventually coaxed into his first reconnaissance sailing, more than six months after arriving in the village, a privateer set upon the excise boat. Henderson, who had ventured out less than a mile, tacked back immediately with his mainsail peppered with shot from the swivel guns and blunderbusses of the pirates.

Enough was enough. The King's Boat Commander refused further entreaties to leave port, and all but abandoned any pretence of his real work. He spent so much time in the inns and bars that his own subordinates could stand it no longer. They reported Henderson's drunken incompetence to Edinburgh and the man was at last removed from his post.

His replacement, William Abernethie, fared little better. Time and again his men were caught up in fights on the quay. In September 1776 for example, they were pelted with stones from the massed ranks of villagers as they tried to impound a load of spirits from the sloop the *George and Betty*. It was a bloody affair. 'While making the seizure we were insulted by a mob from the shore who threw stones at the boatmen', he wrote in his log book. 'William Ferrier got a stroke from a hand spoke upon the back which has almost disabled him from duty'. Eventually William Abernethie – like George Henderson before him – took to spending more of his time consuming drink than chasing those who were trying to land the stuff. In the spring of 1778 his junior colleagues again disowned their commander who was once more removed.

The new boss was no stranger brought in from a distant place, but Abernethie's own deputy David Moncur. He made an immediate impact with a sensational seizure from the sloop the *Euphemia and Peggy*. Included amongst the '158 choppin* bottles and 76 stone bottles with 134 gallons Geneva; 12 choppin bottles containing cinnamon waters; 1 grey beard containing 2 and a half gallons of brandy; 1 choppin bottle of rum; 10 choppin bottles of red French wine, 8 choppin bottles of white Spanish wine; 18 pounds weight tea; 16 pounds raw coffee beans' were the presumably scarce yet much prized, '514 pairs of spectacles.'

If this load brought a smile to Moncur's face and an appreciable bounty into his pocket, his comeuppance was not far away. Days after this seizure Moncur was ambushed as he approached a party of smugglers two miles

---

* A choppin was a measure equivalent to four imperial pints.

from the village. They 'after knocking him from his horse, otherwise abused him, and robbed him of his watch, pocket book, money and the saddle of his horse – and stripped him of all his clothes, except his britches'. Moncur had a long and cold walk home that night. His colleagues, rather curiously, were nowhere to be found.

Several Berwickshire officers were investigated for alleged collusion. Local people would never publicly disown them, but anonymous letters were regularly received by officials in Dunbar and Edinburgh. 'James Crawford has carried on a correspondence with the smugglers and merchants for more than a year gone by,' wrote one. 'And he has misled and deceived the government some hundreds of pounds. He has got some seizures but they're all collusive and not in the Right way.'

To look good, Crawford, who was tidesman at Coldingham, did sometimes try to grab a few of the minor players. On at least one occasion this went spectacularly wrong. In September 1778 he was badly scarred by a mob of five women when attempting to seize gin which had been washed ashore at St Abbs and which they were helping themselves to.

The glory days for the Berwickshire free traders came in the 1770s and early 1780s. Ships like the *Ann and Peggy*, the *Pretty Nymph*, the *Catherine and Magdalen* and the *Betty* were regularly being stopped en route to and from the Continent. For every chance meeting with the revenue, many more crossings must have been trouble-free. But any seizure of highly profitable cargoes was a potential disaster and increasingly heavily armed escorts were employed. These privateers usually came off much the better of any exchanges – and the sea battles which took place off the Berwickshire and Northumberland coast further added to the sinister reputation of the Eyemouth smuggling fraternity.

One of the most dramatic exchanges took place in April 1776 when Captain James Kydd, commander of the *Princess Ann Hoop*, seized a small lugger with an illicit cargo south of Holy Island. Kydd was on his way to Berwick when he reported being

> Chased by an armed cutter of superior size and force, mounting 16 carriage guns, four pounders and 26 swivvels with upwards of fifty men, which came up to him and fired upon him, the master threatening to sink him, whereupon he was obliged to surrender the said vessel. Captain Kyd also met with a large armed lugger mounting 10 carriage and 16 swivvel guns with 42 men which lugger and cutter it is understood are not only employed to smuggle on this coast, but to protect other small vessels in such illicit proceedings, seven of which the master of the cutter acknowledged were expected and that he intended lying six weeks or two months on the coast to protect them.

This ability to be able to commission an escort of pirate ships for upwards of two months gives some idea of the money that was being made and the extent of organised smuggling in the south-east corner of Scotland. It was an acutely dangerous place. In September 1779 a squadron commanded by the American naval commander John Paul Jones audaciously sailed through the pirate waters of the southern Forth, with ships clearly visible from Gunsgreen and Fort Point.

Is there a coincidence in the fact that a Masonic Lodge was established just as smuggling began to take a hold in Eyemouth? The principal brethren, including all of the major office bearers, were almost always the same men who feature in the lists of real or suspected smugglers. In evening meetings they rubbed shoulders with the very excise men they ought to be avoiding.

The Nisbet brothers were certainly at the head of the queue when Lodge St Ebbe was set up in 1757 in the home of James Simpson, an Eyemouth vintner. They dominated the early years of the organisation – Patrick was Secretary in 1757–8 and his brother David succeeded him in 1759. William Henderson, a brother-in-law to one of the Nisbets was the first Master Mason in 1757 and 1758. Another brother-in-law, William Graeme, succeeded to that charge in 1759, and all retained senior positions within St Ebbe.

None of this confirms the charge that the Masonic Order in Eyemouth was a front for illegal activities. Primarily it was a religious institution, but lodge meetings did provide a chance to talk with others of a like mind and business outlook, and to sup heavily in closed company. If nothing else, the monthly gatherings offered opportunity. Merchants from Eyemouth and inland Berwickshire, and visiting brethren from the towns and cities may well have sealed deals in the aftermath of Temple activities. Such agreements strayed beyond the legitimate and profitable business of grain to the more colourful and yet more lucrative trade in brandy, tea and tobacco.

Scotland's national bard was made a Royal Arch Mason when he visited Eyemouth in 1787 and is remembered still as possibly the only exciseman to receive a warm welcome in the town, though Robbie Burns did not actually join the service until 1791.

Freemasonry added considerably to the colour of the village. Meetings were held on the first Thursday of every month, as well as on the three Festival Days of St John the Baptist on 24 June, St Andrew on 30 November and St John the Evangelist on 27 December. Though these were held behind the closed door of the temple, very public displays of freemasonry were seen in regular processions through the village. On 2 May 1758 to mark the laying of the foundation stone of the lodge building, more than a hundred brethren from near and far marched through the narrow lanes of Eyemouth.

All of the masons were dressed in black, with white aprons, gloves and stockings and arranged in order and carrying the symbols of their craft.

Though the meetings rarely degenerated from over indulgence, the masons of Eyemouth did get through a remarkable amount of liquor, with hearty meals and many rounds of boozy toasts made at the end of an evening's business. Music was also important, and in contrast to bland services held in the Kirk, lodge meetings often included bands of various description, sometimes involving the military units stationed at Eyemouth or Berwick. Of course they could not always appear and in 1775 a move was made to procure an organ. With insufficient funds to buy one outright, the brethren latched on to a novel idea. They allotted part of their reserves to gamble for one.

> 31 March 1775 – This day a committee being called in order to take into consideration concerning an organ to be disposed of by Thomas Aitchison of Chirnside by throwing dice at the rate of 5/– each throw, it being agreed that the Lodge should subscribe £1/15/– the Master and Brother James Renton took it upon them to throw the dice at the appointed day at Chirnside, and threw too few – good day to the Organ

By the time of this comical attempt, the Nisbets were starting to feel the chill of old age. They were still actively engaged in trade in the mid 1770s, and still under suspicion as smugglers, but none of the three brothers had any male heirs and around the year 1780 they sold their magnificent creation of Gunsgreen House. Why is unclear. Had they lost their fortune? Had that wealth been squandered on the folly which was Gunsgreen? Had they simply grown weary and soft? Patrick was already dead by the time of the sale. He was followed by David, who died at the age of seventy-seven in 1788, and by John, who passed away in the following year. The residue of the estate of the Nisbets passed to their grandsons and great-grandsons and their own place in Eyemouth history into legend.

Gunsgreen House and its grounds were bought by the Rev George Home, minister of Ayton and cousin of Patrick Home of Wedderburn. As Patrick had bought the estate of Eyemouth in 1766 it meant the entire harbour and its environs were once again controlled by the Wedderburns. They could not have been deaf or blind to the goings on at the quayside and along the shore. Whether they took an active part in the business is more difficult to prove. Just why Patrick in particular was so interested in the little village and so keen to acquire the estate which his family had lost more than a century before requires some explanation. He was, to some degree, an Eyemouth man himself.

Patrick's father was none other than Ninian Home, the Sproutston minister who had saved the family from potential ruin in 1716. After hoodwinking the Hanoverians, Ninian handed back the Wedderburn titles and property and then tried to manoeuvre his son Alexander into wooing the 10th Lord's eldest daughter, Margaret. His machinations almost worked ... but not quite. Alexander did not care for Margaret, but did romance, and marry, her younger, more attractive sister Isabel. The two families were now joined, but not sufficiently to combine the lineage.

Whether from true love or true avarice Ninian, by then a widower, took it upon himself to wed Margaret, a woman many years his junior. After their marriage in 1726 they moved to Linthill House on the outskirts of the episcopal stronghold of Eyemouth. There, Ninian enjoyed many years of marriage before his death in 1744. 'Enjoy' is most definitely apt for the old minister. He may have been a man of the cloth, but Ninian, like many of his ancestors, was extremely fecund and demanding. Margaret bore him nine children. The eldest, Patrick, succeeded first to his father's estate of Billie, and then to the greater title of Wedderburn when his uncle, also Patrick, died without issue in 1766. This fusion of the lines was the culmination of Ninian's dream. He was of course dead by the time it happened ... and so was his wife. Margaret Home was brutally murdered in her own bedchamber in 1751.

The family butler, an Invernessian called Normand Ross had, in the summer of 1750 become involved with a local Eyemouth girl who fell pregnant. She demanded money and threatened to tell his employer of the affair, something that might well have led to his dismissal. The butler had little cash of his own and in desperation decided to rob Lady Billie. Margaret was in the habit of counting rent money from her tenants in front of Ross before locking it away in a cupboard in her bedroom. It would have been difficult enough to gain access to this, but the lady of the house was both canny and careful. To provide privacy and security she had ordered the building of a strong lock for her door with a wire cable that led to her bedside. Once the sneb was bolted, entry was well nigh impossible, and any attempt would certainly have woken Margaret.

But on 12 August 1751, after watching Lady Billie count out more than £70 sterling into her strongbox, Ross decided he had to take his chance. Sometime after supper when Margaret had left for her usual evening stroll down to Eyemouth, the butler slid himself under her bed. There he waited. When she eventually returned, Margaret undressed and placed the keys to her cupboard on a bedside table. Hours passed before Ross was certain that it was safe to creep out from his hiding place. As his hand edged slowly towards the table it knocked into a plate left from the evening meal. As the dish and cutlery clanked on to the floor, Margaret jumped up, crying out 'Who's there'? Instinctively, Ross grabbed at the knife, which had tumbled to the floor, and, as the lurid accounts of the time reported he 'instantly made a furious attack upon her. Cut her across the throat, and upon the Lady's grasping his hair, and making other efforts to save her life, he mangled her with the knife in the arms and other parts of her body.'

The commotion roused the family and the other servants, who rushed to the first floor bedroom, but because of Margaret's lock could not gain entry. Ross jumped out of the window, breaking his leg as he fell, and made off as far as he could. A manhunt ensued. Dozens of tenants and labourers, some with dogs, combing the countryside and he was quickly apprehended. Ross was found guilty of murder at the High Court in Edinburgh on 18 November 1751. His execution has the distinction of being the last to take place under the Old Scots Criminal Code that ordered that the guilty man's right hand be first struck off before the hanging.

Ross expressed contrition on the scaffold and his death-speech in some ways echoed that of George Sprott almost a century and half earlier. 'I acknowledge the justice of the sentence pronounced against me' he said 'and in particular that my right hand, with which I own to have committed the cruel murder, is justly to be cut off, to deter others from such villainous attempts in time coming.' Street theatre Georgian style then took over, and in front of a massive crowd Ross's arm was sliced off before he was strung up on a gibbet.

With the death of both parents Patrick, at the age of twenty-three, was head of the family and heir to the Wedderburn title, which he eventually gained in 1766. One of his first acts as thirteenth laird was to purchase Eyemouth from Henry Trotter.

It was an astute piece of business. From corn to fish, but above all from smuggled luxuries, the village throbbed with trade. Unfortunately for Patrick the ink on the bill of sale was barely dry when the very root of Eyemouth's prosperity was almost pulled apart. Weeks after negotiating the estate's purchase, William Crowe's pier was badly weakened by a massive spate of the River Eye. Patrick attended to this at once and commissioned one of Britain's most celebrated engineers not just to repair the breakwater, but build another pier on the opposite side of the bay. James Smeaton was suitably impressed with the potential of the port, which he surveyed in May 1766. 'The harbour of Eyemouth' he wrote, ' lies at the corner of a bay at which ships can work in and out at all times of tide, or lie at an anchor secure from all winds, except the northerly or north easterly. From this circumstance its situation seems very advantageous.'

But Smeaton's army of labourers had barely started their work, when the North Sea again attacked the harbour. On New Year's Day 1767, barely seven months since the storm which had weakened the old pier, another hurricane lashed down on the whole east coast, affecting ports from London to Aberdeen. The stone walls were buffeted from the seaward side, with high winds and rolling breakers thumping over them. The tide was so high that at that time it almost broke into the lanes. Such seas were normal in winter and no undue alarm was felt. It was New Year's Day and most villagers were too senseless from drink to bother about the weather. But the winds kept up and the waves thundered through the afternoon, returning in a second tide late in the evening. Around midnight the entire pier gave way and a massive flood rushed into the harbour basin, overflowing the flatlands and breaching the flimsy defences in front of the little cottages.

Panic ensued as the storm drove the sea up the gouged Eye valley as far as the gardens of Netherbyres, almost a mile from the beach. The suddenness of the collapse of the pier, and the speed of the encroachment of the ocean caught everyone, quite literally, asleep. Many of the low-lying houses were swept away in the torrent.

Debris was strewn along the shoreline, the harbour moorings torn out and the wharf walls largely demolished. The incursion of the ocean washed more silt from the river down into the entrance to the port. There it joined an accumulation of sand and gravel, swept in by the tides.

Thankfully for Eyemouth, Smeaton's men were still in the village and, using more of the scattered pudding stone from the Fort, they first patched up the broken wall of the old pier before resuming work on the new wharf on the southern shore of the river at Gunsgreen. This was finally completed in 1772, providing the haven with vastly increased shipping space and much improved shelter. The great engineer then headed north, and began work at Peterhead, using many of the techniques he had employed at Eyemouth.

Harbour repairs did not come cheap, and though Patrick Home was happy to contribute he still expected the bulk of the money to come – as it did – from the gentlemen of the shire. Smeaton's work cost another two and a half thousand pounds.

It was obvious that for Eyemouth to continue to develop, regular attention – and that meant regular amounts of cash – would have to be expended on the harbour. Elsewhere harbour trusts were being established to carry out this work. If Patrick gave this consideration at the time of the Smeaton improvements he did nothing beyond that. It would take another calamity, more than twenty years later, when the poorly maintained piers finally collapsed, for that step to be taken.

Wedderburn ought not to be condemned for this. The improvements of 1772 were enough to cause a dramatic increase in the already prodigious business of the port. Between that time and 1790 the number of vessels

using the port trebled. Shipwrecks, common before, became unheard of
and only one man lost his life in the twenty years after Smeaton's improvements.

The new facilities were a boon to everyone who used the port and that
of course included the smugglers. Patrick was not unaware of what was
going on. He might have been an infrequent visitor, concentrating his time
at his main estate of Paxton House and later when an MP in Westminster,
but he had eyes and ears in the village. His baron baillie David Renton and
above all the Rev George Home of Gunsgreen kept up a regular correspondence.

These letters confirm that if the Homes were not themselves directly
involved in smuggling, they certainly knew of the extent of the business
on the coast. In 1767 Patrick had used his influence to procure a position
at Coldingham for his lazy kinsman John Home. This help was not well
rewarded. John Home quickly saw that much more could be made from
engaging with the smugglers than suppressing them. He probably took his
lead from James Crawford, his official boss, and a man well known to be
in league with the criminals. When John was accused of similar complicity
he tried to pin the blame on another colleague, John Swanston. The minister
of Ayton took up John Home's case 'Not so much from a conviction of
his innocence as from a belief he might *possibly* be innocent.' But, wrote
Rev Home rather sadly, 'The result was something approaching a letter of
thanks for his activity, and a promise of protection against the smugglers.
In a few months he threw up the excise and entered into partnership with
these very smugglers'.

The riches, or presumed riches, which could be made from smuggling,
also had a baneful impact on the estates, which had so recently been
enclosed. In another note to Patrick, George Home acerbically commented:
'Frances has taken to smuggling and cannot pay his rents. There is this
disadvantage in new improven lands, that if they are not indisciously and
even tenderly managed, they suffer an injury that cannot be repaired
without a considerable expense'.

George Home would have watched nocturnal landings from the broad
windows of Gunsgreen which keek out to the sea and wink across to the
little village across the bay – landings which sometimes took place on his
own Gunsgreen shore. These goods were then moved inland or secreted
in some of the storerooms and garrets of Eyemouth. His reports hint at
danger and the consequences for anyone who crossed the smugglers and
their handlers. Mr Home was presumably also a consumer of their wares.
It is easy to imagine the picture – the fevered activity of ordinary folk,
carting kegs in the darkness along the muddy lanes of Eyemouth, whilst

Home's windows danced with roaring fires, smoking candelabra and the stumbling silhouettes of the 'unco' guid' roaring into their cups of tax-free brandy and gin, and bottles of home-produced Scotch.

A frequent dinner guest at Gunsgreen was George Tod, who took over as Eyemouth parish minister in 1785. He was another member of the extended border clan, related to both George and Patrick, and promoted to the post through the usual means. Nepotism was not an evil, it was the norm. Tod, though, was discreet in his public assessments of the major business of the town. When he had to write up Eyemouth's entry in the *Old Statistical Account* in 1791, he brushed over the importance of smuggling, acknowledging only that 'Owing to its vicinity to England, [Eyemouth] became remarkable for smuggling; but that pernicious trade' was now 'much quashed'.

This judgement was written more from wariness of who might read the account than from the facts of the case. It is true that smuggling had declined by the 1790s, but it still went on. It was still a money-spinner. George Home's letters, written at the same time as Tod was compiling his entry for the *Statistical Account*, confirm as much.

As the century drew to a close, and war erupted once more with France, the heyday of smuggling came to an end. Some would continue to operate outwith the law until the rates of duty between England and Scotland were equalised, which would not happen until the middle of the nineteenth century. For the most part, however, the Berwickshire free traders found the business ever more dangerous and increasingly difficult to organise. Some spectacular cargoes continued to be loaded and big money made, at least until the overall tax on spirits was reduced in 1823. In April 1820 for example, a schooner was apprehended off St Abbs Head carrying a cargo of brandy, tea and tobacco valued at more than £4,000.

But the opportunities afforded by smuggling were becoming harder and more dangerous. The majority of people on the south east coast had to look to less lucrative legal employment, back to the corn trade and to fishing for a living. Elsewhere in the Merse, where enclosure was now complete, the new age was finally closing in on the old. Contemporary writers usually applauded the transformation, but some showed genuine concern for the effects on ordinary people. 'The farms in Berwickshire are generally large,' wrote one commentator 'which though it proves lucrative to individuals, is hurtful to the country, depriving it of many useful and enterprising young men, who find it necessary to seek for farms elsewhere'.

There were no other farms to be found – none at least that the former cottars and sub-tenants could afford. They had to make do with labouring work or leave the land for the towns and cities of the central belt, and the smaller communities springing up along the border rivers. A few chose to strike out for the coast.

One such family was the Spears. They had been small-scale farmers in the Tweed Valley for generations. When the runrigs were taken away, John Spears, with his wife Catharine Johnston and at least one child, headed down through Berwickshire, ending up at Eyemouth around the year 1770. There was already a family with the name Spears living there – relations of John who had moved to the village some years before.

When the shoals of herring returned again in millions around 1780, John Spears became a full time fisherman. Family connections helped in this. His distant kinsman George, who had been born in Eyemouth in 1743, had a share in one of the haddock boats and worked in the herring drave.

Blood and marriage would have counted for nothing if the incomer could not sail or find fish, swear and stand his ground in a fistfight, or drink with a death wish. John Spears apparently did not disappoint in any of this. By 1788 not only was he apparently accepted as an Eyemouth man; he was also doing very well. This former pauper now skippered and had a part share in his own boat.

Chapter Four

Ministers, Men, Merchants and the Sea

I cannot help thinking that your purchase of the estate of Eyemouth was a good bargain

John Renton, Baron Ballie of Eyemouth to
Patrick Home MP, 25 March 1794

The place that John Crawford Spears and Catharine Johnston made their home was not initially a welcoming one. Notwithstanding their vague family links, Eyemouth folk even to this day are suspicious of those not born and bred in the town. The Spears settled in a cheap hovel near the water's edge, one of the little dwellings thrown up after the great storm of 1767: two rooms, with earthen floors and a single window for a family that quickly grew. At least six children and probably many more came into the world in this damp, dirty and cold lean-to. If an old sail were available, it would be laid down over the bare ground. Otherwise sand from the beach was used as a basic covering, and swept out when it was too foul to bear.

The Spears were not especially god-fearing. Both had been baptised in the Church of Scotland before their enforced move to the coast, and they gave little thought when christening their own children in the established Kirk. But it was obvious from the moment the young couple set up home, that the minister in Eyemouth was less revered, less feared even than the clergy they were used to in rural Berwickshire.

John and Catharine were not alone in striking out a new life in Eyemouth. The population of the parish had trebled in less than a century, and by the early 1780s around nine hundred people packed into the narrow confines of the community. Some occupied new properties on the western tip of the village which, from the stimulus of smuggling, had started to stretch out along the banks of the River Eye. It was not long before these joined up with the substantial three storey Chester House, formerly isolated on a sanitised spot on the Burnmouth road, and home to David Renton, Baron Baillie for the Wedderburns. David's kinsman John Renton of Lamberton was, like Patrick Home, wedded to the notion of progress and 'a zealous promoter of the agriculture of the county of Berwick'. As a lay contributor to the *Old Statistical Account*, John Renton put down the dramatic changes in the countryside to, as he put it, 'a few individuals of more than ordinary

71

penetration and discernment': people like himself who had racked up rents, cleared folk from the land and laid out vast new estates.

In time the track where David lived would be named Church Street. It was set back from the sea and was not a place for the fisher folk. Poor immigrants did not settle there. They had no choice but to take space in the old crumbling beachside shacks, or to construct simple shelters on the flatlands where the river met the sea. This was the worst area of the whole place. No pavements, no cobbles, only open sewers and stagnant pools.

The shacks along the river Eye were juxtaposed to warehouses and granaries. At the edge of this crowded thoroughfare was a gable-ended inn. Built in the middle of the eighteenth century it bore witness to a continental influence. Known today as the Ship it was a tolerable and spacious bar, frequented even by the wealthy. To the dismay of the minister it was only one of around twenty liquor shops that were available in 1791, one for every thirty-five parishioners. Most were drinking dens for the common folk, for visiting fishermen and migrant labourers. They supplied the roughest of moonshine for a few pennies.

The Spears arrived at a turning point in the history of the village. After more than thirty years as minister, James Allan passed away in May 1767. On the day of the funeral, work stopped on Smeaton's new pier, and the community was quiet for the burial of a man who, in spite of all the problems, had wielded enormous influence over their lives. Allan's successor Thomas Tait occupied the pulpit for ten years before his death in 1776, but by then time had marched on, and the power of the parish minister was much reduced.

During Tait's time the fishing industry revived. In the 1770s the herring shoals suddenly dived once more towards the Berwickshire coast. This time, unlike half a century before, everything was in place to exploit the potential riches of the silver darlings. There were strong stone piers to protect the boats from all but the fiercest wind and waves; a merchant class well used to business risks; a government bounty to further entice tradesmen to venture; a population swollen both by the displaced and by those who sought adventure in smuggling. Most of all there was a market. The urban sprawl of Edinburgh was within reach, and Eyemouth herring came to be shipped to continental Europe and to the Caribbean to feed plantation slaves.

Boats, this time hundreds of them, were drawn south from Lothian and Fife and they stayed, not for two weeks but three months. In place of the ground-drave a float drave was tried with immediate and conspicuous success. The village creaked under the weight of the incomers, and the bars and common lodging houses did a roaring trade. Fishing for herring became

central to the summer economy of the village – so much so that the
Freemasons stopped parading on the festival of St John the Baptist, which
fell at the height of the season, on 24 June. The minds of the merchant
brethren were on other, more temporal matters. On a practical level there
was no room for them to proceed down the quayside, unless they traipsed
in Indian-file. The wharf was too crowded with curing equipment, shoogly
high-stacked barrels, stinking, discarded offal, chubby fishwives in striped
aprons, and screeching gulls.

The herring fleet sailed in the evening and two or three hauls were made
in drift nets that were attached to each other in a nocturnal daisy chain.
When the fish entangled themselves in the sheets their fluorescent sheen
turned the blackest night to a winking dawn. Tens of thousands of herring
were shovelled into the open boats at every haul. It was not unheard of
for the flimsy craft to tip over under the sheer weight of the herring. No
lives were lost, however ... at least not at this time.

The boats returned in the early morning, prompting a magnificent collage
of activity. Some of the little vessels bobbed at anchor in the bay while
others struggled to cross the harbour bar, and all the while the race was
on to get the precious cargo ashore before it went bad. It was the job of
the women to hitch up their skirts and wade out to the fleet, taking first
the herring, and then returning to carry their men on broad backs and
strong shoulders. A slender lass was considered gaunt and inadequate – of
no use to a fisherman.

If they had wavered before, men like John Spears were now able to make
fishing their full time profession. The narrow rigs of fisher's lands that they
still held became kitchen gardens to be worked by wives and bairns –
ground to keep pigs for slaughter.

James Allan had not lived to see it, but within ten years of his passing,
the industry that he had prayed for finally became established. By 1777
Spears had a full share in his own boat. The family was now a fishing unit,
alongside those with longer associations with the sea – the Dougals,
Maltmans, Pattersons and Whillases. Some of the Whillases later left the
shallow inshore waters of Berwickshire for the greater adventure of the
wider ocean. One of their number, Eyemouth born John 'Jock' Whillas
made a packet of money and became famous as the owner of the mighty
Cutty Sark.

The growing importance of the drave encouraged landsmen to the beach.
But, hanging like a shadow – a big black minister's cloak of a shadow –
over the whole future of the fishing was the obligation to pay fish teind.
It was bad enough that local crews were each supposed to give the minister
£20 Scots a year. If the hauls were even only fair, that amount split between

four or five men was manageable, though bitterly resented. But stranger boats, those which gathered in the port for the float-drave were liable not for a fixed payment, but an actual percentage, a full twentieth of their landings. James Allan had never asked for anything like this, and nor had Tom Tait. There was a lot of interest as to what stance his successor, James Williamson, would take when Tait died in 1776.

The people of the village, so many of whom disdained religion and so few of whom were regular worshipers at the dilapidated Church, turned out in their droves to see the new man. Like the induction of James Ramsay, the service for Williamson was held not in the Church but in the kirkyard. This time it was not because the doors to the building were locked. It simply could not accommodate the crowds.

One of Mr Williamson's first official duties was the christening of a son to John Spears and Catharine Johnston. William, the couple's fourth child, was baptised on 17 November 1776. He was the first boy to survive childbirth, his elder brother, also William, having died in infancy in 1773. The lad would grow up to know nothing else but fishing. Like other callants he was taken to sea almost as soon as he could walk and was made a working, earning cabin boy before he was a teenager.

The new minister, like the previous two incumbents, was not greedy in his demands. Williamson never threatened a rouping and only ever asked for the established £20 Scots teind from local boats, which seemed to cover both the winter hunting of cod and haddock and the new herring float-drave. He did not demand anything from the migrant fishermen who arrived for the summer season. Fishing boomed, and relations between people and pastor were settled. Indeed all five skippers signed a petition presented to the local Presbytery in 1781 pleading for the neglected Kirk to be either urgently repaired or completely replaced. The poor state of the fabric did, though, provide a neat excuse for a lie-in on a Sunday. 'Not only was the roof of the church uncapable of defending the seats from the rains, the east and west side are in a ruinous and dangerous condition' Williamson told the Presbytery. 'Inhabitants of the Parish are induced from apprehension of danger not to attend the public worship of the Church in stormy weather.'

A bit of patching was done, but the landowners, called heritors, seemed to have short hands and deep pockets. Williamson managed to wring a new Manse out of them in 1777, but it was hardly spacious or comfortable. When a new Kirk was refused he gave up and in 1785 moved to Dunbar.

His replacement was another young minister who had come from a preaching post in Berwick-upon-Tweed. George Tod may have been equally green in the pulpit, but he had rather more obvious credentials to be in

Eyemouth. He was also much more determined to take all that was due from the stipend.

George's father the Rev John Tod of Ladykirk had been tutor to Ninian Home. His mother was one of the daughters of George Home, the tenth laird of Wedderburn who had narrowly escaped execution after the crushing of the '15. The new Eyemouth minister was a minor aristocrat. Indeed, as the years passed and Patrick, the thirteenth laird showed no signs of delivering an heir, John Tod's chances of succeeding as the next head of the Wedderburn clan increased.

Tod's time in Eyemouth was not a happy one. He inherited his father's truculence and had an overbearing air that sat ill in the community. Unlike his three immediate predecessors the minister did not join Lodge St Ebbe. James Allan had been one of the founding brethren in 1757, Thomas Tait was elected Secretary in 1773 while James Williamson was made Master in 1777–8. Being part of the lodge was important. The monthly meetings were as much a chance for a good blether as they were for the more ritual aspects of the craft. In showing diffidence to freemasonry, Tod lost out on these evenings, and on the chat amongst the merchants of the prospects for the town.

The minister was an inveterate complainer who always felt short changed. He was not happy with the Kirk that was falling to bits, his house was too cold and too small, the stipend was inadequate and the people brazen. For an aspiring cleric with Tod's pedigree this was a sorry state of affairs. Worse still when he looked across the harbour he saw the fine elegance of Gunsgreen House, where his kinsman, George Home, the minister of Ayton, virtually held court. What did the Eyemouth minister have to offer visitors and dinner guests? A rickety manse much more in keeping with the fisher-folk's shacks, a far cry from a plush mansion. The humiliation was complete when he noted the pennies in his plate, yet saw the money thrown away by the fishermen in the Ship Inn. Was it right that a man of God should have to live in poverty? Was it right that a close relative of the Wedderburn Homes should be treated with such disrespect?

A few months after his ordination, the rising herring trade was given another boost when the government improved the bounty regime. Local merchants had previously sent the vast bulk of landings 'fresh' to market, but, encouraged by this new inducement, traders began to preserve some of the fish by pickling and smoking. This, in turn, encouraged more boats to land bigger catches. John Turnbull was one of the first to erect temporary smokehouses and sheds in the early 1770s. He ensured a ready supply by making deals with the crews based on a fixed price for a set amount of their catch.

Herring fishing was different from the winter pursuit of haddock. Bigger boats, and many more than were in the usual fleet, were required for the drave. To work them, the full time crews broke up in the early summer, with one or two full time fishermen picking two or three hired landsmen for the season.

In past decades linen-weavers, the independent artisans of eastern Berwickshire, had looked down on the coarse folk who made a living from the sea. But by the close of the eighteenth century these outworkers were coming under pressure from the new towns and their factories. Soon the weavers of Coldingham would struggle to produce a yard for every mile that emerged from the mills. Young men still took to the loom, but a population drift, accentuated by the consequences of enclosure, was clearly happening. Writing in 1791, John Renton said of Coldingham 'Our supernumerary young men go partly to England and partly to Edinburgh and other populous towns in Scotland in quest of employment.'

Some also moved to the coast. In 1786 houses were built on the cliffs above St Abbs for the four fishing crews who pushed their cobbles out from the shingle, past the razor-sharp rocks. Before this they had tramped back and forth from Coldingham village. Other families loaded up their possessions for the adventure of a two-mile drive south to the expanding village of Eyemouth. The Purves, the Swanstons, the Raes, the Gillies and the Craigs abandoned past lives and settled by the sea at this time.

There was plenty work in the gutting sheds and curing houses as well as on the boats. Employment was also available in the corn trade and at the boatyard, which was set up over the rise of the beach in 1800.

The expense of additional boats, nets and lines was considerable. Each new drave vessel cost about ten pounds sterling, and to this had to be added the outlay of about twenty-five pounds for a winter haddock boat. The merchants helped with the finance – it was in their own interest to ensure the fleet remained solid and seaworthy. John Turnbull owned at least one drave-boat and had a share in a winter yawl.

Against this background of activity and speculation George Tod began to cast covetous eyes. In 1787 he issued the expected and traditional bills for fish tithe of £1 13s. 4d. per boat, *and* tried to insist that the visiting herring fleets deliver to his door a full twentieth of their catch. Tod then went further. He scanned the musty documents relating to the teind in Eyemouth, especially the decreets of 1675 and 1763, and decided that the annual fee paid by the local fishermen *only* covered the winter season. They were still liable to deliver a full tenth of their summer herring catch to him, and merchants, like John Turnbull, who owned boats but did not themselves fish, had to pay full teind.

Tod's demands came as a bombshell to the community. The minister was ready for the predictable backlash, and told the merchants and the fishermen that he was quite willing to re-negotiate a financial compromise. After all, what use were hundreds of crans of herring to him? He also pointed out that the money was not for him alone. The Kirk organised and funded education and poor relief. A vastly increased population in the parish had overwhelmed the existing structures. It was time for the fishermen to give a little of their new-found prosperity to help others in Eyemouth. Did that sound unreasonable?

Todd talked a good game. He told Chirnside Presbytery that he 'Would certainly never take any measures to hurt that fishery, which it is so much in his interest to encourage.' But thanks to inflation the modus, which had been fixed for well over a century and a half, had tumbled in real value. George Tod could see that he was not getting anywhere like the same worth from the teind as that enjoyed even by James Allan, a minister who had been far too complacent, far too lackadaisical. It was time to tighten things up. 'When even in its infant state this fishing could afford his predecessors the whole demand which he now claims, certainly in its present flourishing situation, it should with cheerfulness pay his lawful and customary dues.'

Of course that was not how matters were viewed along the quayside. This minister had been in the parish less than two years, yet in this bold and unprecedented move he might ruin everything. Folk now fondly recalled the 'enlightened' days of James Allan, conveniently forgetting that even he had seized the effects of fishermen who would not pay the teind.

The little matter of George Tod's relationship with Patrick of Wedderburn complicated matters. Presumably the laird had been consulted and presumably there would be no shyness in involving the courts and sheriff officers if Tod's demands were refused? Agitated meetings followed, and a collective decision was reached. The five skippers of the place, along with the merchant-owner John Turnbull, opted to ignore the new bills, though the crews would still pay their traditional modus-money of £1 13s. 4d.

This defiance had a history. Eyemouth's reputation for violence and lawlessness was well established. They were the smugglers who had defied the law; they were the Borderers who had been virtually beyond the pale of justice for centuries. If the minister wanted to take them on, then fine. But he ought not to expect their attendance at his Kirk – or even civility in the street. John Spears, who, in October 1786, a few months before the bills were issued, had entrusted the baptism of his second son Robert to the minister, never again crossed the church step. Robert was the last

bearing the surname Spears to be christened at the Church of Scotland in
Eyemouth.

The minister faced down the boycott. Through the summer of 1787 Tod
watched as the boats offloaded and asked, always politely, for his legitimate
share of the herring catch. He would have spent many long hours on the
pier for it was by far the best season ever experienced in Berwickshire.
Hundreds of crans went bad in the high-summer heat, and heartbreakingly
had to be dumped in the bay. Tod, meticulous in his note taking, estimated
that Turnbull alone had made more than a hundred pounds in the three
month drave. A huge sum. A third as much again as the minister's entire
annual stipend.

The Eyemouth boats were heavy-laden crossing the bar, and smuggling
was momentarily forgotten as gold tumbled into the pockets of the fishermen from the landing of silver darlings. Boats from other ports swarmed
southwards and artisans, who had otherwise no connection with fishing,
came down to the sea. Two men from nearby Ayton, merchant Robert
Liddle and joiner Robert Aitchison, set up a makeshift curing station on
the lip of the harbour along the Salt Greens. As Turnbull and his cronies
had already 'engaged' most of the local crews to fish for them, Aitchison
and Liddell instead sealed deals with the stranger boats, and were likewise
kept busy through the whole of the drave.

In the midst of all this activity, Scotland's national bard 'cam up a bold
shore and over a wild country to Eyemouth'. Robert Burns dined, supped
and slept at William Grieves', another merchant who had started to dabble
in fishing. He gladly accepted an invitation to take a sail around the bay
and observed, almost as a throwaway in his journal, 'Fishing of all kinds
pay tithe at Eyemouth'.

But many didn't that summer, despite their heavy landings. George Tod
felt as a pauper to these common fisherfolk. He was insulted by their
continued refusal to entertain his claims for additional herring teind, and
affronted by their insolence on the street. Worse still, emboldened by the
stance they had taken, and with the silent support of the merchants, some
fishermen even began to refuse to pay the traditional modus.

It was all too much for the minister who initiated three civil actions –
one against the fishermen for herring teind and the sums of whitefish teind
which had been withheld; a second against John Turnbull, for full herring
teind as a merchant boat owner; and a third suit for half herring teind
against Liddle and Aitchison, on the grounds that they had been importing
fish into the village from stranger craft.

Any hope Tod had entertained that legal action would bring swift
surrender quickly evaporated. The herring drave, as had been proved by

earnings from 1787, was now an important element of the local economy. The three cases, which came to be conjoined, were vigorously contested and eventually reached the Court of Session in Edinburgh.

The minister's claims were simple enough. The Eyemouth men who hunted cod and haddock in the winter had historically paid £1 13s. 4d. per crew in lieu of fish teind. That was long established and accepted. But that was not the only element they should pay. Todd argued that the fishermen were also liable for a full tenth of their earnings from the new summer herring fishing. Moreover those who had been withholding the modus laid themselves open to further demands. He referred back to a statement made by James Allan in 1764:

> The practice [of accepting a fixed annual payment] seems to have arose from conveniency and lenity; whether established by length of time is unknown ... yet <u>on the agreement being refused or broke, he has the right to draw the tenth fish</u> from them

As for merchants like John Turnbull, who did not themselves fish but who owned boats crewed by landsmen, they should likewise deliver a tenth of their catch, or the cash equivalent. Boats visiting and discharging herring in the port at any time of the year were due to pay half teind, or the monetary value of a twentieth of their catch.

A verdict in Tod's action was eventually delivered in 1793. It confirmed that Eyemouth men, who normally worked all year round on whitefish boats were liable by *'use and wont'* to pay £20 Scots per crew, but that this *did* exempt full time fishermen from any further exaction. The five crews who had withheld payment from the minister were ordered to deliver what they owed to Mr Tod, which after much grumbling they duly did.

The Court of Session further decided that visiting boats should pay half teind – that is a twentieth of their catch – or whatever the minister would agree to accept. Tod, in spite of the legal bluster, had never in fact asked for very much from the stranger crews, basing his demands more on the profits they might have made rather than their gross catch. Nonetheless, the judgement was a worry. Would it persuade the dozens of little craft that crowded Eyemouth Bay in the summer, bringing work and money to the community, that they should opt for somewhere else, somewhere where the minister might not bother them?

Perhaps most disconcerting was the decision to impose full teind on 'interested parties' who were resident in the parish but were not themselves full time fishermen. Did this mean that any merchant who financed all or part of the expensive new boats would have to pay a proportion of the landings of that craft to the minister? The answer appeared to be 'yes', and

John Turnbull was the living proof. He was ordered to give a tenth of what he had taken, or what had been taken on his behalf, in 1787. In a spirit of conciliation, George Tod agreed not to press for anything more than £10 sterling. It hardly conciliated a furious John Turnbull.

Finally, the court decided that no teind could be claimed on fish brought into the village for processing. Aitchison and Liddle had therefore nothing to pay and were the only clear winners.

In effect the rulings restored the status quo on the tithe, but left an area of doubt hanging over the obligations of the curers. John Turnbull felt aggrieved at being taxed so heavily for risking so much. Eyemouth merchants would be careful in future. They would cure and sell but not help to catch the fish. They would offer inducements, but not openly take shares in the summer herring fleet, something that was pretty well general along the whole of the rest of the Scottish East Coast.

To the fishermen the Court of Session action was a stupendous victory. They had managed to rebut Tod's claims for part of their earnings at the highest civil court in the land. But the five years of legal argument further alienated the people from their pastor. Moreover the decision of the judges to confirm payment of the winter teind – the modus – rankled. Resentment against George Tod was unanimous. But at least it persuaded him against any further legal action.

The judgement was delivered just as the herring again twisted towards the Berwickshire coast. The boom would be more sustained than that of the late 1780s, lasting well into the new century and affecting stations in Fife and along the southern shores of the Forth. Eyemouth had the advantage of already being a commercial harbour, and the herring fleet jostled for space with trading luggers. 'Improvements of all kinds are going on' David Renton wrote to Patrick Home in the Spring of 1794. 'You will think me partial to Eyemouth, so I am. I cannot help wishing to see it flourish and become the seaport town worthy of the county to which it belongs.'

But this seaport was crumbling. Its wharves and piers seemed solid enough from the roadstead approaches, but as the little ships and herring boats nudged closer, the dilapidated nature of Eyemouth harbour was plain to see. The North Sea squalls regularly punched holes in the sea defences, ripped out palings and dragged sand and gravel across the bar. Who authorised, who carried out and, most important of all, who paid for repairs was contentious. As far back as September 1773 a survey by engineer Robert Cramond had recommended urgent action to prevent the entrance from silting up. But nobody came forward to meet the estimated three hundred pounds cost. The farmers of Berwickshire had had their fill of bailing out

Eyemouth – especially since it now seemed more important to fish merchants than grain traders. Nothing was raised. Nothing was done.

Wedderburn, taking his lead from David Renton, decided the time had come to offload responsibility for the port to a Harbour Trust. This was far from a cheap option, requiring a Private Act of Parliament which Patrick himself paid for. As he charted this through Westminster the laird asked once more for help from the Berwickshire gentry and from the Convention of Royal Burghs of Scotland. A delegation from the Convention hurried down to Eyemouth, arriving on 8 July 1794. They were shocked at the state of affairs. 'We are of the opinion that if the breaches are not soon repaired, the harbour will become totally ruinous'.

Renton drew up a memorial to the Convention, which presented Eyemouth as core to the prosperity of East Coast trade, vital to the national war effort against France and to the suppression of smuggling. The effrontery of this was quite shameless for a community which had so recently prospered from illegal trade, and which still echoed to nocturnal landings of contraband.

> It is well known that the enemy's privateers, as well as smuggling vessels have been in these seas when the King's ships and yachts are either confined by contrary winds in the Firth of Forth, or by being at such a distance, the mischief has been done before they could come out to prevent it ... whereas no enemy's ship, or smuggling vessel can appear between Holy Island scares and the red head, without being discovered from Eyemouth. It is certain that if the King's Ships and yachts were stationed there, the enemy's privateers durst not appear to annoy the trade, and smuggling in those parts would be totally suppressed.

Positing Eyemouth as a bastion against freebooters was a good joke. Playing the patriotic card was almost as hilarious. The navy had never been welcome in Berwickshire. His majesty's ships were feared because they hunted down smugglers. They also carried off men, who often did not return. The press gang regularly 'recruited' in Eyemouth. John Spears' cousin was one those taken in the 1770s. John gave his name to his first son, who died as a baby, and his second, who became a fisherman of renown. The man both were christened after neither saw nor held them. Once snatched for service William Spears never returned to walk the streets of Eyemouth or crew the family boat. He died for a King and cause of which he knew little.

In late July 1794, three weeks after their visit, the Convention signalled its willingness to give a generous grant of three hundred pounds, proof of the importance it attached to Eyemouth harbour. But a warning was also sounded that the support from the Royal Burghs and, more importantly, from Berwickshire's farmers could no longer be taken for granted.

One condition attached to the grant was the formation of a committee to take a long hard look at the port's affairs. As this considered its work, a parallel local group convened in emergency session. After all the warnings and sure signs of fatigue, the old pier had finally given up its struggle. A lashing midnight gale pushed brickwork onto the berthing spots, and dragged a dune of sand and gravel over the main channel. It was a calamity for the port, and one that Cramond had predicted more than twenty years before. For a short period Eyemouth harbour was once more closed.

Another drive was made to solicit funds, and, including the £300 already promised, around £1,500 was raised. But as the Convention had warned, the farmers of Berwickshire did not offer a shilling. Wedderburn sent £100, but most of the funding came from the merchants and traders of Eyemouth. It was now a mercantile port. That was evident from the opening session of the Harbour Trust, which was inaugurated on 15 May 1797.

The members estimated that around 200 ships annually used the harbour, which ought to generate net revenue of around £70 a year. The first schedule of dues did not even mention fishing boats. Apart from the fact that these were usually drawn up on the beach, rather than tethered at the pier, there was also an appreciation they were liable to pay the minister's teind.

At first traffic at the harbour exceeded the trust's expectations. Because of the French war, imports of foreign grain were banned and this stimulated production at home. Berwickshire was the breadbasket of Scotland. Grain prices doubled between 1795–7 and vast quantities were shifted through Eyemouth. In the period up to 1815 port income exceeded the predicted £70 p.a. in all but three years. In 1814 it amounted to more £154.

Thomas Purves, the harbour master, was rushed off his feet and he petitioned – successfully – for an increase in his salary. His family had once spun linen in Coldingham, now they all lived from the sea. Many would die on the ocean, including Thomas's great-nephew James, who was destined to drown while strapped to the tiller of the *Myrtle* in the Disaster of 1881.

As with the close of the seventeenth century, the dying years of the eighteenth offered much promise to Eyemouth. The village was a commercial and increasingly a fishery centre. There was plenty of berthing space along three substantial stone piers. Street coverings were being put down throughout the village and a bridge was erected across the river Eye providing a link with the Great North Road. New businesses were providing employment, including a commercial boatyard. There was ambition in the place and a sense of drive from the Harbour Trust, from David Renton the baron baillie and from the resident heritors in the parish. The laird, though absent in London or at his inland estates, at least did not interfere. All of this made Eyemouth *potentially* significant. It *might* be on the cusp of great things. Then again, it might regress into little more than a tidal creek with a handful of cobbles and a thin pretence of trade. All hinged on decisions yet to be taken.

The minister ought to have rejoiced at these prospects for the community that he served. Perhaps he did. But the dawning of the new century brought a fresh challenge for George Tod. He had endured long years of poor attendance at his Sunday services, he had preached till he was blue in the face of the moral outrages many in his parish were guilty of – fornication, Sabbath breaking, drunkenness, some were even opting to be married by a lay-priest at nearby Lamberton. The Kirk he used was falling to bits and regardless of his protests nothing was done. Tod leapt at the chance when Ladykirk parish became vacant. It was the charge of his long-dead father, it offered an improved stipend, it promised peace, respect and much overdue deference. After sixteen troubled years, George Tod couldn't get out of Eyemouth quickly enough.

Chapter Five

A Cultured Man in a Cultural Desert

Frae Farthest Merse and Lammermuir
Frae ditch and dyke and drain
Our country lads o' ilk degree
To work an honest 'dale' at sea
Are hurrying east again

They raced horses for sport on the Berwickshire border. A long straight gallop opened out a little to the south of Burnmouth, pointing downwards to the last settlement before England. Here at the tiny Kirk of Lamberton the regal union of implacable enemies was cemented with the handing over by English plenipotentiaries of Margaret Tudor, daughter of Henry VII and bride-to-be of James IV. A century later, in 1603, their great-grandson, along with a massive courtly retinue passed by the hamlet en route to pick up the crown of England.

Lamberton became used to hurried weddings, though none would ever involve individuals of quite such high rank, in a match that would be so significant. A tradition developed that James IV, in recognition of the part the Kirk had played in his own marriage, decreed that weddings could take place within the parish without proclamation of the banns. It was poor history, but it was believed. The old toll house was the Gretna Green of the east, a place where lay priests said vows over runaway lovers, shotgun brides and those disinclined for whatever reason to involve a man of the cloth. A sanctuary for rich and poor alike which by the middle of the nineteenth century annually hosted more than three hundred marriages. Once a year it also thundered to the sound of lathered horses. Lamberton Races attracted substantial crowds to a tented village that served as a feeing fair for landless hinds. Lairds and lords, peasants and paupers rubbed shoulders and drank in a heady mixture of holiday excitement and turpentine brew. They came from all the airts of eastern Berwickshire and north Northumberland. On little ponies, in rickety traps and on foot. They boozed and gambled, sang and fought. It was an occasion many looked forward to, and it even endured the austere years of the long French Wars.

The fisherfolk of Berwickshire relished the races. The event provided a break from the summer herring season, and for the Eyemouth contingent it followed on from their own fair on the first Thursday in June, and foreshadowed the late Autumn one, held on the last Thursday in October. Lamberton was also important to many of the landsmen who helped crew the boats. From the 1780s when the drave revived, and especially from the mid 1790s when the shoals danced to the shore, part time 'hands' were taken on to crew up the summer vessels. Weavers, tailors and shoemakers were amongst those who dipped their toes in the German Ocean, but above all the fleet depended on an army of landless labourers. For some the drave would become an essential part of their living. The new methods of agriculture and gradual introduction of machinery meant that by the 1820s an acre of barley, oats or wheat could be cultivated with only half the labour required in 1760. Life on the land became hard. The drave was a seasonal diversion and potentially a good earner, especially for single men. But it was only seen as a supplement to their meagre living from the soil. Most continued to bargain their labour at hiring fairs. They still legged it down to the gallops of Lamberton.

John Spears was an old man at the start of the nineteenth century. He lent heavily on his eldest boy William and, as the first decade wore on, it was the son who inherited the family portion of the winter haddock and summer drave boats. The role of skipper went to Spears' nephew and namesake. These two cousins, John and William, were Haimoothers born and bred, their futures rested on the fickle nature of shoaling fish and the mood swings of the elements.

The homage old John had once paid to his betters – to the lords in the land of his ancestors who took away the little ground he had and forced him out, and to the minister in the Kirk of his nation who demanded a share in his earnings from the sea – was now dilute. The Spears did not attend Sabbath worship. They did not take the sacrament. They did not invite the minister to their home or use his services in their daily lives. When William decided to marry Ellen Dougal, there could be only one route. The couple opted for a Lamberton wedding, conducted by a layman who asked only that they abide by the law and accept each other. Tops of bottles were smashed, and Ellen dashed after her man with an open blade, intent on cutting through the bands of the creel he had hooked onto his shoulders. Then back by fast cart to Eyemouth, their family and friends from the quayside and a night-time shindig in one of the warehouses.

The celebrations of William and Ellen's wedding would have been pretty wild, with plenty of fine contraband and even rougher whisky downed. The company danced late into the night in the summer of 1802, perhaps with too much exuberance – the girl Ellen was carrying was born soon afterwards. Too premature for the age, and too tiny to survive long in the dirty, exposed conditions of Eyemouth, little Janet hardly drew breathe, hardly opened her eyes before life left her body. The minister, for once, was needed. Burials still required that degree of Christian reverence.

The baptism of William Spears had been one of the first services conducted by James Williamson after he was inducted at Eyemouth in 1776. The burial of that boy's first born was likewise an early duty for the new minister, the Rev, later Rev Dr James Smith who arrived in April 1802.

Smith did not approve of the excesses of Lamberton Races and still less 'irregular marriages' conducted at the toll house. He frowned on the heavy drinking, and deplored the habits of the fisherfolk in language, dress and hygiene. Dr Smith was a dour gentleman but an accomplished scholar who edited and revised Schrevelli's Greek lexicon, gaining a doctorate from Edinburgh University in the process. What on earth was he doing in Eyemouth? How uncomfortable did he feel as he opened his little prayer book to speak over the tiny coffin of Janet Spears, surrounded by the commonality of the village?

Like past ministers, James Smith's appointment aroused a lot of attention. How would he approach the pulpit, what lessons would he read and above all, what would he say and do about his stipend? James Smith was being closely watched in 1802. His seemed an awkward charge.

On the other hand things had to be set in context. Dr Smith lived two lives in Eyemouth. He had his books, his writings, his society soirées and civilised philosophic debate, often at Gunsgreen House. There was a group of genteel friends, the good and the almost grand in border society. Unlike George Tod, he joined Lodge St Ebbe and rubbed shoulders with fellow brethren including the Homes of Gunsgreen. Dr Smith courted and in 1805 married the very well connected Jane Forman Home. Jane was the niece of George Tod, and made up another strand of the complicated Wedderburn web.

By the early 1800s, with the death without issue of many of the Homes, it did indeed seem that the estates would come the way of George Tod. As events panned out the minister died in 1819, the year before the sixteenth laird, and it was his brother James who inherited as the next Lord of Wedderburn. James, who changed his name to 'Home' only enjoyed the status for a year before he too passed away, and everything then passed to Jane Forman Home's brother John. Though John was married he did not leave any legal issue, and his heir was his own – and Jane's – brother William. To further complicate an already tortuous, not to say almost incestuous family tree, William married Jean Home, the daughter of George of Gunsgreen. Their daughter Jean, the niece of Jane Forman Home, would eventually inherit everything under entail. That was not until the 1850s and by then Jean was the wife of David Milne, son of Admiral Sir David Milne, who had been in charge of the coastal defences of Lothian and Berwickshire in the Napoleonic Wars. Much of this would stretch away into the future, but the links were evident when Smith first walked the potholed streets of the village. Like George Tod he felt he was not only spiritually above the people, but a class apart as well. Smith, the Tods, the Homes, the Milnes and their like were the elite in eastern Berwickshire. The aristocracy of the Merse.

All that was fine for gay parties and social get-togethers. The work of ministering to the poor of Eyemouth was another thing altogether. Smith doubtless did try to do his best for the community. If the fishing people would not come to his Kirk, did not wish his visitations, were recalcitrant when admonished by the minister or the session for their shortcomings, then what more could he do? A man of God should not have to struggle to deliver the Good News message. He was a minister not a missionary.

The frustrations soon sunk in. Non-attendance he might stomach; lack of respect was an annoyance. Christ-like he might turn the other cheek. One thing that Dr Smith could not ignore, however, was the maintenance of his living. The Presbytery was watching and it did not take long for the fish tithe issue to rear up once again. It was as though the early days of George Tod were being repeated. 'No, no, he must have been misinformed. They were no longer liable', 'The matter had been settled many years before', 'some might still have to pay, but not them', 'Here, have a few fish for the pot ... and plenty more to come when he was hungry, but money? Not a chance. They didn't pay money to the m*inister*'. So many excuses. Such ingenuity.

James Smith showed that despite his aesthetic leanings he could be just as tough as Tod had been. He not only insisted on the prompt payment of the modus of £1 13s. 4d. In 1803 Smith also tried to revive the Church's claim to part of the summer drave.

Why a man of letters and learning should have fired up the community seems, at first, hard to understand. He must have been aware from George Tod of the nature and extent of previous litigation and the trouble that it had caused.

But a cultured man could not live on a paltry eighty pounds a year. Smith could not entertain in a tiny Manse. He could not afford a fine cloak when delivering his Sabbath erudition or a pretty trousseau for his bride-to-be, or the wherewithal for trips to the country and runs to the towns. Unless, that is, he tapped into the growing profits from the herring trade in the parish – profits that Tod had been sure the minister was lawfully obliged to take; profits which if he did not now demand, might be lost forever to the Church. Smith spoke with the session, consulted his lawyers and prepared his case.

There were other matters distracting the minds of men, indeed consuming the entire country from the Dover Straits to Cape Wrath as these missives were sent up to Edinburgh. It was a time of national emergency and potential French invasion.

Coastal stations were put on alert and volunteer companies formed into a makeshift home guard. At Eyemouth the handful of soldiers garrisoned at a barracks just below Fort Point was increased. The bairns joined in pretend drills on the beach, as infantrymen marched along the shore and into the bulbous market place for inspection. Two and a half centuries before, it had been French regulars who had used the village to stand against the English. Now redcoats with shouldered muskets strutted behind the Union flag, defying Bonaparte to attack.

Those who made their living from the sea had a particular interest in the progress of the war. As the needs of the navy increased the press gang reappeared with a vengeance. A number of Eyemouth men were snatched in one big raid made on the village on New Year's Day 1806. The fate of the unfortunates was effectively sealed when the Customs Board received another anonymous letter from someone in the village alleging that some had returned to their old habits. The customs records duly note what followed as a double benefit to the nation 'Certain fishermen who were lately concerned with the smuggling have now been impressed into the navy'. Perhaps the men were jumped as they made their way from house to house on what was normally the happiest, haziest day of their year. Thumped on the head, to wake up with the mother of all hangovers in the bilge of a King's man-o'-war.

Reports of what might have happened to these men and to the few who actually volunteered for service in the forces came via the pages of the *British Gazette and Berwick Advertiser* which rolled off the presses for the first time in 1807. Prior to this news was obtained from the infrequent mail coach, through gossip from visiting ship's captains and, of course, from whatever the minister could tell them. British victories were always proclaimed with all the ostentation that could locally be conjured up. In 1798 for example, musket rounds fizzed into the air when it was learned that Nelson had destroyed the French fleet at the Battle of the Nile. The canon recently plugged on the earthworks of the old Fort thundered shot for the first time into the bay. It was a carnival for the community and the Freemasons even offered to reimburse the soldiers for the ammunition they had used.

Three years later and news of another massive British victory at Aboukir Bay near Alexandria was marked in even grander style. The triumph of the

Scots Pack on 21 March 1801 was all the more sweet because of the part a local man played in the capture of the first eagle standard to be prised from the crack French Invincible Legion.

James Sinclair won fame with the Black Watch in the scorching sands of Egypt. His name was shouted through the cooler streets of home, and toasted, along with that of Nelson, Pitt and Wellington when word of Sinclair's heroism eventually reached Eyemouth. Such was the sense of patriotism that James McIntosh, who worked a small farm on the edge of the parish, named his first-born son after the Prime Minister. William Pitt McIntosh, born at the start of the nineteenth century, would live to a ripe old age, see the rise of the town and enjoy the riches of the fishing. In his twilight years he also witnessed the death of the place, when the hurricane came down on Black Friday.

British victories in Egypt aside, the French threat to the island fortress was real enough. Commander Milne who set to work organising the sea defences of Berwickshire and Lothian inevitably came into contact with the Wedderburns. When Milne decided to put roots down in Berwickshire he bought an estate close to Paxton called Graden. Thereafter it was known as Milne Graden.

The southern-Forth watch should have been a quiet posting, and for most of the time it was. The chances of the French mounting an attack through the underbelly of Scotland were about as likely as Rev Smith attracting a capacity congregation on a Sunday. Yet for a few hours on the last day of January 1804 it seemed as though Napoleon had taken leave of his senses and ordered an attack on Lothian, the Merse and North Northumberland.

As dusk was pulling down the day on 31 January 1804 beaconsmen at Hume Castle, far inland, ignited their bonfire on sighting the flames of another from the English side of the Cheviots. The French were on their way! All freemen were called to arms!

What they had actually seen was the reflected glow of a housewarming. A family had just moved in to their new home atop a hillside in Northumberland, and, as was the custom, had lit fires in every room of the building, to literally warm up the house and offer an open invitation to friends and family to visit. The nervous militiamen at Hume Castle were not to know this, and their signal set in train all the beacons along the border. Foot soldiers and horsemen raced first to their muster points and then began a dash to the coast. Within two hours the Roxburgh yeomanry filled the market place at Kelso. The men of Liddesdale had been so afraid of being late in the field that they had commandeered every available horse and rode into the town at full pelt chanting Reiver-style

We'll gie them a welcome,
Well gie them a grave.
O Wha Daur Meddle wi me
An Wha Daur Meddle wi me
My name it is little Jock Elliot
And Wha daur meddle wi me?

Before dawn on the following day militiamen had streamed to the coast, arriving at Haddington, Dalkeith and Dunbar. In Eyemouth the little troop of soldiers lay prone in the grass on Fort Point, anxiously peeking at the sea for any glimpse of French transport ships. Bombardiers hunched over their tiny, polished artillery pieces, whilst down below along the Street, bemused villagers wondered about the commotion. Throughout the day volunteers poured into the place, as the wait went on for an attack which never came. Had the beacon at St Abbs been fired it is likely that the whole of Scotland would have joined in the false alarm. The canny watchers there were more circumspect. They tarried from setting alight their pyre on the very reasonable basis that any invasion alarm would come from the *coast* and not from inland. By the evening of February 1 the order to stand down was circulated. The threat had been real enough to convince some from Berwick to flee the town, especially after a joker trundled a wheelbarrow at high speed across the cobbled streets in the early hours of the morning. The echoing sounds persuaded many that the French had arrived and were taking up position.

This excitement over, life went back to normal. Attention in Eyemouth switched from the potential depredations of the French to the very real threat of an enemy much closer to home. James Smith's legal action for herring teind entered the Court of Session in Edinburgh. The amount he was demanding staggered even those who remembered the avarice of George Tod. To ask for a full tenth of the catch was an outrage, but the minister's estimation of the cash equivalent was even more unbearable. Smith calculated that each boat should give him £20 *sterling,* not Scots, even though he later admitted that Tod never managed to collect any more than £22 sterling a year for *all* the teind, whitefish and herring combined. Even if some of the boats had grossed £200 in the summer of 1804, and none would admit to it, such sums could not be borne.

The real target for the minister was not the fishermen but the merchants who had moved from the corn trade and smuggling to curing and selling fish. They sheltered behind the modus exemption, pretending they too should only pay £1 13s. 4d. sterling as tithe, rather than the full tenth of the catch landed in boats which they owned, but did not declare, or by men who they employed, but would not acknowledge. It was a well-worn dodge, and potentially robbed the manse of tens if not hundreds of pounds in a very good season. The imperative to plug this loophole was made all the more apparent when the demands of the French war forced Britain to abandon the Gold Standard in 1797. The printing of paper money caused prices to soar. The real value of the modus declined even further.

In 1788 it had been John Turnbull who had engaged lawyers to represent both himself and the five skippers in the Court of Session. In 1804 the fishermen apparently acted by themselves. There can be no doubt, however, that it was merchants like Thomas Hill, Richard Turnbull, Thomas Forrest, William Robertson and Robert Alexander who were shifting the chess pieces behind the scenes. Little doubt either that they paid the legal bills. How else could the fisherfolk, already in hock for the new boats which were being delivered from the beachside yard, afford an expensive action in Edinburgh? How else might they comprehend the importance of defending the suit?

Everyone connected with the fishing stood to lose if Smith was successful. Home crews might desert the place while skippers from other ports had already made clear they would not be hounded for teind but would sail instead to Berwick or to Dunbar. Without a substantial drave the wages paid to the women who worked in the yards would be lost, recently established sail and rope makers go out of business and trade at the bars and lodging houses drop off. Many of the new buildings, which had been thrown up for gutting and curing, would fall empty. It was a near doomsday scenario – how many other little fishing creeks along the coast had shown promise only to wither at the first hint of difficulties? There was no God-given right for Eyemouth to succeed. In fact, it seemed that God, or at least His agent in the village, was intent on destroying the place.

Smith was sanguine about all of this. As a commercial port Eyemouth was booming. The fish trade though more important than ever was still eclipsed by commercial traffic. Nor did the minister accept that his demands would lead to the demise of the drave. He simply wanted to restore the value of the teind delivered to the Manse and take a little of the additional profit that was so evidently being made.

Once again the case took years to trickle through the courts. Smith kept a close note on what he felt he was due during this hiatus, but was sensible enough not to press his claims on the quayside. A reckoning would be made when the legal judgement was delivered. All the while the fishing continued to prosper, the fleet grow and the population increase. In 1811, 962 people were noted within the parish, reversing a slight dip that had occurred in the 1790s.

The year of the census started badly for James Smith. In January, in the

Court of Session, Lord Glenlee rejected the arguments that had been based on the 1793 judgement. After seven long years of litigation it seemed that the fishermen had no case to answer, and the merchants no cause to worry. Celebratory toddies were downed in the bars for what seemed to be another famous victory. But the joy proved premature. Smith was a stubborn character and would not accept this as the end of the matter. The action continued. Many more months of uncertainty followed, involving more expense for both sides, more acrimony in the village.

At least the minister had a new Kirk to look forward to. The heritors were finally persuaded that the old building was beyond repair after receiving a petition from all the ministers of the Merse. 'The Presbytery do condemn Eyemouth church as in a ruinous state and unfit for a place of public worship'. James Williamson had been saying that thirty years before. A patch of ground along the Ayton Road, mid way between the marketplace and Chester House, was acquired and on 24 June 1811 the foundation stone of the new Parish Church was solemnly put in place. Members of Lodge St Ebbe paraded through the lanes and down to the site, near what had once been the village rubbish tip. Operative masons when digging the foundations would have come within a few yards of the body of a teenage girl who had lain in the rancid sands for four centuries. Was she murdered? Had she perhaps been buried in a pagan ritual? The remains would not be uncovered until the site was examined by archaeologists in 1982.

The stone laying which ought to have been a joyful coming together of all the people of the parish was marred somewhat by the highjinks of John Dangerfield. He was one of the few smugglers who still operated along the Berwickshire coast and was a rough character not to be crossed. Dangerfield openly ran the blockade imposed during the French Wars, sometimes discharging cargoes of wine and tobacco quite openly on the quay, but more generally landing at tiny inlets which only he and his associates knew about.

As a Freemason Dangerfield was entitled to be at the event, but he and his crew were obviously much the worse for drink. The smuggler raised up his sword and staggered towards the official party. He rambled and spluttered and offered to fight any man who dared to take him on. None did. There was instead an embarrassed silence, save for the sound of the shuffling feet of men staring purposefully at the ground. After making his point, very loudly, Dangerfield cursed at the crowd again before tottering away presumably towards the Ship bar. For the dubious entertainment he provided this brother Freemason was ejected from Lodge St Ebbe.

Work on the new Church took three years to complete. During this time, as the bricks stretched out and the tower began to thrust skywards,

James Smith's protracted teind case inched forward in Edinburgh. The heritors might have financed the Kirk, but the fishermen felt they were being robbed to pay for the pews. This minister was now even more unpopular than Tod had been, and that was saying something.

Dr Smith didn't even have the ability to stage manage the formal opening of the new building. It was ready by the early summer of 1814, and the minister tried to make the occasion even grander by offering to officiate at a service in Lodge St Ebbe. The Freemasons curtly turned him down. They would be parading through Eyemouth to the Church, but would do so in traditional manner, and would not require Dr Smith's involvement. It was an embarrassing rebuff. Smith, because of his determination to see the legal action through, had few friends in the community.

Just days before the consecration news emerged from the Court of Session that cast even more gloom over the pallid features of James Smith. His latest ploy had been rejected. The Court agreed that fish teind was due from the fishermen, but would not accept that separate and additional payment could be claimed from them on their summer herring earnings. Nor was it proven that merchants or others were liable in any regard. It was up to Smith to offer further evidence that they were. The minister pondered his options as he pulled on his cloak and strode from the manse to dedicate the Kirk.

The event drew crowds the like of which Eyemouth had not seen for many a long year, including even those fishermen, like William Spears, who were at loggerheads with Smith and who felt no bonding with the established Church of Scotland. Of course, their attendance did not signal willingness to compromise. They had come for the show. Maybe they hoped for more theatre from John Dangerfield. Instead they got a rather tedious religious ceremony.

Spears was as affected as most of the rest of the town with 'the ague' from the dank environment in which he and his family lived. They were certainly more comfortable than they had been in the years before 1780, and the scourge of typhus, so long endemic in the community, was now becoming little more than a bad memory. But conditions were not easy and for fishermen life on the sea was becoming ever more risky. They were now venturing further and further offshore, and some boats had even started to migrate as far as Caithness for the late spring herring season.

Life was generally just as unpleasant and as perilous for the wives and bairns left at home. Of the seven children Ellen had borne John Spears by the time of the Kirk's opening, only two lived beyond infancy. Dr Smith's early work in burying Janet was followed with the laying to rest of another baby girl, also called Janet, a third, named Catharine, and a pair of boys in quick succession, both called John after their paternal grandfather. The family seemed fated to lose all of their bairns until Andrew arrived in January 1806, and somehow made it through the winter. He looked like being the couple's only child, when Ellen was again confined and delivered of another boy on 12 November 1812. Named after his father, William also survived childhood, though he was always a sickly bairn. Ill health would dog his later years, though it would be a very long and quite remarkable life. Despite the relentless pregnancies, which would yet involve one more birth, that of a little girl, who was given her own name, Ellen Dougal also lived to a grand old age.

A few months after the opening of his new Kirk, James Smith bowed to the inevitable in the Court of Session. He was not going to win the action and agreed to accept a judicial minute lodged by the fishermen, which, like the judgement of 1793, offered a kind of victory to both sides. The five skippers confirmed they were free to fish all year round for a fixed annual payment of £20 Scots, that is £1 13s. 4d. Smith was provided with a clear statement that this privilege was available to full time fishermen only. But, and this remained the massive imponderable for years to come, on what basis would proof be accepted of a man's occupation? And what of the position of halfdalesmen who were not full time fishermen? The minute read:

> On behalf of John Spears, Robert Collins, William Maltman, James Noble and Alexander Paterson. The defenders humbly submit that they are entitled to catch as many herrings as they can, in their own proper boats, with their ordinary boats' crews, and for their own proper behoof, and are not liable for teind upon such herrings. They do not wish to transfer their privilege to merchants and others, or to allow their names and rights to be a cover for others for withholding teind from the minister. All they desire is the above exemption, which they have offered to prove has been their prescriptive right.

Another eleven long years of legal debate had ended without a formal judgement and with matters apparently returned to the way they had been in 1804. But Smith, now armed with this judicial minute, felt vindicated. It clarified who was exempt from herring teind, therefore by implication it established who was not.

The judicial minute was agreed in the summer of 1815, at exactly the time when the government doubled the bounty on herring from two shillings to four shillings a barrel. It made marginal activity profitable, and already profitable business lucrative. With the French Wars over, export trade to the slave estates of the West Indies, the traditional market for pickled herring, picked up once more. A new market on the Continent was also developing, with branded Scotch cured herring acquiring a formidable reputation, even amongst the fastidious Germans. The establishment of the Fishery Board in 1807 helped in this, with fishery officers domiciled in every sizeable port, including Eyemouth.

Large numbers of stranger boats from the Forth and from Fife again arrived off Berwickshire. Smith was diligent in issuing teind bills to them all. Quite often he joined his tallyman at the head of the pier, noting the number of crans that were being landed. What the merchants had feared and warned of now came to pass. The visiting crews had no need for a fight with the Eyemouth minister, they could go elsewhere. In successive seasons that is precisely what they did.

By the summer of 1818 landings had dipped alarmingly and even local crews were boycotting the pier. They did not have to leave the village to do this. Instead they fraternised with the erstwhile enemy. Large French ships took up position in the bay and offered ready money for herring. Here was an international solution to the fishermen's domestic tussle with the Kirk. If they did not actually *land* their catch, how could they be charged teind on it? Of course it was not only Dr Smith who lost out from this ingenious deal. If less fish were landed what would the merchants cure or the salesmen sell?

The timing could not have been worse for Eyemouth. The close of the Napoleonic Wars led to a slump in the grain trade as prices readjusted to peacetime conditions. Coastal business tailed off and dues at the harbour tumbled from £154 in 1814 to a meagre £23 six years later. The trust, which in 1796 expected a healthy annual surplus of revenue over expenditure, somehow managed to rack up a debt of more than £300 by 1819.

The decline in commercial revenue ought to have been more than compensated by the increased fishing activity. But at Eyemouth fishing boats paid no dues. They had been specifically exempted when the Orders were drawn up in the 1790s, *because of their obligation to pay tithe to the Kirk*. If this demand now led to the ruination of the herring business, Eyemouth would be totally sunk.

Surely there had to be a way to satisfy Dr Smith before this happened? It was like 1788 and 1804 all over again – except this time there was no looming legal action. This time the fishermen, or to be more precise, the fish merchants, took the initiative. In the late autumn of 1818 the ten leading curers in the village called at the Manse. Thomas Hill led them but included in the group was a young man called John Dickson who had only just started a smoking business on the quay. In later years Dickson would become the most celebrated trader in the town. More significantly for the meeting with Smith was the presence of Richard Turnbull, son of the merchant who had stood his ground in the legal tussle with the Kirk in 1788. His was a conciliatory voice and Smith was inclined to listen – not least because for all the trouble that the family had caused to the Kirk, one of their number, John Turnbull, had recently enrolled as a divinity student at Edinburgh University. Though the fishermen shunned the Kirk because of its demands on their pockets, some merchants were clearly happy to return to the Establishment, especially if it helped shore up their social pretensions.

The minister's parlour strained to accommodate the visitors, though at least their body heat warmed up the chilly room, which reeked from the smoking grate every time the door was opened. The curers crowded in, and Dr Smith, doubtless enjoying the occasion, asked what he could do for them. Thomas Hill, speaking for the party, said they had a proposal, which they hoped would end the fish teind problem. That summer some of the Fife men had spoken of a similar tax which had once been demanded in the East Neuk. To forestall the very kind of trouble now being experienced in Eyemouth, the minister there had negotiated to lease his rights to a tacksman for an agreed sum over a specified period. That deal and the Fife tithe had long since died away, but might it point towards a possible compromise in Eyemouth?

Dr Smith, who was in ill health and assuredly tired of the ructions over the tithe, could barely contain his glee. He embraced the idea with gusto, but drove a hard bargain when it came to the nitty gritty of agreeing a price. Whatever was offered he demanded double; whatever concession was given, he asked for more. Eventually the deal was done and from the summer of 1819 the right to fish tithe was assigned to the ten merchants, for an annual rent of £57 10s. 0d. That was in addition to the modus payments from the home-based crews, now eight in number. The deal, which cost each curer less than £6, effectively trebled the amount the minister took in from the tithe. More importantly for the community, it offered a permanent solution to what had for so long been an intractable problem.

The agreement complete, Smith then successfully petitioned the Presbytery for permission to spend lengthy periods away from the parish on the grounds of his age and ill health. The old minister had hit the clerical jackpot. A massive increase in his salary, four or five months in the year absence from a place he had never really liked, and an end to the long running trouble of the tithe. In February 1820, an assistant was appointed to help Dr Smith and to take on all pastoral duties in the periods he was not at home. The choice was made by Smith himself and was obvious. John Turnbull, his studies at Edinburgh now at an end, returned to Eyemouth as both assistant and successor to the minister.

Smith then played an ace from the nap hand he had suddenly been dealt.

The minister proposed, and it was accepted, that his new assistant should take half the fish teinds of Eyemouth as the major element in *his* salary. It gave Turnbull a personal stake in the lease deal and ensured that any future annoyance from the fishermen or the merchants would be directed at a native of the parish. Smith may have been a Greek scholar, but the web he drew around his closing days was positively Byzantine.

Larger fleets than ever before were now drawn to Berwickshire. The merchant-lessees who reaped the rewards could well afford to absorb the costs of the money paid to the minister, but altruism was not a quality they cared for. Boats were never charged too much, but anyone who showed reluctance to pay what *they* asked for got a crack over the head from one of their burly coopers.

Fishing was now the number one business in Eyemouth. It gave work to all that needed it – including those who lost their jobs when the old kelp works in Mason's Wynd closed. The factory had been part of the village for several decades, taking seaweed from Eyemouth and the neighbouring coastal parishes of Cockburnspath, Coldingham, Ayton and Mordington. It provided work for the very poor, the infirm and the elderly and operated on extremely tight margins. It could not survive after duty was reduced on Barilla in 1820. The shack, which had housed the works, was taken over by the most indigent in the village, and continued to house paupers late into the nineteenth century. Shortly before the demise of kelping a bone mill was opened at Brownsbank, close to the distillery on the southern shore of the River Eye. It would eventually take over the entire site, processing bones, rags and coal from all parts of the East Coast, and material imported from Germany.

A few individuals tried to make money from an Old Faithful. Shebeening of whisky at least to supply a local need went on even after a general reduction in duties in the early 1820s made taxed spirits affordable. The fact that rates were lower in Scotland than England ensured that smuggling across the border still went on until that particular anomaly ended in the 1850s.

Berwickshire stills suffered from the changes to the Scottish duties. Small distilleries, like that at Brownsbank, suddenly faced massive and now quite legal competition from much larger operations in other parts of Scotland. 'The smugglers from the northern and middle districts of Scotland have marched almost together to the borders' commented the *Berwick Advertiser* in 1823, 'where a fine field is open to their talent and industry, in introducing spirits legally made into England. The difference of the duty is 3/6 per gallon.'

Eventually, the owners of Brownsbank changed its use, and Scotland's most southern distillery became first a brewery and then a chemical works producing artificial camphor and vitriol. Some locals who had been brought up on Brownsbank Best might hardly have noticed the difference. The whisky was remembered in the early 1900s as 'cut-throat stuff'.

But, regardless of quality, strong drink was needed not just to inebriate, but to settle deals, solemnise births and marriages, say farewell to the dead and celebrate anything that was worth celebrating. Like the coming of age of young fisher-callants.

Before a lad was admitted to a boat's crew at the age of ten or eleven, tradition demanded a 'brothering'. It mirrored Freemasonry in ritual, and was entered into with equal reverence. The elements were almost as secret as those practised by the St Ebbe brethren and though boys knew something would happen, they were never told the details or advised of the timing. The origins of this 'rite-into-manhood' are obscure, but it probably evolved at the same time as the Freemasons set up in the town and was certainly an established feature by the early years of the nineteenth century.

In or about 1823 just before the start of the summer herring drave, young William Spears, along with some other boys, including his best friend and cousin, William Dougal, were grabbed from behind and dragged towards a granary on the Salt Greens. Each had their head covered either with a lint bag, or simply the heavy hands of the assailants, usually their elder brother or cousin. In Spears' case it was probably his brother Andrew, a veteran seventeen-year-old who ambushed and pulled him along the lanes. The group of lads, including Spears' contemporaries Robert Angus, Peter Mack, Alexander Purves and James Lough, were flung into a quayside building. Awaiting them were the men they would soon be joining at sea. No women were ever privy to a brothering. It was, though, a proud moment for every mother, and kept them gabbing for weeks at the common well and bleaching green at the base of Fort Point.

Their heads uncovered, the lads blinked into the eerie candlelit world of men perched on benches and beams amidst the airless stench of rancid tobacco, stale grain and the detritus from the fish trade. That, and the pervasive odour of whisky. Spears, Dougal and the rest were forced to the far wall, dingy and darker still than the rest of the storehouse. Stepping from the shadows, the skippers lunged at each lad, grabbing their soft chins and forcing their heads upward to gaze into the loft. Above, dangling from the ceiling joist was a block and tackle with a noose attached. This was yanked down and placed around each boy's neck in turn. Whoever was first suffered most. The anticipation, the unnerving uncertainty of what would happen next was part of the test. Pity the bairn who wept or filled his breeks at that point.

A salt roll and a jug of beer were brought forward and the unfortunate callant barked at by his skipper to 'swalley the breid'. Any hesitation, any attempt to spit out the brackish loaf, and the noose rope, held by a 'hangman' to the side of the lad, was pulled taut around his neck. There was no way out but to eat the roll, and as each boy did so the skipper sprinkled beer across his face while another crewman threw ale over his legs and britches, each shouting alternatively 'weather' and 'Lee'. This symbolised a fisherman's life; the life these young boys were about to enter. A dangerous existence where crews had to work as one or the whole boat might be imperilled. The wreck in November 1821 of a Banff lugger in the Eyemouth roadsteads, with the loss of five of the six-man crew had recently underlined just how unforgiving the sea could be.

For the privilege of being petrified with fear, part hanged, drenched with beer and gagged to the point of vomit on a putrid salt roll, each lad had to hand over five shillings. When all had been 'brothered', the ubiquitous whisky jar was brought out and fiddles and whistles played the men and boys a dance into unconsciousness. Spears, William Dougal, Robert Angus, James Lough and the rest of their crews became fishermen in the summer of 1823, even though they were not yet teenagers.

All had attained some formal education up to then. A new parochial school had been built by the heritors in 1821, and a lending library was set up in the same year. Books and learning were never very important to fishing folk, though, and teaching standards at the school were woefully low. William Landels, who began life as the son of a poor tenant farmer in the Parish and later became a renowned minister in London and Birmingham, reflected that although lessons were based on scripture, education in Eyemouth was far from that of the Christian ideal. 'The parish school was neither opened nor closed with prayer' he remembered, 'and the religious instruction the children received was thrashed into the dull by the taws of the master, or into the very obtuse with his fists forcibly applied to the sides of the head.'

It was all enough to drive a good man to drink – and that's exactly the effect it had on the poor schoolmaster James Trotter. Like the excisemen of old, Eyemouth eventually beat the Dominie. After almost a decade of battling with rough boys, rude girls and their indifferent parents, Trotter sought solace in a bottle. He was often drunk in class and after one almighty bender an exasperated John Turnbull finally complained to the Presbytery. This body rebuked Trotter, putting on record that he 'had been guilty of various acts of gross intoxication and having otherwise conducted himself in a most scandalous manner'. He might have expected worse. Of one hundred and thirty-nine cases brought against schoolmasters in Scotland in the period 1791–1853 more than a hundred resulted in dismissals. Only seventeen were let off with a reprimand.

It was unusual for boys to continue at school beyond the age of nine or ten. Once brothered they itched to go on their first trip as a man. William Spears joined James Dugald and his crew of William Angus, George Craig and Robert Young. Willie's father would not take the lad out on the family boat, at least not to begin with. Callants were placed with others so they could learn about the sea and about fishing with no fear of family favour. That said, all of them were interconnected in this insular place, some several times over. The fishing folk were a race apart because they were a race together. This gave them strength and a sense of their own worth, which was important both in their daily lives on the precarious ocean, and in their continuing battles with the Kirk and the laird over issues like the tithe.

The early 1820s was a decent enough time for these young boys to enter the harsh world of the Berwickshire fleet. Good money was possible from the herring fishing. Between 1809 and 1820 at least 10,000 barrels were exported from Eyemouth alone, in a trade that was worth a minimum of five thousand pounds a year. But as had been periodically the case, herring shoals might suddenly, and without explanation, disappear. The local crews therefore put as much reliance on the less lucrative, but certainly more dependable winter fishing for cod, haddock, whiting and saithe. They exploited the town's geography, supplying the nearby urban centre of Edinburgh and even took their fish by canal to Glasgow and the west of Scotland.

In the years after he appointed John Turnbull, Dr Smith became a stranger to the village. When he was not away he was bedridden in the Manse. Fish teind, which had been such an issue for Smith, George Tod and even James Allan, seemed settled forever. But this not did improve the mores of fishermen who continued to shun worship and even fish on the Sabbath.

John Wares, the resident Fishery Officer from 1817 frequently complained about the crime of setting nets on a Sunday, something that was all but general in his patch. Wares did what he could to discourage the practice but his district was too large and the fishermen ran rings around him. Those he caught did not appreciate his interference. The fishery officer faced the hazard of physical assault every single herring season of his long tenure in the district. As late as 1839, when Wares was in his early sixties, one encounter with the men of Dunbar led him to report that 'I was in great danger of my life'.

By then Dunbar, once the jewel of the southern Forth fishing industry was fast being overtaken by Eyemouth. The village was now a fish town of growing size and increasing importance.

Chapter Six

Dodges and Death and California Days

The village itself was a scene of spiritual indifference and death. A conversion was never known to have taken place in it. The very possibility of such a thing was denied

Rev. Dr William Landels

Shortly before Dr Smith slipped away from this earthly world a fisherman called James Dougal called at the rundown Manse. The Dougals were thrang with all of the families in the village, and James, a particularly fly character, was kin to the Spears, having married William's sister Agnes. He explained to the minister's wife that he had come to pay his annual tithe dues, told her that he worked the sea all year round and thrust his modus payment of £1 13s. 4d. into her hands. The fisherman then tarried a while, and seemed slightly over anxious that he should get a receipt for the money. With the minister ill, Dougal pressed Mrs Smith to do the necessary and when she duly wrote out a one line bill, he grabbed at the paper and was off like a shot.

James Dougal had deceived her. He had not been named under the terms of the 1818 tithe lease as one of the full time skippers. He should therefore not have paid the minister – or his wife – £1 13s. 4d. as exemption for herring tithe, but ought to have given whatever the leaseholders asked for in the summer season.

When the drave closed the merchant-lessees presented Dougal with a bill for an element of tithe to cover their costs. With a flourish Dougal produced his receipt from Mrs Smith, proof that he too belonged to the privileged class of fishermen. The episode caused much mirth in the community, and a lot of admiration for the sheer nerve of the man. Dougal justified his deception because he said he was discriminated against. He had not been named in the 1818 lease as he was then a raw youth. Now that he was a skipper in his own right, who in the summer took on two landsmen to crew his herring boat, Dougal felt it was his right to join those who only paid the modus. He did not want to be bothered for any tithe whatsoever, but if he had to pay anything it should be no more than £1 13s. 4d. for the whole year. There were others like him who were keenly watching for what might happen next. Would Dougal get away with it?

The ten leaseholders met in a bar and made it known to all that whilst

Mrs Smith had acted in good faith, they could not be out of pocket from her error. They decided against pursuing James Dougal, but instead held back £7 3s. 8d. from the lease money to the minister. This was the amount they estimated they *could* have charged had they been able to levy tithe against the fisherman and his crew. With the minister failing fast, they expected his wife to accept this as the inevitable consequence of her own foolishness. There was also the temptation to inflate Dougal's alleged liability to their own advantage. The merchants may even have been party to the entire episode, as a means of getting rid both of the tithe and the annual cost of the lease. By muddying the waters in the final days of Dr Smith they might have hoped that his successor John Turnbull would, as an Eyemouth man born and bred, abandon the Kirk's claims altogether.

In all of this they were profoundly mistaken. The minister rallied sufficiently from his sickbed to demand that the full amount be paid as normal. When this was refused James Smith again went to law. It was to be his final act. The old man died on 9 October 1825 a full month before the case came before Duns Sheriff Court. His widow pursued the matter, and though the court initially declared that the minister's estate was liable for the error, it later accepted that the proportion should only relate to the two landsmen and not the two Eyemouth men who, along with Dougal, crewed up the herring boat. The leaseholders were therefore awarded only half of what they had claimed, that is £3 11s. 10d. Their annoyance at what they believed to be the partiality of the judge boiled over into anger when Sheriff Boswell added that the merchants should pay two thirds of the costs of Mrs Smith. Added to their own legal bill, they had to expend more than £65 to gain less than £4.

The lease had seemed a neat, possibly permanent solution to the issue of the tithe. Sheriff Boswell's decision consigned it to history. Fresh negotiations had not been entered into when John Turnbull took over as full-time minister in the late autumn of 1825. These would have been pointless with the legal dispute continuing. In any case the herring were once more bypassing the Berwickshire shore. In the first year of the lease more than 20,000 barrels were cured in Eyemouth and a lot more sent fresh to market. A little over a tenth of that trade was being done at the time of the judgement on Dougal. Halfdalesmen arrived to be told there was no work for them, and that some of the boats were not even being launched from the beachside. Fourteen fewer curers set up business in 1827 than had done in the previous summer. All of the coopers were either laid off or given general labouring work. The loss of income was sorely felt in the community. There was scant consolation in the fact that the minister suffered as well.

With the herring gone, the fishermen focused their efforts, and most of their investment, on the winter white fishing. To maximise profits some even took large hauls along the Forth and Clyde canal to sell direct in Glasgow. In June 1825 John Wilson, one of a returning crew of four, fell from his boat near lock sixteen and was drowned. It was ironic that he had braved the ocean all of his life only to die on a narrow, becalmed inland waterway, after bingeing on cheap liquor at a waterside inn. Wilson's death came a fortnight after a ferocious storm ripped apart the fleet berthed at the pier-less harbour of Coldingham Shore. Four of the boats were badly damaged, and one, the *Merry Wives* completely wrecked. The total loss to the fishermen of St Abbs was more than £90. Only one of the 24 men affected had any savings to speak of. It was a bleak summer for Coldingham Shore.

Aid was sought from the Fishery Board in Edinburgh to part pay for a new boat which was ordered from the carpenters of Eyemouth. The boatyard, which had operated on an ad hoc basis at the side of the beach, was on the verge of moving. It had outgrown the site and the materials piled up on the Salt Greens quay got in the way and hindered trade. James Tate, who doubled as harbour master and ship builder, obtained land at Brownsbank on the other side of the harbour and on 29 March 1827 the first vessel was launched from the new yard. A large crowd was drawn to watch the sloop *Good Design* bound into the water before being hauled around to the dry dock for fitting out. In celebration of the day, a ball was held in the Mason's Lodge room, with dancing and drinking which went on well into the early hours of the next morning.

Three weeks after this famous celebration, and in spite of grim weather, the Berwickshire fleet cast off as usual for the haddock grounds. Each of the eight open boats had four men on board, and one or two also carried a cabin boy gaining experience and sea legs.

Another man by the name of James Dougal directed his crew towards a favoured spot about a mile off Gunsgreen Point, close enough to the shore to cut a dash for home. They had only just reached the place where they were to play out their lines, when a freak surge of water upturned the boat. The four men and the boy were flung into the dark and freezing seas. The drama was clearly visible from land, where the distance to the floundering crew appeared deceptively short. Some tried to fling rope out, and others made for a cobble that was lying in the shingle. By the time this was launched and had been rowed over the swells to the upturned hull, there was no sign of Dougal, or his crew of George Craig, William Angus and Robert Young.

Suddenly from behind a wave, one of the discarded oars surged forward.

Clinging on was a barely conscious boy, his eyes bulging in a face already 'sooked' by the sea. The rescue party grabbed at the lad and pulled him to safety. He was totally spent and for a while lay motionless in the bilge, as the boat sped away from that pool of death. Fourteen-year-old William Spears was carried to his home where his mother had been told to expect a corpse. Anyone who saw the boy believed that is what she would have come the morning. But William revived and against the odds eventually recovered. It was his first but would be far from his final taste of tragedy. Another, more personally painful disaster was being prepared by the hand of fate. It would soon envelop the whole Spears family.

The four drowned men were all married and left twenty-eight children behind. These families were rendered destitute. They had no savings and with the wreck of the boat, no assets to speak of. Some help was given from the recently formed Eyemouth Seaman's Friends Society, and assistance also came from parish relief. At least one of the widows, that of George Craig, remained on the poor roll until her death in the 1860s, almost forty years after her husband had been lost.

The shipwreck of 1827 was the first to hit Eyemouth for many years. It rocked the place and reminded the folk of the dangers of their calling. They would not have to wait long for the next tragedy to strike.

On 12 December 1828 the boats sailed out at first light and scattered towards the inshore banks. The weather was sinister and black clouds had already broken before the men were fully three miles from shore. The flashing lightning and heaving waves tossed the tiny boats about, and without even attempting to cast lines, they all pulled around for home.

Fifty-one-year-old William Spears, father of the young lad who had been miraculously saved two years before, had trouble tacking. His boat was overmanned. For some reason a vessel which could only comfortably accommodate four men that day carried a crew of six. The seas chucked the boat up and scooped the men under. The other skippers managed to make it home, taking with them the news of the loss of Spears' vessel. It was another hammer blow to the town. The local paper described the legacy of the shipwreck in the following way. 'The unfortunate sufferers are William Spears senior, William Spears junior; Joseph Collin senior, Joseph Collin junior; Andrew Dougal and David Dougal. As it is only about twenty-one months since Andrew Dougal's father was drowned by a similar accident, it may be literally said that in three families, father and son have perished.'

But the reporter had mixed up his facts. William Spears had sailed with his son alright, but it was his eldest boy and not his namesake who died with him. Andrew Spears was taken at the prime age of twenty-two. William, the boy of sixteen still sickly from the ducking and the trauma of the 1827 shipwreck had not been on board. He had scarcely sailed since that day. Now he was left to fend for his five-year-old sister Helen and their mother, Ellen Dougal. The Spears had been a big family in more ways than one. Others in the community had looked up to them. Now all that was left was a callow boy who didn't look as though he would outlive his teens, a baby girl and a weeping woman.

Berwickshire folk did not mark Christmas. The long anticipated Auld Year's Night was a morbid and quiet occasion in 1828, with the streets thin of people and short on revelry as time ticked over into 1829. Though none of the drowned had been of his Kirk, John Turnbull launched a subscription fund for the many dependants of the drowned men. He also persuaded other ministers to take a collection across the county. It was a Christian act from a minister who cared deeply and who was above all else an Eyemouth man. Turnbull emerged from the gloom and lamentation with an enhanced measure of respect. Some of the people, young Willie Spears included, began to think better of this man, if not yet of his Church.

Turnbull believed passionately in personal self-reliance and in the notion of communities helping themselves through times of trouble. This was the credo of the evangelical wing of the Kirk, and is best shown in Thomas Chalmer's attempts to replicate the rural parochial structure in slum ridden Glasgow. Fishing villages like Eyemouth, where all pulled together, ought to have provided a template for others to follow. Turnbull's actions in the wake of the 1828 Disaster were a perfect example of neighbourliness.

Yet while the people were glad to accept help in times of trouble, to the consternation of the minister they showed no shame in continuing to ask for handouts when life was relatively good. Eyemouth people were the dole scroungers of their day. John Turnbull bleakly accepted in his contribution to the *New Statistical Account* in 1835 that 'so far from there now being an aversion to apply for parochial relief, there is rather a disposition to demand it as a right.'

The Spears were grateful for the small amount they received from the relief fund. As well as the death of the men there was also the economic disaster of the wrecked family boat to consider. Young William had to start again. Along with his mother he stooped for hours at the shore picking whelks with which to bait lines borrowed from others in the village. He worked an abandoned and leaking herring boat in the summer, crewing up with his cousin Willie Dougal and two halfdalesmen. The boy quickly became a man, winning admiration for his courage and his enterprise. Turnbull might have seen in William Spears the epitome of all that he preached. But the fisher lad had no time for the Kirk and no interest in ideas. His only purpose was the sea and what it could provide.

Yet even the infidels of Eyemouth found it hard to resist the quickening pace of religious change that swept Scotland in the 1830s. They might have had little regard for the Established Church, but other denominations did slowly win the support of some. The first to arrive were the Primitive Methodists who held services in private houses and then later in the old Soap Works. William Landels recalled that as a boy he was encouraged to speak up for his faith. Landels' experience of preaching began in front of a scattering of people in the tiny home of fisherman William Purves. Playing by the mantel was a bairn who could barely crawl and would not remember the experience. While William Landels left to study theology James Purves was thrown a haddock line. The preacher became famous as a bishop and the fisherman wise on the ocean as skipper of the *Myrtle*.

By 1835 the Methodists had enough adherents and sufficient funds to build a little chapel in St Ella's Place. Like the boy Landels, other members stood up in front of the congregation to say what Christ had done for them. William Dougal's father George became so accomplished as a lay-preacher that the new chapel acquired the moniker 'Old Barque' in tribute to his simple oratory. This, though, was no religious revival. The converted were devout but still few in number. The fishermen were too busy making money and catching fish to bother about God.

Within five years of the death of his father William Spears had amassed enough capital to put down money on a new boat at Tate's yard. He pooled his cash with his cousin Willie Dougal and together they bought *Adventure*. It might have been bigger and more robust than the vessel that sank in the cruel waters off Eyemouth in December 1828, but it was still without decks, still a flimsy bit of matchwood to launch in defiance of the waves. Ellen Dougal pined when her son strode down the wooden staircase from their upper storey home in the centre of the village. She never took another husband, despite being widowed at a relatively young age. William was her chief concern. He was also her pride. As the years rolled on the lad became known as the 'Kingfisher'. Experienced crews followed him to the hunting grounds, and when Spears did not sail through periodic bouts of ill health men still chapped at his door for advice.

When the herring failed to show off the coast, Spears searched for other opportunities to put bread on the table of his mother's kitchen. He took premises on the Salt Greens, dabbled a bit in smoking fish and in selling direct into the markets. In particular Spears dealt with the young Coldingham curer John Dickson, who moved down to Eyemouth in 1828, and with John Cormack who started a cod liver oil business in the town at about the same time. Spears and William Dougal, John Dickson and John Cormack were the talk of the town. In joint ventures they worked well together.

More boats were added to the winter fleet with fishing vessels often outnumbering coastal craft in the harbour. Anyone walking the lanes with the gutting sheds and smokehouses constantly active would be left in little doubt that Eyemouth was now a fishing port, first and foremost. Voices were beginning to be raised in favour of state help for fishermen, at least to provide better berthing facilities and asylum harbours. There was an appreciation that the boats were now lunging further out into the deep and not just paddling around in inshore lagoons. From 1824 Westminster allocated an annual sum of £2,500 for harbour development in Scotland. It was a pitifully small amount that was spread thinly amongst a plethora of little havens.

Some of these grants came the way of Berwickshire. Stone piers were erected at Cove near Cockburnspath and at Burnmouth in 1831 and at Coldingham Shore two years later. They may not necessarily have made the lives of the sea going folk any safer. As at Eyemouth the new harbours gave an impression of safety and encouraged the fishermen to be more daring.

In November 1835 the first Coldingham Shore boat to be lost in living memory was swamped just short of home. All six crewmen were drowned – Alexander Cormack, Peter Johnston, John Wilson and his son, also John, and two brothers, Alexander and Robert Johnston.

Burnmouth and St Abbs each received around fifteen hundred pounds from the Fishery Board, but Eyemouth got nothing. In the year that the foundation stone was dropped into place at Burnmouth, prompting a day long celebration involving musical bands and processions of freemasons from across the county, Eyemouth Harbour Trust made a solitary investment requiring a degree less pomp. A new privy was erected on the pier. Costs were kept to a minimum. There would be no need to clean it out: the wooden structure was precariously balanced over the side, so that everything dropped into the listless waters of the Eye.

This lack of attention at Eyemouth was only superficial. Influential figures were arguing with verve that the port should become a harbour of refuge, perhaps even a naval base. Admiral Sir David Milne, who had first come to know the place when organising the coastal volunteers during the French Wars was the most active enthusiast. In 1832 he had another reason to take an interest. His son David married Jean Home, the granddaughter and heiress of George of Wedderburn and the burgh's feudal superior.

Both the Milnes and the Homes therefore had profound interests in Eyemouth. David Milne-Home – as he was now known – was made baron baillie of the coastal estate. It did not take a genius to work out that the harbour needed attention. In 1836 Milne-Home forwarded a memorial to the harbour trust from more than thirty ship's captains, from all over Scotland and England, complaining of the cramped accommodation and poor state of Eyemouth. He attached his own note, advising that they consider an application for a state grant. His father, Admiral Milne, backed the notion that Eyemouth 'could be so improved at a comparatively trifling expense as to render it a complete and safe harbour in all kinds of weather'.

James Jardine, an Edinburgh based civil engineer, was engaged to survey the harbour and suggest improvements. His initial report recommended that at a cost of £1,500 significant widening and deepening of the existing basin could be achieved. The trust approved of the proposals and petitioned the Fishery Board for a grant of two thirds of the cost.

The Fishery Commissioners were enthusiastic, but would make no decision until they had seen the detail of Jardine's work. This was produced in 1837 but what had started as a medium sized project to consolidate a tidal creek, had curiously changed into a massive scheme to enclose the whole bay. Jardine, taking on board urgings from Admiral Milne, now proposed the construction of a breakwater across the Hurkur rocks, joined by a pier from the Luffhard skerries to the shore at Fort Point.

The trustees were overwhelmed by the sheer scale of the scheme, but Milne and Milne-Home chipped away at their exasperation. Two months after Jardine submitted his final plan the Admiral gave it a public endorsement, stressing the national advantages that would accrue from the development. 'Were Eyemouth made a port of refuge, it would become a safe anchorage in bad weather, and would be the means of saving many vessels, much property and many lives'. As well as providing a refuge for windblown ships, under the scheme 'Eyemouth would become the first fishing station in the Kingdom, both for the herring and deep sea fisheries, where now, under all its present disadvantages, considerable quantities of fish are caught, cured and exported to foreign countries.'

Jardine had not attached a detailed estimate to his revised scheme, but clearly it was going to be many times more expensive than the initial proposals. The Fishery Board in Edinburgh considered the plan in November and December of 1837. It was now clearly beyond the means at their disposal, but they were suitably impressed and urged Eyemouth Harbour Trust to pursue central funding from London. They also contacted David Milne-Home to offer the services of their own engineer to cost Jardine's plans and to advise on any changes which might make the proposal more viable.

Ambition now knew no bounds and the trust lept ahead infected by wild exaggerations of what the future might hold. Without even waiting for a hint of Whitehall's response, the Harbour Board moved to radically overhaul its scale of dues. There was pragmatism in this. Members, especially the clerk Thomas Bowhill, were all too aware that before a grant was given there would be scrutiny of the accounts and questions asked as to the profitability of the port. It had been forty years since the last schedule had been published and it urgently required revision. Discussions on this had been going on since the 1820s, but a decision had always been avoided because of the high cost of amending the regulations. In 1838 payback looked assured, not only from additional boats using the port, but also by attracting the honey-pot of state money to construct a whole new harbour.

At a special meeting in early 1838 agreement was reached to press ahead with a Private Act of Parliament to change the constitution of the Trust. Under the proposed Bill, additional charges were to be levied on ships of a certain length and tonnage. Fishing boats, however, continued to be exempted from harbour dues, once more because of their continuing obligation to pay tithe to the Kirk. The attention of the Trust to that detail would have been heightened by the first legal action over tithe in more than a quarter of a century.

Some of the fishermen had started to protest that despite having their own new stone piers, the Burnmouth crews were effectively using Eyemouth all year round, yet were not being charged anything at all in fish teind. John Turnbull was forced, against his better judgement, to demand a few shillings from these boats. The last thing he wanted to do was open up old wounds, yet even Turnbull was pushed into taking legal action when one recalcitrant Burnmouth skipper simply refused all of his entreaties.

In the spring of 1837 a case against John Aitchison for alleged tithe arrears was heard at Ayton JP court. The skipper argued that the money had not been asked for at the proper time and consequently he had divided all of the earnings from the boat amongst the crew. Turnbull's tallyman disputed this and said that Aitchison had simply refused to pay, and that he had stirred up others also to withhold the tithe. The Burnmouth man was duly ordered to stump up the money. The significance lay not in the amount paid – no more than a pound or two – but in the fact that fish tithe was back as an issue. Moreover the influential Willie Spears was involved, albeit indirectly. His only living sibling Helen was courting John Aitchison and they would marry in November 1837, a matter of weeks after the judgement against the Burnmouth man. The wedding was not celebrated in the bride's home of Eyemouth. Aitchison would not enter the Kirk of John Turnbull. The match was made down the coast in his village.

The new scale of dues at Eyemouth was expected to revive the Trust's flagging financial fortunes. The cost of rushing pell-mell with a private Harbour Bill was not fully appreciated however. Debts of around £500 were incurred within a matter of months. With no financial assistance seemingly imminent from Whitehall or from Edinburgh, the Trustees fretted on their own personal liability. Bankruptcy loomed. In desperation they negotiated a bank loan to cover their legal fees. More debt, more interest to be paid, and the anticipated increase in traffic yet to materialise. Had they been sold a pup?

Alarmed at this lack of constancy, David Milne-Home spent more time in the village and chaired Trust meetings. He arranged for the visit of the Fishery Board's engineer in the late spring of 1840 in an attempt to kick-start the moribund development. James Mitchell felt the Jardine scheme was indeed too big to contemplate in a single leap. Instead he proposed an ongoing scheme of works beginning with the expansion of the existing wharves and quays then a deepening of the basin to provide additional water and the construction of a third, or middle pier, to provide much greater berthing space.

Milne-Home viewed none of this as optional. The only way to increase the revenue of the port was to attract more vessels by offering better facilities, including deep-water anchorages. A momentum had to be generated which would firstly wipe out the Trust's liabilities and then provide a surplus to press on with the grander scheme to enclose the bay. They had to speculate to accumulate.

What was axiomatic to the baron baillie was seriously scary to most of the other members of the Trust. The mood at another special gathering called in July 1840 was sombre. Few present were keen on contemplating Milne-Home's vision of a possible future. What about the harsh reality of the present?

The risks were too great and the Trustees bottled out. They would not be bullied into endorsing Jardine's plan to enclose the bay and neither would they back Mitchell's cheaper scheme. Bowhill scribbled in the minute book 'In the present state of the harbour funds they cannot undertake to execute even the more limited plan'. Nothing would be done unless or until the Trust had built up a sinking fund of at least £800–£1000. That amount was preposterous, and everyone present knew it. Milne-Home who, perhaps crucially, had been unable to attend the special meeting, was thoroughly depressed at a great opportunity missed. Apart from the fear of debt, there was parochialism aplenty in the Trustees' decision. No grant or loan meant no interference from Edinburgh or London. Eyemouth Harbour remained in the hands of local men who knew what was best. That, at least, is what these men of worth truly felt as they trooped out from the little office along to the Ship Inn and the Lodge Rooms.

They had to watch their step. It was the Trust's decision not to provide lamps along the Salt Greens that made the quay a dangerous place to walk at night. Darkness, broken paving stones and the lack of any fencing led to many a nocturnal ducking. It was not really a laughing matter. Several people, meandering out of the bars into the unlit, uneven, and – post-booze – unsteady world of the pier had drowned when falling into the water, or died from injuries when they struck the boards of boats. The trustees, ever displaying the real values of the middle-classes they so wished to be a part of, would not spend money improving safety. 'Nothing but a stone wall round the quay could prevent drunken persons from falling in the harbour' was how they curtly responded to demands for action. The death of inebriates was something Eyemouth would just have to endure.

In the same fashion, the old harbour walls were expected to endure the incessant pounding of the North Sea from one side, and the sudden spates of the River Eye from the other. The port managers would not take a chance with the Jardine-Mitchell schemes, and they would not spend more than a few pounds on basic maintenance. It was a false economy. Less than a year after fudging what to do, and with another coastal vessel having foundered in the bay trying to make the inadequate passageway into the port, the Trustees were called again to yet another emergency meeting. A fierce storm in June 1841 had brought massive sandbanks to the mouth of the harbour. The port was once more closed.

The accumulation of silt was an age-old problem. The tides, aided by the sweeping motion of the Eye water as it reached the sea, always seemed to bring back more than time or the actions of man could remove. Labourers had been employed since the 1790s to dig out the banks. In 1837 a more permanent arrangement was reached with two carters. It was steady work for Alexander Craig and Peter Mack, the latter of whom had moved down from Ayton in the late 1820s. Mack, and his extended family, including five sisters, lived in a garret off the Long Entry. Catherine, the eldest girl, married a sailor called Peter Waddell. The other four lingered for a long time without husbands. Jane would eventually tie the knot with a mischievous young fisherman called James Purves – the infant who had played while the Methodists preached in his home. The wedding only came after Jane had borne Pur'es at least two children.

Canute-like, Mack and Craig toiled to funnel up the sediment, even though it was obvious that the gravel and sand left in the wake of the 1841 storms was well beyond their limited capabilities. They did their best, even to the extent of bringing along another wagon and two additional horses.

With a sense of panic the trust looked again at the plans they had so recently rejected and a decision was reluctantly taken to press ahead with some of Mitchell's proposals. Off the agenda was any suggestion of a bid for aid from any other outside body. In another stunning example of small-town myopia, the members believed they could carry out the work cheaper, quicker and most important of all, without any external interference.

The folk of Dunbar showed no such reluctance. Just as the trustees at Eyemouth drew back from the brink, their counterparts there finalised a deal with the Fishery Board. At an estimated cost of £12,990 the new Victoria harbour was expected to provide safe accommodation for all kinds of boats. It, not Eyemouth, would be the refuge that many on the East Coast had been demanding.

Sadly for Dunbar, and by implication for Eyemouth, the money proved insufficient and over the next thirty years around £60,000, much of it state funding, was wasted on the port. Any improvements were marginal, and by the time the work was finished the fishing fleets had gone elsewhere. The Fishery Board had its fingers burned at Dunbar. Expensive lessons were also learned from other developments at Wick and Anstruther.

By the time Eyemouth finally did got its act together it would have to deal with the scepticism of civil servants who had seen so many harbour failures. It had as strong a case as any other creek in the 1830s and 1840s. But the Trust chose first to be timid, then worried, and ultimately weak. When it reluctantly agreed to press ahead with part of the Jardine-Mitchell scheme a decision was made to keep it local. Instead of a government advance and with it the removal of some of their power, the Trustees took out a bank loan and protected their independence. Estimates were sought and the metropolitan firms passed over when a builder from Ayton lodged a competitive bid. Balfour Balsillie was given the work. He assured the trust that he would deliver on time, to budget and that his wharves would be of the highest quality.

Balsillie's men, like Smeaton's labourers seventy-five years before, used the pudding stone from the Fort as a base material, exhausting the last of the supplies. Any hope that this would further reduce the cost proved as hollow as Milne-Home's eleventh hour plea that the Trust again seek help from the Fishery Board. The new middle pier was a fine addition to the harbour, and the quays were at last properly paved and laid out. But Balsillie kept demanding more and more money. The initial advance from the Commercial Bank for £1,200 was soon used up, then another £500, and finally a private loan from a local landowner for a further £1,000. All this was secured against the harbour dues. In the end more was paid out to Balsillie for his modified, scaled down version of Mitchell's development than the engineer had estimated would have been needed to complete the entire scheme.

It was finished in 1844 and, to the great satisfaction of all, the new harbour began to pay its way. There was a major jump in port revenues over the next couple of years, with a welcome return of freight boats docking at the harbour. Heavy lifting machinery, bogeys and loads of metal and wood made up the bulk of the landings. Eyemouth was the drop off point for the materials to build the Berwickshire section of the Great Northern Railway Line. Nobody guessed that this would signal the death knell for most of the coastal trade on which the harbour depended.

The ancient walls of Berwick Castle were, as one observer put it, 'demolished to make way for the modern improvement' of a rail terminal for the town. This was completed in 1846 as the mainline link between London and Scotland began to slot together. No move was made to get a rail connection to Eyemouth. What was the point? The harbour there was of much greater use. When the last sleepers were unloaded on to the quay the penny perhaps dropped. Within a very short space of time revenues plummeted as rail became the chosen mode of transport for freight. Eyemouth harbour had helped in its own commercial demise.

The situation in 1846 was grim indeed. It was made worse when claims were made against the harbour for damage inflicted by Balsillie's labourers at the Fort, and when Alexander Herriot suddenly, and without warning, called in his £1,000 loan. In desperation the Trust unsuccessfully petitioned the Treasury for help, and with total ruin looking all but certain, offered Herriot a generous deal. He agreed to continue his credit, but at a much greater annual rate of interest. Desperate now to maximise revenue, the Trustees authorised the harbour master to take as much sand and gravel from the beach for ballast as was required, in spite of repeated warnings of legal action from David Milne-Home, acting as factor for the Wedderburn estate. In 1850 he forwarded a petition from the occupiers and proprietors of houses along the shore, who claimed the foundations were being undermined. 'To my eyes' he wrote, 'and to those of the fishermen who are good judges, it is quite apparent that the surface of the beach has during the last year become much steeper than it ever was before'.

But the Trustees argued they had a prescriptive right to take whatever they wanted from the beach. At least one member cautioned prudence, but his unease was dismissed and the practice continued. So did the warnings from Milne-Home. Two decades would elapse before the Harbour Trust had to come to terms with the consequence of yet another poor decision. It was one that seemed fairly innocuous at the time, yet it would lead to the Trust's own ruin.

The demise of the shipping trade did not mean the new piers were deserted. Paradoxically, they were busier than ever. With far away markets now accessible by rail in hours rather than days the fish trade blossomed. As the newspapers relayed tales of the Gold Rush in exotic California, the fishermen of Berwickshire toasted health, wealth and silver darlings. 'Our fishermen have nothing to do but catch herrings to make gold glitter, there being a hungry market' wrote the correspondent of the *Berwick Advertiser*. 'There are six Yarmouth luggers, with buyers from Manchester, Glasgow and Edinburgh, and all our own curers, anxious for herrings.'

The fishermen who continued to grumble about the modus as they jangled money-filled pockets and crowded into the Ship Bar did not pay a farthing in landing dues. The fish tithe they so hated was a tiny tax which, had they only stopped to think, actually saved the fleet a fortune.

Along the Salt Greens quay, the clerk to the Harbour Trust wrung his hands in despair when filling in the account books. What was to be done?

FIGURE 1. Eyemouth Harbour, 1840.

FIGURE 2. Eyemouth Harbour on the eve of the Disaster.

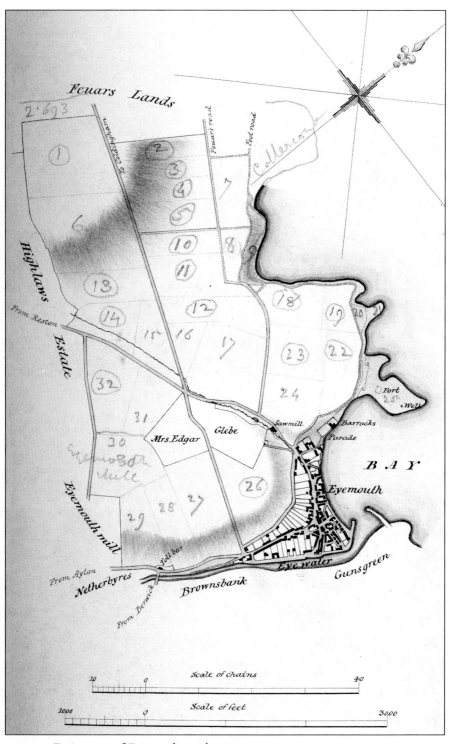

FIGURE 3. Feuing map of Eyemouth parish, 1846.

FIGURE 4. The old dead-house. Built from gravestones in 1823 to ward off resurrectionists.

FIGURE 5. Eyemouth fleet in the roadsteads. Waiting for water to enter the harbour.

FIGURE 6. Contemporary etchings of Disaster Day 1881 and the forlorn attempts at rescue of boats and drowning men. (*Mary Evans Picture Library*)

FIGURE 7. Agnes Aitchison. Her husband survived the Disaster. She is pictured here in 1922 at the great age of 84.

FIGURE 8. An old fisherman who rejoiced in the nickname 'Auld-Youngy'.

FIGURE 9. Fisherman James Lough, the author's great-great-grandfather.

FIGURE 10. Gunsgreen House and the harbour.

FIGURE 11. The railway station in the 1890s.

FIGURE 12. Eyemouth harbour before the works of 1885.

FIGURE 13. The fishing trade revives after the First World War.

FIGURE 14. Packing the herring.

FIGURE 15. Old men at the Weatherglass.

FIGURE 16. Robertson's curing yard, Eyemouth.

FIGURE 17. George Robertson and his herring packers.

FIGURE 18. Deep water was at last achieved in the developments of the 1960s.

FIGURE 19. Modern Eyemouth showing the harbour improvements of the 1990s.

FIGURE 20. Memorial to the lost of Black Friday.

FIGURE 21. William Spears, 'The Kingfisher' (inset)
and the statue of him erected in 1998.

FIGURE 22. The author and his wife being creeled on their wedding day.

FIGURE 23. Fishing boats coming home through the roadsteads.

Chapter Seven

The Gathering Storm

When Satan showed our Lord all the Kingdoms and the glory of them, he put his thumb over Eyemouth

Popular jibe made against Eyemouth by inland folk,
especially those from Duns

The decline in commercial traffic was difficult to arrest. The Board tried to attract some of the new steamboats which had begun to operate between Leith and Newcastle by offering free berthing spots for a trial period. It wasn't much of an inducement. The craft drew too much water and could not always enter the shallow harbour.

A more realistic approach was the decision to recruit fishermen as pilots to assist trading ships and windblown vessels. The local men were well used to saving foundering crews from boats that had inadvertently come too close to the Hurkurs or the Fort. Now they were to be paid escorts. The first intake of course included Willie Spears and William Dougal from their own boat *Adventure*. Four other pairs were licensed – Thomas Swanston and Richard Paterson from *Isabella*; George Dougal and Alexander Collin of *Dandy*; John Burgon and William Swanston who owned *Delight*; and Robert Gillie and James Cowe from *Bon Accord*.

In a sensible, if canny move, the Harbour Board explicitly stated on each man's licence 'the Trustees shall not be and do not hold themselves liable for the consequences of any damage that may arise through the neglect or mismanagement of the bearer'.

The money paid out was not as great as the salvage rewards pocketed from wrecks, but it was certainly more regular and there were plenty who queued up for a certificate. In 1839, just two years after the first batch had been granted, thirty-two fishermen from each of the now sixteen winter boats were given licenses.

The pilots were not lacking in bravery. In January 1841 the men made a rush to the beach when the brig *Hythe* from Newcastle suddenly tumbled from nowhere and started listing heavily two miles off Gunsgreen Point. In foul conditions Spears, Dougal and a half dozen others piled into two of the bigger boats and slammed through the waves to the sinking vessel. All were rescued, and on the way back to the bay, the fishermen even took off their own clothes to give to the drenched sailors.

Piloting was an alternative source of income, and since the men were most in demand when the weather was poor, which generally meant they could not themselves get out of the bay to work their nets and lines, the arrangement was very satisfactory. It was fishing, though, that continued to be the real money-spinner. In 1839, after six lean years, millions of herring arrived once more on the Berwickshire banks. A freak shoal even appeared in the roadsteads in March of that year, something unheard of in living memory. The fish swarmed upwards towards the harbour, and as boys pelted them with stones from the pier head, Willie Spears and William Dougal leapt into the water and manually dragged a heavy-laden net to the shoreline. Within minutes every man was doing the same, and by the end of the day more than a hundred barrels had been caught, gutted and packed. It was a good omen for what would be a fabulous summer season, the best ever for Eyemouth. More than 30,000 barrels were cured, some finding its way to Stettin in the Baltic, and much more went fresh to the home market. Demand could not be met, curers jostled for space on the quay and salesmen grew hoarse shouting their top prices to the boats as they lurched across the harbour bar. The best fished boats averaged more than five hundred crans for the drave and were paid about ten shillings a cran. Even allowing for expenses and the wages of the hired half-dalesmen, a lot of fishermen were handed in excess of fifty pounds when the reckonings were made at the end of the drave.

As usual the French had arrived in May. But foreigners were not needed that summer, and they were not welcome. The sheer size of the ships, and the way in which they cut across the Scottish boats, damaging gear and threatening safety led to loud complaints. Rusty cutlasses from smuggling days and the occasional blunderbuss were unearthed in Eyemouth, and the men went to sea prepared for a fight. There were plenty of skirmishes, but no reported loss of life, and by early September a fishery protection vessel, rather belatedly, arrived to offer reassurance. The French had left by then, but would return the following summer and for several years thereafter, prompting the same complaints and the same resort to arms.

If the three-month herring season had been good, the winter fishing was even better. Quality was excellent, quantity unsurpassed and prices at the quayside hard to believe. In the winter of 1840–41 some Eyemouth men were earning up to £4 a week.

The reputation of Berwickshire herring, and increasingly of fine haddock, added to the premiums the merchants could mark up. It is at this time that John Dickson, now firmly established as the leading curer in the town, perfected the Eyemouth haddock-smoke. Findon, a tiny haven south of Aberdeen, had already shown how a distinctive cure could be marketed.

Arbroath smokies are famous to this day. Dickson's 'Eyemouth flavour' were equally prized from the 1840s. In recognition of his role in greatly boosting the haddock business, Spears organised a whip-round amongst the fishermen, and at a very liquid supper John Dickson was presented with a silver snuffcase.

There had never been such good times. The lanes leading off from the Salt Greens were a hive of activity. There were fifteen herring yards, eight smoking houses, thirteen gutting sheds, eleven granaries, two massive warehouses and far too many whisky shops. A tempting prospect for men with money to burn. A few were provident enough to put a little money into the recently established Ayton, Eyemouth and Coldingham Savings Bank and one or two even took to building or buying their own homes.

There was also something of a revolution going on in the approach to safety at sea. For as long as anyone could remember each man had been entitled – expected even – to take on board three pints of whisky a week. Spears, as ever, led the way in substituting jugs of warm coffee for strong drink. Others followed his lead, though the Kingfisher was no temperance maniac. He made up for his long sober hours at sea when *Adventure* was tied up to the quay.

As more people settled in Eyemouth the civic authorities, such as they were, did their best to improve the burgh. Pavings were laid down in most of the lanes, scavengers contracted to remove some of the rubbish which was just dumped in the gutter, a company formed to provide gas lamps in the village and an attempt made to improve the putrid water supply. Key in this was the arrival in 1840 of an English-born plumber Timothy Statham and his family.

Statham seized on the opportunities he saw in the village and soon diversified into house building. He was responsible for large chunks of new dwellings constructed on the western approaches of the town, in places like the Houndlaw and Paxton Terrace. He rubbed shoulders with the other self-made men, including William Spears who regularly invited Statham to join him and his crew in boisterous Friday night suppers.

Just about the only bit of Eyemouth which was not doing well from the money swilling through the harbour was the Harbour Trust itself – that, and the minister. The new schedule of dues, which put a heavy debt of burden on the Trustees, had of course exempted the fishing boats that crowded around the basin. John Turnbull had been quiet in his demands for fish tithe, in spite of the clear opportunities the increased trade offered the Manse. He was only ever drawn to a single legal process, that against John Aitchison of Burnmouth. The Eyemouth minister, unlike so many of those who had occupied his pulpit in the past, was extremely reluctant to become embroiled in a battle with his parishioners. It would not have looked good.

Turnbull was himself involved in the church/state turmoil which history has recorded as the Ten Years' Conflict. He was destined to leave the Establishment along with a third of all Kirk ministers in Scotland in the Disruption of 1843 – the culmination of many decades of trouble over secular involvement in the Kirk. It would have been difficult for him to argue against lay patrons imposing ministers on reluctant congregations, which was at the heart of the dispute, yet use the civil courts himself to extract a clerical tax rooted in 'Romanism'. The minister preached at non-intrusion meetings, which demanded an end to lay patronage. Turnbull was also the lead organiser for the local branch of the Church Defence Fund, a body established to support the Evangelicals and lay the ground for the financing of the Free Church of Scotland.

Remarkably, and for the first time in many a long year, Sabbath attendance at the Kirk actually increased. Some were curious as to what Turnbull was up to, and others admired the minister's principles. For two years Willie Spears and William Dougal even entered their names on the heads of family register. Whatever the motivation, the novelty had worn off by 1842. The Presbytery, rather foolishly, tried to proselytise. They set up a committee under John Turnbull to 'promote the observance of the Sabbath among the fishermen, and of their spiritual interests generally at the time of the herring fishing.' There was no surer way to alienate the fisher folk than by banging a bible in their faces. Those who retained an interest in religion gravitated towards one of the other sects in the town. The Methodists, in their tidy chapel in St Ella's Place, or the United Secessionists (later the United Presbyterians) who arrived in 1841.

Chirnside Presbytery did not totally give up on Eyemouth. In fact it spent a bit of money in the parish. Alterations were made to the bell tower and a new Manse was put up adjacent to the Kirk, with a garden that stretched down towards the harbour. Turnbull had lobbied for a different location, perhaps on the grassy brae overlooking the Main Street, but he was overruled. Fishermen and especially fish curers shook their heads as they passed the workmen on the site. What idiot would choose to put a house and garden back-to-back with a long row of curing sheds? The noise, and the smell, would only increase as the fish trade developed, as surely it must.

The recovery of the herring drave in the late 1830s had an unusual by-product. Engaged couples no longer married in the summer. There was simply no time. Everything was put off until after the herring had gone. Most weddings were conducted in September at the close of the season.

But the late autumn of 1841 was sadly thin on celebrations. Any that were planned were postponed. The folk had no stomach for a party. The place was again in mourning for a boat lost, for men drowned, for an extended family ruined.

On 3 September 1841 Thomas Dougal and his crew set sail on a windy, but far from wild, afternoon and steered for the herring banks off Berwick-upon-Tweed. What exactly happened to the *Jabez* is not known. An alarm went through the town when the boat did not return, and the next day a party found the little vessel, heaved on its side and with waves washing over it, on the sands of Marshall Meadows beside the English border. All the men were lost. The skipper, aged fifty-two, left a wife and five children – the sixth, their eldest son, fifteen-year-old John was a cabin boy on the *Jabez*. It was a family boat, and two of Thomas' cousins, both called George Dougall, also perished. One left a widow and five bairns, the other a heavily pregnant wife and seven young orphans, the oldest of which was only ten. The other crewman was John Grieve, a waged half-dalesman who normally worked at Highlaws farm.

The whole of Eyemouth was touched by the tragedy. Most of the fishing folk were related to the Dougals, and all rallied around the bereaved and those who were now left destitute. A subscription list was printed in the *Berwick Advertiser* and The Shipwrecked Mariner's Society sent £25, even though no Eyemouth men were members.

The three widows had one asset left. The herring boat might have been lost, but the winter haddock yawl, newly built and only just paid for, was still tethered to the beach. There were five shares in *Big Dandy*: three for the men who had been drowned and one each for James and William Dougal, who had sailed on another of the boats the day that their father and brother had been lost from the *Jabez*. Plenty of young lads wanted experience at sea and were willing to give part of their earnings to the widows in exchange for a half share in the haddock fishing. This money sustained the families until another tragedy hammered down on the Dougals.

In November 1844 high seas lunged over the Hurkurs and pummelled up the beach to where the winter boats had been hauled. Two were lying lower than the rest: *Trusty* owned by David Johnston and crew, and *Big Dandy* the breadwinner of the Dougals. The mooring pegs snapped like sugar-candy and the wooden vessels were dragged down and cracked open on the rocks. There was nobody awake to try and drag them back and the boats were flung about the bay until the storm abated and the seas returned them, limp and ragged, to the clawed sands. When light came up the sight on the shore was pitiful. Repairs were estimated at more than £15 for *Trusty*, twice that for *Big Dandy*.

The families had already spent the funds raised through the *Jabez* subscription lists and were getting a few pennies from the parish. For black fate to strike twice at the Dougals brought a delegation to the door of the Fishery Office. William Dougal, who had been cousin and nephew to those lost in 1841, the Kingfisher and two of the Patterson boys were well received by John Coupar. He had only recently arrived in Eyemouth as replacement for old John Wares. Coupar duly wrote out an application for aid and forwarded it to Edinburgh. 'The petitioners', he wrote, 'are in very destitute circumstances, the widows and orphans having nothing to depend upon but their own industry and a small allowance from the poor funds of the parish.'

The November storm had been the culmination of a year of near misses for Eyemouth. In February the haddock fleet was obliged to scatter when a sudden storm came down. Five of the vessels managed to steer south to the relative safety of Burnmouth, while the other eight somehow scrambled a line past the Hurkur rocks and across the bar to calm water. One boat newly delivered to John Dougal was driven past the entrance and on to the beach. Losses of gear, if not of life, were expected to be high. But in fact there was relatively little damage caused and nobody was injured. They were lucky. Prophetic words were written in the *Berwick Advertiser*, words which all endorsed. 'Many lives and much valuable property might be saved by the enlargement of Eyemouth harbour'. The harbour was inadequate, inconveniently shallow, impossible to make on an ebbing tide. Not for much longer though ... Surely?

That February gale was as nothing, and the fishermen hardly tested, compared to what took place a fortnight later. Again the fleet was at sea when virtually every other on the East Coast remained in port. When the anticipated blast came crashing down, accompanied by billowing snow and nerve-freezing temperatures, a general move was made for home. Two boats failed to follow. The whole population made for the beach, the cliffs and the piers to await the return of the missing craft. As the afternoon wore on, messengers were saddled up and sent both north and south in the hope of finding the overdue boats beached in deserted coves. At about eight o'clock in the evening, with tar barrels burning on the headland and torches winking all along the shore, Robert Lough and his wearied crew steered their battered boat past the skerries and into the calmer waters of the bay. There seemed little hope for the other missing craft. It was skippered by Robert Angus, the lad who had gone through 'brothering' with Spears, Willie Dougal and the rest. The womenfolk – the young wives and mothers of the lost men – wept at the harbour-side, and ran around the lanes and the wynds in despair, seeking comfort but seeing only pity in the eyes of others.

The fires were kept burning all night. Men sat huddled around them, passing bottles and preparing to face the fact of another lost boat, of more drowned comrades. Then, as dawn kicked in, came the unexpected cry of a lookout, followed by a 'holler' and a 'huzzah' and a rousing of the whole community. 'The long looked for object came into view, to the joy and at the same time the consternation of all, and tears of gratitude as well as anxiety filled many an eye'. But could the boat make harbour without being dashed on the razor-sharp rocks? 'She was to the leeward of this harbour, combating against the unabated storm, and continued so for nearly three hours, within sight of hundreds of spectators, when, by a kind of providence, the crew reached their desired haven in safety ... The crew had been in an open boat for twenty-nine hours amidst such a storm that can be more easily imagined than described'.

Robert Lough and Robert Angus won a reputation that day. The tales told in the bars and to their children and grandchildren did not need any exaggerating.

John Turnbull had stood with the people on the shore, trying to comfort the distressed and calm the distraught. But he was no longer John Turnbull, minister of the Established Kirk. When the crisis in the Church of Scotland came to a head, as all knew it must, Turnbull was one of those who walked out. He took with him one hundred and sixty out of two hundred and thirty who professed a connection with the Kirk in Eyemouth. Turnbull gained instant appeal and unprecedented popularity. Hundreds flocked to hear him preach in an old barn near the Well Braes. Did they imagine they would get a different, more interesting, more uplifting sermon than those which Turnbull had been delivering for more than twenty years in the Church of Scotland?

The schism of May 1843 had much more profound implications for the nation than sermons and religious dogma. Free Kirk ministers moved to duplicate all of the social and welfare functions of the established Church. They built and ran schools, organised charitable giving as a form of poor relief and created a structure for life in each parish. The split dissipated effort and blurred effectiveness in a system that had already shown itself to be ineffective in the new towns and cities. Inevitably, the state began to encroach even further on areas previously left to the Church. This would be seen as early as 1845 with the passing of a new Scots Poor Law, and as late as 1872 in the Education Act.

This process was massively significant in Eyemouth. Up until 1843 there was logic in the Kirk taxing the fishermen. It could – it did – argue that this money went not just to the stipend, but to benefit all the people of the parish. After the Disruption this justification lost its moral sheen. In schooling, for example, even old James Trotter, the drunken teacher who had been Eyemouth headmaster for thirty-five years, was drawn away with Turnbull.

The minister's replacement was ill at ease from the very moment he arrived, and he didn't stay long. John Murdoch was wooed away to Kirkpatrick Fleming after little more than a year. He left in such haste that the Eyemouth charge was rendered vacant for three months, with the hard-pressed Presbytery unable to supply locum preachers. Then, on the last day of July 1845, a new man arrived. Stephen Bell came from a parish in Lanarkshire carrying a conviction that the Disruption was wrong. The Church of Scotland was, and would forever be, the *national* Kirk. It could yet reach out to the thousands of souls who felt lost and abandoned. His mission was to bring God to these people, wherever they were, whatever they initially said or believed, and however base they might appear to be. He was as a whirlwind compared to the thin soughs of previous pastors. The timing of his arrival, though, was unfortunate to say the least.

A matter of days after Stephen Bell had humped his cases and trunks into the new Manse, the Kirk tallyman issued, as he had always done at the close of the white fishing season, the traditional modus tithe bills of £1 13s. 4d. a boat. There was more than the usual moaning when these were handed out. Meetings were held in pubs and men talked in little groups along the quayside. One spoke up more than any of the others. Willie Spears questioned whether there was any justification for the tithe now that the Kirk was broken in two. At the very least there was a chance to test the mettle of the new minister. An anonymous letter was posted off to the local paper. The author, it later emerged, was William Spears.

> The fishermen of Eyemouth who are almost to a man members of a
> Secession meeting, were last week served with a summons for refusing to
> pay teinds to the minister of a church by the door of which they have no
> communion ... Can they see in him the pastor whom they ought to love?
> No! To them he is the Oppressor who is now in the very act of depriving
> them of the means of earning their living; the individual who robs them,
> forcibly, compelling them to give a portion of their hard earned and scanty
> income to prop up a system their conscience condemns – a system that must
> be supported by sheriffs' officers with ejectments in their hands. Is it fair, is
> it honest, is it consistent with the spirit of Christianity that such things
> should be done?

Taken on its own the letter was bad enough, but the editorial support which the fishermen received from the *Berwick Advertiser* nonplussed the minister. The editor sensed a cause. He wrote of a 'monstrous injustice' an 'evil system' a 'relic of Romanism'. It stoked up a circulation war with the other local journal, the Tory supporting *Berwick Warder*.

What had Stephen Bell walked into? His congregation was small, he had to endure the traditional 'non-welcome' in the Market Place and especially along the Salt Greens when the boats were landing. Yet if Bell believed in anything, he believed in adherence to the established order, both in church and state. If the tithe bills were legitimate – and they were – they simply had to be delivered. He gave his authority to the tallyman, and told the fishermen they would have to pay. Privately, though, Stephen Bell was as convinced as William Spears that the fish teind should go. But how could it be removed without injuring the assets of his beloved Kirk?

As he pondered on this, Bell also sent out demands for arrears that had been brought to his attention. These again involved Burnmouth fishermen, and to make sure they realised he meant business, the minister added a covering note. Failure to pay would involve legal action and the confiscation of their property.

The Kingfisher was directly involved in this assault on his comrades from Burnmouth. One of them was his brother-in-law, John Aitchison, who had previous experience of tithe persecution. After a flurry of articles in the local press, and with the minister adamant that sheriffs officers would be employed, the fishermen pulled back from the brink. They paid their dues and settled their arrears.

Concerned at the bad start he had apparently made with an important section of his flock, Bell tried to show what a conscientious pastor could do for them. They needed to appreciate his worth, and that had to go deeper than being preached at on a Sunday. He set about reforming the savings bank, he revived the lending library, and changed the Sunday school into something more meaningful than a crèche. For those who came to Kirk, his sermons were a powerful change from the dirge of previous incumbents. Bell spoke with passion, but in a language that was easy to understand.

Slowly, but perceptibly, Stephen Bell noticed a difference in his life, if not in the numbers who attended worship in the Old Kirk. People were almost becoming civil to him. William Spears made this happen from the moment that he crossed the street to pass the time of day with the minister. The man's job would never be liked, but perhaps he could be tolerated. Bell even found large and enthusiastic audiences turning up for some of his evening lectures on history, philosophy, and the climate.

With a temporary halt to hostilities, Spears tried to coax Stephen Bell into acknowledging the nonsense of the tithe and invited him to one of his renowned suppers. Bell must have felt uneasy when he first gingerly climbed up the creaky wooden outside staircase that led from a vennel folk called Spears' Place. But it was *the* place to be on a Friday night in Eyemouth. Mind you, if the minister was uncomfortable, others in the company were equally restless. What on earth was Spears thinking to bring this man amongst them?

Bell took a good glass and spoke sense at the table. On that December night in 1845 he candidly said he had great sympathy with the fishermen. How to remove the tithe without affecting the stipend and alienating an important part of the living in Eyemouth ... well, that was the issue he had to confront.

Spears and the rest drank heavily and toasted loudly to the name of Stephen Bell. Along with John Dickson, Timothy Statham and William Dougal, Bell was invited to dip his loaf in the sauce left from the carcass of a massive cod which they smothered in butter and then picked clean to the bone. When they had done, Ellen Spears-Dougal brought in clay pipes and yet more claret. It was a night to remember: a night some of those present would later recall with crystal clarity in less harmonious times.

Outside on the Street, and along the quay and in the smoking bar of the Ship others muttered. There was talk that Spears' real intent was not to do away with the tithe for everyone, but rather to convince Stephen Bell to stop bothering him for dues. Ill health, which dated back to his near drowning in 1827, regularly kept Spears ashore. If he did not fish in the winter, as he often could not, why should he then be entitled to launch his herring boats for free in the summer? Those who went only to the drave and who were asked to pay a good deal more to the Kirk than the modus of £1 13s. 4d. were especially loud in their moaning.

Stephen Bell held true to his word at Spears' dinner table. He approached David Milne-Home and asked for support in trying to find a way of getting rid of the impost. Milne-Home backed the call but urged caution. Any action that might harm the Kirk living could not be agreed. Bell, in publicly floating the idea of abolition, was encouraging the fishermen into believing the tithe's days were numbered. Milne-Home chided the minister for his loose tongue. But there was no going back now.

Accordingly a special meeting of the heritors was convened in Eyemouth on 3 December 1846. With some reservations they supported Bell. Two days before this, Chirnside Presbytery had likewise agreed to consider abolition, but on the proviso that an alternative source of finance for the minister's stipend was found. Stephen Bell had given this plenty of thought. Everyone agreed that the removal of the tithe could only boost the fishing industry at Eyemouth, surely the fishery board would make up the deficiency?

Bell's memorial to the Fisheries Commissioners reached Edinburgh in late 1846 and was immediately sent before a powerful committee including both the Lord Advocate and the Solicitor General. They agreed the impost was unsustainable and in turn petitioned the treasury for an annual grant of around £70 – significantly Bell said this represented just a fraction of what he could demand every year. The memorial concluded:

> This impost is extremely odious to the fishermen – it has estranged them from the ministrations of the clergymen, and has been the chief cause of the irreligious and improvident habits which prevail to a lamentable extent among the seafaring population of the parish. Mr Bell observes that it is also very injurious to the fishery carried on at that port and that in consequence of it many of the boats encounter the hazard of delivering their fish into French vessels lying off the coast instead of bringing them into the safe harbour of Eyemouth. Fishermen who earn an uncertain livelihood must be greatly irritated on every occasion when they are forced to resign a tenth of their precarious earnings to any person ... This very peculiar tithe, which is so local that most persons in Scotland are not aware of its existence ... The Memorialists do not believe that the Bounty of the Crown could be more beneficially employed than to the removal of this severe and oppressive impost.

As David Milne-Home had predicted, a belief went abroad that the tithe was now dead. Yet even if the Treasury agreed to an annual subvention it might take years to organise. The baron baillie, soon to be laird on the death of his father-in-law, told Bell that he must continue to demand at least the modus payment until all matters were settled.

In the very month that the Fishery Board endorsed the tithe application to the Treasury, the common folk of Eyemouth celebrated another legal victory, this time one involving David Milne-Home. In 1843 as judicial factor for the Wedderburn estate he had raised a civil action against some of the inhabitants who were using land at the Well Braes, to the northwest of the town. For years they had utilised the water of the North Burn to wash clothes and to bleach their fishing nets. It became a landmark case because to defend the action the villagers had to be admitted to the poor roll. In late January 1847 Milne-Home's case was thrown out. It was the first time a court had judged that a burgh of barony was a corporate body entitled to acquire certain rights even against its own superior.

As word was awaited from the Treasury on Bell's tithe-grant application another government official paid a visit to Eyemouth. Captain Washington, head of the Tidal Commission, arrived in April 1847 to take evidence for an official report into the state of coastal harbours. He spent several days at Miss Jane Allanshaw's Inn and listened as successive witnesses, both sea captains and fishing folk, spoke of the importance of Eyemouth harbour to all shipping between the Forth and Tyne. It should be deepened, it ought to be made a harbour of refuge, accessible at all states of the tide. Like earlier reports, and future plans, the talk was loud and ambitious, the subsequent action negligible.

It took the Treasury almost a year to reply to the detailed memorial sent on behalf of Stephen Bell. It rejected the notion of an annual grant of seventy pounds a year in three brusque lines. Had it agreed to the request a lot of future trouble would have been avoided. This important obstacle to the development of the harbour would have been removed and Eyemouth might have received thousands of pounds in grant aid. The money instead went elsewhere to Dunbar, Anstruther, Fraserburgh and a necklace of other ports.

Stephen Bell was now truly caught on the horns of a dilemma. He had badly miscalculated in making public his own views on the tithe. It was also a mistake to put a figure on the potential revenue the Church could demand. The issue, kept quiet during the long ministry of John Turnbull, had now been brought to the attention of Chirnside Presbytery. Resources were squeezed as a result of the Disruption. Bell was instructed to be more attentive to the collection of fish tithe.

But confusion reigned on who paid what and on the amounts that ought to be demanded from various categories of fishermen. Stephen Bell was sure that Eyemouth men could be forced to pay the annual modus of £1 13s. 4d., as had been established by long precedent and practice. But what about those who only fished for herring in the drave, which was now a major money-spinner?

That very summer the minister had been harangued by a squad of local fishermen who pointed out half-a-dozen boats that should not be covered by the privilege of the modus. One was easily identified as belonging to John Cormack, a curer who also had a cod liver oil plant in the town. Bell dispatched his tallyman John Nisbet (how that mighty family had fallen from the days when they built and owned Gunsgreen) to talk to Cormack. He got no more than a few shillings and an earful of abuse. The curer demanded to know why he was being unfairly picked upon? Why not target Eyemouth fishermen who did not always put to sea? If Cormack had to pay, then the minister *had* to demand tithe from this group, which included the Kingfisher.

Bell came to the inescapable conclusion that there were many loopholes in the tithe law that were being exploited. Though it pained him, he knew that he had to do his duty. He wrote out a note requesting that William Spears attend at the Manse at his earliest convenience. Nisbet hurried through the lanes to Spears' Place to deliver it to the home of the Kingfisher.

Bell thought there might yet be an amicable way out of the mess. If he could make an arrangement with Spears, the whole of the community might be won round. The Kingfisher was initially sympathetic: the minister had, after all, tried his best. An agreement of sorts was reached whereby Bell would continue to collect the modus from Eyemouth fishermen and in addition would seek ten shillings from local crews who only fished in the herring season. The minister said he would be prudent in any demands he made on visiting boats, though Spears urged Bell to forget this potential source of revenue altogether.

It was a compromise that, like all such settlements, was open to abuse and unlikely to endure. Worse than that, the terms of the deal were interpreted differently by home and stranger crews and even by Bell and Spears. What ought to have put a lid on the simmering tithe trouble actually lit the touch paper for fifteen years of acrimony. It was back to the old arguments that had exercised the community, demonised the minister and enriched legal teams over decades.

The detail of how the arrangement might work did not overly worry William Spears. Despite his periodic bouts of illness, the Kingfisher continued to do justice to the nickname. In 1846 he ordered the first half-decked fishing boat ever to be built in Eyemouth, possibly the first of its kind in the whole of Scotland. For safety, for speed and above all, for increased capacity to hold fish, *Superior* knew no equal on the shores. Spears and his callants, along with another crew headed by Robert Dougall, then notched up another first. In the winter of that year *Superior* and *Children's Friend* set out from the harbour on a journey that would keep them away for many weeks. They ventured far south to the late autumn herring fishing off Yarmouth and returned with pockets full of coins. The earnings added to what had been the best Spring haddock fishing Eyemouth had ever known.

Construction work was going on all over the town, including a large warehouse which was only half finished when Spears, Dougal and their crews returned from their second season in Norfolk in September 1847. The men held impromptu concerts in the half-finished shell, christening it 'Haimooth's Hippodrome' in honour of the theatre in Yarmouth where they had experienced high-class entertainment and watery beer. The name stuck. To this day the building, which is now home to the Royal National Mission to Deep-Sea Fishermen, is referred to by all as 'The Hippodrome'.

Almost unnoticed in this glorious time for Eyemouth were the first signs of a virulent disease that would almost kill the place. In October 1846 British cholera was detected in the town. It laid low several children and old folk and killed at least one bairn. It was a warning of much worse to follow, and focused attention on the unhygienic state of the streets, lanes, vennels and closes. All fish touns are characterised by their haphazard architecture, but Eyemouth, because of the needs of smuggling in the previous half a century and earlier, was particularly sinister. It was a monstrous carbuncle of a place, which Chambers' Picture of Scotland summed up thus: 'At one time all of the people, high and low, young and old, rich and poor, were more or less engaged in smuggling, and no house was built without a view to accommodations for contraband goods. The whole town has still a dark cunning look, is full of curious alleys, blind and otherwise, and there is not a single house of any standing but what seems as if it could unfold its tales of wonder.'

There was a fear across the whole of Britain that deadly Asiatic cholera, which had swept through the country in 1832, was poised to do so again. With no law in place to force through improvements, dirt and disease remained a fact of life. An ad hoc grouping came into being in 1847, and in October 1848 a committee of six emerged to try and improve the public hygiene of the town. With some of the streets not even three feet apart and most of the lanes in bad repair they had a lot of work to do.

Clearing a few rubbish tips and putting down a bit of quicklime here and there might have improved morale, but it barely addressed the real issue. The fishing community, which crowded into a tiny area, put little emphasis on personal hygiene. Their homes were tiny, ill ventilated and without either running water or sanitation. They could not be forced to wash, persuaded to stop tipping their night-buckets into the street, or prevented from piling fish offal high against their walls.

It is a paradox, then, that with cholera stalking the nation, tourism first emerges in Eyemouth in the summer of 1849. In June of that year the riverside boatyard, now run by the firm of Hall and Weatherhead, launched its first pleasure craft – a yacht commissioned by a well-to-do English family who had started to take holidays on the Berwickshire coast. The following month a few influential men met in the parish schoolroom to plan a summer festival. Taking the lead was David Milne-Home, but of the five co-members William Spears stood out as the only fisherman. He enthusiastically backed plans for a day of sailing, rowing and running events. Without Spears' active support it is unlikely the crews would have shown much interest in spending a day at sea for sport alone.

The inaugural Berwickshire Regatta and Gymnastics were duly opened on 24 July. More than £80 in prize money was pledged, with athletics sited on the Fort promontory – an area which had recently become popular with a few hackers who regularly thumped guppy balls on a rudimentary golf course. Competitors came from as far away as Hawick, and with the band of the 33rd Regiment, then stationed in Eyemouth, providing musical accompaniment, a crowd of several hundred were entertained from dawn to dusk. Though additional police were drafted in, these were not needed: 'By a wise regulation by the committee, no liquor stronger than beer was allowed to be brought to the ground'.

Everyone dressed up in their best clothes and hats – the women wearing striped shawls, and the men in black garb, waistcoats, and tall funnel hats, called Raikie Steps. It was said that Eyemouth had not seen the like since the day Mary Stewart and her entourage of a thousand horsemen traversed the village en route to the Priory of Coldingham.

It was a joyous day, but reports of the competition winners were juxtaposed in the *Advertiser* with dreadful news. Asiatic cholera had now arrived in the borders and was killing with a vengeance.

In September 1849 the pestilence reached Eyemouth. A Dunbar crew became concerned when one of their number, Peter Marr, was violently sick at sea. They steered their boat into the bay in the middle of a chilled but calm night. Marr continued to vomit on shore and his comrades purloined a wheelbarrow with the intention of pushing him to the railway station at Burnmouth. They had barely reached the Toll Brig over the River Eye when the poor man's screams obliged the company to turn back. The doctor, John Dawson, was roused but by then the fisherman was too far gone. Peter Marr, Eyemouth's first cholera victim, expired at 3 a.m.

The news of the illness spread like wildfire, and for several days the streets were empty. People were afraid to venture out. Slowly, though, life returned to normal. Marr's death had brought no epidemic; in fact not one single person was reported as being sick for several weeks. It was as though the cholera incident had provoked an outbreak of good health. Eyemouth appeared to be circled by disease – the epidemic was rife in Kelso, Hawick, Berwick and Duns – yet, as had been the case in 1832, it could not penetrate the parish boundaries. Smugly, and prematurely, Haimoothers watched the cholera fade from other neighbourhoods. The crisis seemed over, when on 30 October cholera crept into Eyemouth. It would kill more than a hundred from a population of around 1,400.

The first few cases were isolated and sent to the biggest and most suitable building in the town, the old barracks, just up from the Well Braes. The soldiers vacated their billet, which was converted into a hospital. But the people simply refused to accept the truth. They hid afflicted relatives and convinced themselves this was just a bad outbreak of sickness and diarrhoea. It allowed the disease to take hold and course through the close-set tenements and overcrowded flats.

John Dawson needed help, and two surgeons in Ayton took the courageous and potentially fatal decision to answer his plea. Some local women were employed and three from Edinburgh were also engaged as nurses. The number of fatalities reached double figures within a week, and the hard-pressed medical staffs were strained further when one of the Ayton doctors contracted cholera. Application was made for a replacement from the Royal College of Physicians, but Eyemouth was by then considered to be a place in quarantine and none were willing to take the death road south.

The dunghills and fulzie heaps were removed, quicklime set down in the vennels every twenty-four hours, and fires lit by the people themselves in seventeen different areas. All business was suspended from early November until the tide had been turned in the middle of December. By then more than 100 individuals had died. A further three hundred were struck down with the malady. The Inspector of the Poor wrote at the time that 'The fishers, as a class, are proverbially improvident – their gains are precious and their notions of comfort low. The wives and children of these men constitute nearly three-fourths of the victims of cholera ... Generally speaking those persons who have perished from the pestilence (indeed, almost without a single exception) have been those of intemperate habits, the aged, the poor, the ill fed'.

Families linked by blood and marriage lived on top of each other. When one fell ill the disease jumped to the others like fleas on a dog. Alex Crives lost his wife Alison Whillis on 5 November. Three of his children were dead within two days, and before the end of the outbreak seven members of the Whillis family were dead.

Others families were equally damned: the Collins, the Purvises, and the Dougals in particular. Spears' cousin William Dougal lost both his sons on a single day. In the sickening six-week spell a whole generation of children was wiped out. The 1849 cholera epidemic claimed proportionately more victims from Eyemouth than virtually any other place in Scotland. 'Acquaintances have been talked with in the morning in the streets, who ere the midnight hour were called to account. One very striking case was that of a person who attended a funeral at midday, and parted with a few friends at seven in the evening, and before day break was numbered among the dead.'

The three ministers, Stephen Bell, John Turnbull and Thomas Pearson of the United Presbyterians spent their days comforting the living and burying the dead, of which there seemed to be no end. The numbers were so overwhelming that the cemetery filled up. No substitute ground was available and those who were still able-bodied shouldered shovels and heaped another layer of earth over the entire graveyard, creating a second tier. That too was soon crowded. The visitation of cholera might have been the end of Eyemouth. All trade and business stopped. Even the Masonic Lodge decided there would be no meetings or festivals through the winter months. This was the worst ravage the place had ever experienced, eclipsing all the horrors of the witch-hunt, the shock of rampaging, raping armies, the fear of the press gang. The list of the dead is a litany of Eyemouth's old families. How could the community claw back from such a disaster?

Some of the dead of Eyemouth from the visitation of the cholera, October 30 – December 13 1849

October 30	John Aitchison, labourer, aged 40
	Peter Gibson McIntosh, aged 4 years
	Alexander Mclean, labourer, aged 44
November 2	Robert, son of Mathew Alexander, aged 19 months
November 3	William, son of Robert Windrum, aged 6 years
November 5	Elizabeth Inglis, aged 15
	Joan Whillis, wife of Joseph Collin (fisher) aged 46
November 6	Alison Whillis, wife of Alex Crives, aged 53
November 8	Agnes Sprout, aged 46
November 9	Agnes Dickson, aged 46
	Mary, daughter of Alex Crives, aged 31
	Richard, son of James Whillis, aged 8
	Jane Hislop, aged 53
	Catherine, daughter of Alex Crives, aged 12
	Helen Collin, aged 10
	Ann Collin, aged 8 Jane Collin, wife of James Cowe, aged 22
November 11	Margaret, daughter of William Angus, fisherman, aged 8
	Joseph, son of Robert Purves, tailor, aged 2
	James, son of Alex Crives, fisherman, aged 17
	Agnes, daughter of Alex Crives, aged 19
	Elizabeth, daughter of Alex. Aitchison, tailor, aged 8
	George Burgan, fisherman, aged 32
	Elizabeth Faid, aged 32
November 12	Janet, sister to James Whillis, harbour master, aged 54
	Jane Hislop, aged 27
November 13	Joseph Robertson, fisherman, aged 29
November 14	Mary, daughter of James Ford, shoemaker, aged 27
	Elizabeth Bookless, aged 64
	Robert Whillis, fisherman, aged 44

Janet B Collin, age unrecorded

November 15   James Aitchison, tailor, aged 21
Alex Aitchison, aged 14

November 16   Robert Lyal, carter, aged 25
Paul Robertson, fisherman, aged 62
William Scott, infant
Mary Reid, infant

November 17   Alexander Cow, infant
Margaret, daughter of William Brodie, mariner, aged 17
John Gibbon, out-pensioner, aged 42

November 18   William, son of William Russell, policeman, aged 4
Thomas, son of James Collin, fisherman, aged 24
Euphemia Scott, infant
Alison Purves, infant

November 19   Margaret, daughter of Robert Crombie, fisherman, infant
Mrs Isabella McIntosh, innkeeper, aged 62

November 20   Mary Ritchie, widow, aged 70
Margaret Collin, widow aged 70
Peter Burgan, infant

November 21   Isabella Laurie, aged 32
Agnes Dougal, wife of Robert Crombie, fisherman, aged 35
Margaret Pollart, wife of Ebeneezer Sanderson, aged 70
Joseph Gibson, mason, aged 48

November 22   Margaret, daughter of late Robert Lyal, carter, aged 33
Mary, sister of late George Burgan, fisherman, aged 56
Peter, son of Alexander Burgan, fisherman, aged 8

November 23   William, son of late James Cowe, fisherman, aged 13

November 24   Margaret Hood, wife of William White, sawer, aged 39
John, son of Walter Douglas, brickmaker, aged 13 months

November 25   Jane, widow of George Craig, fisherman, aged 70
James, son of William Dougal, fisherman, aged 9
Andrew, son of William Dougal, fisherman, aged 6
————, eldest son of John Purvis, sawer

November 26   Margaret Stevenson, wife of Alex Angus, fisher, aged 36
Elizabeth Patterson, wife of J Maltman, fisher, aged 46
Eleanor Swanston, wife of Alex Maltman, fisher, aged 43

November 27   James, son of the late James Collin, fisher, aged 6
Mary, wife of William Purvis, mariner, aged 38

John Cooper, fishery officer, aged 55

November 28 Margaret, daughter of Alex Maltman, aged 9

November 29 Richard, brother of James Whillis, harbour master, aged 61
William Wight, labourer, aged 69

November 30 Alice, daughter of William Shearlaw, cooper, aged 22
Ann Edgar, wife of William Purvis, mariner, aged 64

December 1 John Gray, carpenter, aged 44
Isabella, widow of Robert Gillie, fisherman, aged 52

December 3 Margaret Nesbit, wife of George Landells, farmer, aged 38

December 4 Margaret Gillie, wife of Andrew Leitch, fisher, aged 41

December 7 Jane, mother-in-law to William Dougal, fisherman, aged 74
Sarah, daughter of Alex Burgan, fisherman

December 9 John, son of Peter Brown, aged 19

December 10 Jean, wife of William Brodie, master mariner

December 13 Jane, daughter of William Angus, aged 6

Chapter Eight

The Battle Begins

The Eyemouth men go farthest, longest and in worst weather
John Sutherland, Eyemouth Fishery Officer 16 December 1854

Cholera could strike anybody, anywhere, at any time but it was the poor who died in disproportionate numbers. The epidemic pulled back the population growth of Eyemouth ... Dozens had been wheeled, moaning and gurgling to the makeshift hospital at the old barracks, the morgue as it actually became for all but a very fortunate few. Spears, like most of the fishing folk, saw his own relatives die, and many more of his friends and associates. The man, by then in his mid thirties, had never married and he never would. The Kingfisher cared like a father for the lads who sailed in the fleet. When Spears did not himself sail, for reasons of health or commerce, he was always to be found on the pier, waiting the return of the callants. He certainly doted on his closest relatives: his mother, Ellen Dougal-Spears, his sister Helen and his niece and nephews from her marriage to John Aitchison of Burnmouth, by then a crewman with a share in the *Lively*, one of six deep-sea boats based there.

The first bairns in the Aitchison household were named in classical Berwickshire style. The eldest, William Crawford Aitchison, took that of his paternal grandfather, which was also, by chance, that of his maternal grandfather. The second son, Andrew Spears Aitchison, born in 1840, was a reminder of the brother of Helen and Willie Spears who had perished in the shipwreck of 1828. The first girl, Margaret Aitchison, born in 1842, was called after her paternal grandmother, and the fourth child, John Aitchison, who arrived the following year, received his own father's name.

What Burnmouth did not have, but Eyemouth had been given in the year of the cholera, was a decent gauge of what the men might expect when they threw down their lines and pushed off to the ocean. Two weeks after the last corpse had been laid to rest in the reeking graveyard, David Milne-Home, a keen amateur meteorologist, put up a barometer on the pier-head. It was an immediate talking point, and was later copied at other stations including Dunbar.

The barometer showed its worth almost immediately. In June 1851, despite fair weather, the men refused to sail after looking at the 'gless' which indicated an imminent change and a strong chance of storm. By noon, when some were thinking they had stupidly put their trust in a device, the skies blackened and a tremendous wind lashed and lunged at the coast. Two trading ships broke their moorings and were dashed on the rocks. The warning of the barometer saved the boats, gear and possibly the lives of the fishermen of Eyemouth. Ominously, the lesson learned that day was one which all too quickly most came to disregard. The Eyemouth way had always been to take a chance and win an open market. Risk was part of that equation. The barometer continued to be looked at, but if other conditions were fair, it was ignored. Alternatively, if the weather was foul, but the glass hinted at an improvement, its advice was taken and less willing men chided for their cowardice. All it took was for one crew to throw down the gauntlet and sail. The rest invariably followed.

David Milne-Home was also instrumental in ensuring that despite the trauma of the cholera, the summer Games and Regatta continued in 1850. The event surpassed the previous year's success, with prize money of more than £113 attracting athletes from the Scottish borders and the north of England. Special trains brought more than eight hundred spectators from Kelso and Tyneside to Burnmouth station, where rows of carriages and carts, organised and driven by Peter Mack and his friends, were waiting to thrash down the coastal road to Eyemouth. As in 1849, the main arena was at the Fort, where this time a tented village appeared overnight. Campfires threw smoke high into the lazy sky, the listless conditions making yawl racing hard work for the rowers.

Hot food and beer was laid on at the Fort, but the inns and bars of the town did a better trade from those who wanted something stronger. In fact there was some concern that the carter was deliberately ferrying visitors not directly to the field of play, but to the door of whisky shops. Few then managed to find their way along the shore and up the brae, and most were content supping in sunshine until Peter Mack shook them from a happy, flushed condition for the little drive back to Burnmouth.

The Eyemouth summer games should have become an established event in the border calendar, but those of 1850 were the last for fourteen years. This was not because of a lack of will or public appetite for something which was a potential money-spinner, rather it was because of the growing division between the people and the laird.

In the spiralling dispute over fish tithe, David Milne-Home resolutely backed the Church. He had no wish to do down the fishermen, indeed as had been seen from his actions with the Harbour Trust, he desperately wanted the fishing industry to succeed at Eyemouth. But he, like Stephen Bell, could do no other than support the establishment.

When the minister tried to implement the deal he thought had been done with Spears he did not expect the tithe bills to be greeted with joy, but nor did he envisage the kind of angry, and at times violent reception his tally man recieved. Often Nisbet had to go back three or four times before a skipper would pay his crew's modus of £1 13s. 4d. Those, like Spears, who were asked for herring teind needed even more prodding, despite the fact that they were only asked for ten shillings per boat for the entire season.

It was only a matter of time before the bad feeling boiled over. The catalyst came when Bell, at the insistence of the Presbytery, turned the attention of the tally man to boats from other stations which arrived for the herring drave. Spears had warned him against doing this and word was 'put out' to Nisbet to refuse. It was as good as a community-order and though he carried on asking for modus dues Nisbet was sensible enough to heed the warning not to trouble the herring fleet.

Bell tried to get the information he needed from statistics kept by the Fishery Officer. But John Sutherland, aware of the implications for his own safety if he did as he was asked, side-stepped the request.

At that very moment another more celebrated battle over a tax for the clergy was getting more national attention. The controversy over the Edinburgh Annuity Tax, a levy on all citizens to pay the stipends of Kirk ministers, helped enliven the tithe rebels of Berwickshire and fortified them in what would be their long, expensive and often illegal campaign. In the summer of 1851, when Stephen Bell's ability to collect anything more than a portion of his due tithe was most manifest, the Annuity Tax row made front page headlines. The parallels with Eyemouth were clear, though Mr Bell did not think so. Some of his counterparts in Edinburgh received upwards of £600 a year; he made do with a sixth of that.

As the low-level, phoney war over herring tithe at Eyemouth went on, the fishermen experienced real pitched battles when they again ventured to Yarmouth in May 1851. Enraged by the effrontery of the Scotch who flooded the markets, accepted lower prices and even set their nets on a Sunday, the locals of Gorleston attacked the Eyemouth crews. The fight was a less than honourable draw, but with the Berwickshire boys distracted, a Norfolk boat ran amuck in their nets. Calls for help from the supposedly impartial fishery officer drew no response, and in spite of appeals to the board in Edinburgh the Eyemouth men were left, quite literally, to fight their own battles whenever they sailed south.

Regardless of this trouble, good money was brought home from England adding to earnings from the local drave which expanded continuously until 1857. The fishery was changing in nature, largely because of difficulties recruiting seasonal help. The age of the half-dalesmen, some of whom had come from as far away as the Isle of Skye, was drawing to an end. For a few years this dearth of labour meant that some Eyemouth herring boats had to be laid up.

In 1846 a band of women asked whether they might try their hand at the herring and be allowed to take out one of the beached drave boats. There was plenty of laughing at the very idea but the women, themselves daughters and wives of fishermen, managed to persuade the men to let them sail with the fleet. The laughter died down when they delivered some of the biggest hauls. Not only that but, in contrast to the fishermen, these ladies of the ocean did not hand their catch over to the salesmen, but hawked the fish inland themselves. Whether they felt they had made a point, or whether they were subsequently barred, a woman's crew was never again seen in Eyemouth. Instead the drave became more professionally organised and the boats increasingly crewed with full-time fishermen.

In October 1851 when Spears was reddin' up (preparing) some nets in a little yard off the Salt Greens, he was disturbed by a commotion on the quay. Dozens of youngsters were pelting stones at fish as they shoaled in and around the pier. These were saith, not herring, and considered all but worthless by every curer on the coast. Spears could hardly see water for fish and rushed to talk to John Dickson. After the briefest of conversations, Dickson set to work firing up his smokehouse, while Spears called on his crew of callants to get down on to the shore. A bemused crowd gathered, and watched as the men tumbled into their new boat *Supreme* and hauled a herring net around the bay. In a single shot more than 11,000 saithe, cod, turbot and plaice were landed. By the end of the day in excess of 30,000 fish had been brought ashore, taken to Dickson's yard, smoked and then sent down to the London market. Even after expenses, these 'worthless' fish brought in a healthy profit.

The incident is another telling example of the enterprise of Dickson and the leadership of Spears. Without the Kingfisher's say-so, the very idea of laying nets in the bay to catch saithe would have been derided.

The following year, 1852, was another bumper one for the winter fleet. High prices and splendid catches were celebrated at a dinner held in the Cross-Keys Inn on 8 June. At the head of the table was Spears, surrounded by the forty leading fishermen and merchants of the town. To the strains of 'Caller Herring' and brimfull glasses of claret and whisky (did they wonder why they experienced powerful hangovers?!) the health of Eyemouth was celebrated again and again. One of the toasts was to the 'mussels of the Boston Deeps', an acknowledgement of an important new source of bait now being used.

Every man took with him a line with more than a thousand baited hooks and in past years the winter fishing had been hampered by a lack of shellfish. Limpets and mussels, locally picked, were traditionally used as a lure but with more boats and more men, supplies dwindled at an alarming rate. In 1848 a group of women tramped as far as Cockburnspath, twelve miles from home with mussel baskets on their backs. Their appearance led to a catfight with the fisher-lasses there, and one Eyemouth girl, who was eight months pregnant, was seriously injured in a fracas dubbed the 'battle of the limpet protectionists of the Cove'.

To overcome the bait problem regular consignments of Lincolnshire mussels were shipped into the port from early 1851. There was a fairly obvious downside: the expense. Once lines were baited they had to be used, or the flesh would rot and have to be replaced. Here was another financial imperative to sail, whatever the weather and whatever the outlook.

That was what happened on 24 December 1852. The fleet had not sailed for three days and with the bait becoming putrid they took a chance when a weather window opened. Predictably the boats were exposed when the storm came down. They were also much further out than normal, about twenty miles northeast of St Abbs Head. By mid-afternoon it seemed as though everyone in Eyemouth had decamped to the shore. 'The town was in the greatest state of fear and excitement' wrote one of those who ran with them. 'And amongst the fishing population their wailings were truly heartrending. By this time nearly the whole population were upon the beach and pier heads.'

Ropes secured the first boat when it broke through the surf and across the bar. A second vessel, *Vine* skippered by David Johnston bobbed in and out of view and seemed to be heading safely through the roadsteads when it suddenly rolled, shipped water and appeared lost. The crew managed to steer the boat to the Hurkurs, where they all leapt on to the rocks. Miraculously every man was saved. On the horizon behind, the entire fleet was in sight, heaving to and fro, some pitching towards the rocks at the east and west of the bay, others running straight for the beach. The crowds were distraught.

Running the gauntlet through the surf all the vessels careered past the Hurkurs and into the calmer waters of the bay. The final crew to make port arrived well after dark. *Fisher Lasses* was holed below the water line and clearly sinking. John Cowe and his men would certainly have drowned were it not for the bravery of a crew who had just made it home yet launched their boat again to rescue the hapless crew. No boats and no men were lost on Christmas Eve 1852, but the good fortune could not endure forever.

The December storms continued into January. In the first few days of 1853 more than £180 worth of lines – not counting the value of the bait –

were wrenched to the bottom of the North Sea. As was so often the case in Berwickshire this misery was but a prelude to a greater tragedy.

'Boats put off in terrible seas, such is their endeavour here' was how John Sutherland the fishery officer reported matters to his employers in Edinburgh on 8 January 1853. He wrote this line just a few hours after the greatest loss to the Berwickshire fleet in living memory; a tragedy worse than that of the destruction of *Jabez* in 1842, and one to rival those of 1827 and 1828. It was also a sinking which struck once more at the door of William Spears.

Thomas Lauder and the crew of the *Lively* dallied at Burnmouth pier on the chill Friday morning. Most had been ready for the sea by 6 a.m., but the boat, normally the first out, was that morning the last to leave. Three of the men were from the Spouse family. The oldest on board, John Spouse had fallen ill and had arranged for John Cowe of Eyemouth to take his place. That man, who normally worked on *Fisher Lasses*, the boat which narrowly escaped disaster on Christmas Eve, eventually wandered into view well after the other boats had gone. The crew girned at his timekeeping, and were annoyed too that John Spouse's son James had also called off, claiming that he was suffering from rheumatics. There was no substitute organised for James and the *Lively*, a man short, at last pulled past the rocks and into the darkness of open water. Waving them away were the women folk of the village, amongst them John Aitchison's wife Helen Spears. At her apron were their children, now eight in number.

The *Lively* had just caught up with the bulk of the Burnmouth and Eyemouth fleet and the men had only just started to play out their lines when the gale came on. The boats scattered for home. In the blinding conditions the crew of the *Idis* were to report the last sighting of *Lively*. Crewmen told later that *Lively* was in obvious distress. She was lying with her sail down and had shipped a sea (a lump as it is called) and the crew were employed in bailing it out. The *Lively* then hoisted a small bit of her sail, and they got abreast of her. They had not sailed thus more than five minutes when they saw a heavy sea strike the *Lively*, and she went down instantly ... none of the men were ever seen again.'

This melancholy news was carried home to Burnmouth. By noon there were six more widows and thirty orphans in Berwickshire, twenty of whom were under ten years of age. Once more the sea refused to yield up the bodies of the drowned.

Thomas Lauder, aged 38, who left a widow and seven children
John Aitchison, aged 33, who left a widow and eight children
Alexander Anderson, aged 43, who left a widow and six children
William Martin, aged 36, who left a widow and four children

William Spouse, aged 33, who left a widow and four children
John Cowe, aged 44, who left a widow and one child.

John Spouse and his son James survived by the good fortune of not being on board. John Cowe perished. Meetings were held to set up voluntary subscription lists within forty-eight hours of the disaster, with a lead being given by Captain Alexander Mitchell-Innes of Ayton Castle. Some sent a shilling, others twenty pounds to a fund that would eventually raise almost £500. The remaining five Burnmouth boats gave what they could, but villagers there had never been noted for saving money in good times to use in bad.

A. Wilson and crew	£2 0 0
William Spouse and crew	£2 0 0
Thomas Kerr and crew	£2 0 0
William Martin and crew	£0 7 6
Robert Lauder and crew	£0 2 6

The skippers from Eyemouth were well represented, and somewhat better off. Each sent £1

A. Maltman, skipper and crew of 'Olive Branch'
P. Burgan, skipper and crew of 'Champion'
John Burgan, skipper and crew of 'Flying Fish'
R. Collin, skipper and crew of 'Speedwell'
J. Scott, skipper and crew of 'Middlemiss'
G. Scott, skipper and crew of 'Myrtle'
A. Collin, skipper and crew of 'Favourite'
P. Gibson, skipper and crew of 'Liberty'
James Windram, skipper and crew of 'Border Maid'
J. Cowe, skipper and crew of 'Fisher Lasses'
D. Johnston, skipper and crew of 'Vine'
J. Dougal, skipper and crew of 'Rapid'
J. Dougal, skipper and crew of 'Simon Peter'
W. Maltman, skipper and crew of 'Prosperine'

Captain Washington, who had reported on the fishing industry in the wake of a destructive gale in 1848, had concluded that Scottish fishermen were a cautious breed. 'There are a great many creeks ... Where if it blows the least puff of wind the fishermen tend to draw up their boats above high water mark.' That was clearly not the case in Berwickshire where in the wake of the loss of the *Lively* siren voices were again raised against the all too common practice of boats sailing when storms were virtually certain.

The scale of the 1853 disaster impacted hard on Berwickshire. Willie Spears and his mother had another personal tragedy to deal with, though Helen, now a widow with a large family to keep, did not move back to Eyemouth. She stayed at their garret in Burnmouth, where the Aitchisons, the Martins and the Spouses lived in numbers. Her eldest lad, William Crawford Aitchison, then just fourteen, brought home his own wage. He quit school and joined with his cousin James Martin, whose father William was also one of the drowned. Like Spears and Dougal a quarter of a century before, these boys became fishermen overnight. It was the only way to survive. Helen and her brood looked to the future.

Spears helped out as much as he could and he also provided for the other families left in poverty. In particular he gave the widow of John Cowe run of the rooms underneath his apartment. Spears also paid her to be his housekeeper and to look after his elderly mother.

The year that *Lively* was lost was the most remunerative ever for Berwickshire fishermen. Most boats grossed around £400 for the haddock fishing, good money for the October–May season. The summer herring was even better. Almost 100,000 crans were unloaded on to Eyemouth pier, double that of the previous year. John Sutherland noted that the success also attracted more incomers. 'Eyemouth' he wrote, 'is the favourite port from which to prosecute the white fishing, and fishermen from other stations continue to settle here. Only the want of house room somewhat retards the tide of emigration'.

Sutherland also reported that the fishermen were putting more of their money into new boats and gear. Some were even cutting down on their on-shore drinking, though there was considerable local outrage when draconian new licensing laws were imposed in 1854. Henceforth pubs would be obliged to close at 10 p.m. and would not be allowed to open again before six in the morning. The anger was not just at the unwarranted interference in the right of men to take refreshment after a long night at the herring. Where else would the crew be able to 'divvy-up' their money? Sometimes the skippers might have £300 or more to disperse amongst their crews. If the cash wasn't to be counted in the Ship, with a few rounds of whisky and beer, would they have to dole it out in windy, wet and dark streets? The option of sitting down in the skipper's own home seems never to have been given serious consideration.

The bar owners and innkeepers initially laughed at the dictates of Westminster – but authority stalked the streets at night and in the pre-dawn morning. Police Constable John Dewar did not issue warnings; he pressed for prosecutions. Several miscreants were brought before Ayton JP court and fined by George Home of Gunsgreen. Home was also responsible for hearing cases against the few individuals who continued the tradition of smuggling, though this was now on a tiny scale, nothing like the great days of the 1780s. Like the excise men of old, John Dewar had a thankless job, though his zeal to see the law enforced to its full extent did at times border on the farcical. In July 1855 the constable's nightly rounds took him to the Royal Hotel, and a suspicious light still burning at ten past ten. He tapped on the window, and demanded entry. There the diligent polis-man found John White puffing away on his pipe in the kitchen, neither drunk nor even drinking. These mere details mattered not a jot to Dewar. Both White and the owner were arraigned to appear before George Home, and subsequently fined.

The outrage at this persistence would in past times have resulted in trouble. Perhaps that is why Spears invited Dewar to come along to one of his suppers. If the Kingfisher was trying his hand at diplomacy this time it did not work. Relations between the fishermen and the Kirk over the tithe had again deteriorated. The time was fast drawing near when violence would replace words and riots would erupt on the streets of Eyemouth. John Dewar would be at the thick of it, enjoying the experience of noting the names of all who took part – and quite a few who were not there – for the sake of settling some old scores.

In April 1854 Chirnside Presbytery, irritated by the lack of progress on the fish tithe issue, set up a committee to report on what could be done. It was another opportunity to accept the inevitable and agree to let the tithe lapse. When it reported in June of that year, however, attitudes had clearly hardened. The records do not indicate whether Stephen Bell offered any dissent, but they hardly dressed up their criticism of his lack of endeavour to date. 'The Presbytery do strictly enjoin Mr Bell to be more careful, that no dilapidations of the benefice of Eyemouth occur through his laxity in enforcing his rights, and with that view strongly recommend to Mr Bell to lease to a tacksman all his rights to fish tithe.'

The committee believed that these rights included a portion of the earnings from the herring fishing of *all* Eyemouth men – even those who paid the modus for the white fishing season. Proper attention to the fish tithe would at least treble the stipend at Eyemouth. Moreover, unless the minister demanded and received herring tithe money from the fishermen who were already paying him £1 13s. 4d. a year, 'the right to that tithe will lapse by prescription in the course of three years.'

He had to act and act quickly. Stephen Bell was now put on a collision course which could only end in confrontation. Any respect or authority he might have had in Eyemouth was certain to disappear. All of this was in marked contrast to the standing enjoyed by William Spears who was at the height of his powers and unmatched in influence.

The most compelling piece of evidence to Spears' stature can be seen from an incident that took place in February 1854. An attempt to recruit volunteers for the naval reserve ended in dismal failure. A packed audience in the Masonic Hall listened in stony silence to appeals from Captain Craigie. There was not even polite applause to his entreaties, just blank stares and steady chairs. Barely fifty years had elapsed since men in similar uniforms had come into Eyemouth to seize lads in the pressgang. How dare Craigie ask their grandsons to wear the same jackets? As the naval officer prepared to leave, Spears softly suggested that at this time of conflict with Russia over the Crimea, Britain needed Haimooth lads. Craigie had barely removed his overcoat again when he was swamped with 'enthusiastic recruits', and by the end of the evening sixty-four men had signed up. Craigie had much less success at Burnmouth. Perhaps he should have taken Spears with him. When the naval party appeared at the head of the brae all the men, convinced the pressgang was back, disappeared out of the other end of the village.

Why did Spears decide to offer his callants to Craigie? Was it a shrewd move to underline the respectability and patriotism of Eyemouth at exactly the moment when the church was again making vigorous demands for fish tithe?

Stephen Bell did as he was told by the Presbytery, but he had no luck in recruiting a tacksman either in 1854 or in the following year. It was not from the want of effort. He circulated letters amongst his fellow ministers in other coastal parishes and placed advertisements in the Berwick, Edinburgh and Fife newspapers. One merchant did offer terms, but wanted a five-year deal with a break midway through the contract and with the Church guaranteeing any losses that might be incurred. It was changed days indeed from 1818 and the harmonious and lucrative deal negotiated by the late Rev Dr Smith.

Eventually an Eyemouth man rapped at the Manse door. He would give £25 for the 1855 summer season alone. It was a paltry amount. But as the only serious offer, Bell was inclined to accept it. Even this was scuppered when word leaked out and the prospective lessee was given unequivocal 'advice'. 'He withdrew when the fishermen insisted I deal with them directly' Bell told Chirnside Presbytery. ' I was induced to comply with their request both from a desire for peace and also from an apprehension that the tacksman would fail in his attempt to collect the dues'.

Another meeting with William Spears was arranged in late July 1855. The minister was frank. He had completely run out of patience and the trouble had to stop. His final pitch was an annual payment of £1 from all the Eyemouth crews who fished herring. Those who carried on fishing in the winter would still have to pay the modus of £1 13s. 4d. And he would also be levying tithe on the visiting herring boats.

Spears shook his head, but did not argue with the minister. He agreed to put Bell's final offer to the community, though there was never any doubt as to what the view of the fishermen would be. William Dougal, the Angus brothers and the Windrams shouted it down. The merchants and curers, led by Dickson, Statham and Cormack added their voices to the dissent. Their anger was as full as their pocket books empty. Bell might talk of the prosperity of the fishing, but the news that tithe was again to be charged on boats visiting Eyemouth had led to a boycott of the port.

Not one single drave boat from other parts came to the harbour in the summer of 1855. Instead they headed for Dunbar, Burnmouth or Berwick. The slump affected everyone, and wagging fingers pointed towards the Manse of the minister.

Bell had made his position clear to Spears. Now the fishermen reciprocated. They would pay nothing at all during the drave. A few went further and gave John Nisbet something of a kicking. The tallyman was not badly hurt, but he had had his fill and resigned. Bell was furious. He had tried and failed to engage a tacksman, thanks in the main to the obstruction of the fishermen. He had then tried to offer a generous deal, which probably equated to less than a night's drinking in the Ship. That too had been eschewed by lads who thought it fun to call him names, abuse his office and attack his servant. On 3 August 1855 the minister wrote a curt letter to the Kingfisher. It was now time for the law to take a view on proceedings in Eyemouth.

> Sir – I hereby intimate to you, that in consequence of the conduct of the fishermen, no compromise can be entered into regarding the herring teind with any Eyemouth boat. All proposed arrangements with this view must now be considered at an end, and the legal course pursued.

While he prepared this legal action, Bell, to his great credit, continued to tread along the pier, noting the landings as they were heaped ashore. But dedication to the demands of the Kirk could go only so far. When the Drave reached its peak in mid-August he was warned that he too risked being set upon. Stephen Bell knew this was no idle talk and contracted 'two determined men' to come down from Edinburgh, take over the duties of John Nisbet and extract the tithe in a more forceful manner.

It was another miscalculation which stoked up an already volatile situation. On Saturday 11 August 1855 a mob of hotheads, well lubricated from a day's drinking, pounced on the Edinburgh 'toughs', gave them a good hiding and threw the pair into the harbour. When the bedraggled would-be collectors clawed up the pierside ladders, they were again assaulted. This time it was the turn of the women who clawed at their hair and spat in their faces. Bruised, bloodied, drenched and humiliated they were hounded to the very edge of town, not even being given time to collect their belongings.

The crowd then made for the Kirk. Two fishermen, James Maltman and Alexander Anderson broke down the door and in their drunken revelry began ringing the church bell, alternating the clanks with loud and blasphemous obscenities. The noise and commotion brought even more folk on to the street, some in their nightshirts and goonies. It would be a travesty to call what took place a riot, but it was hardly an advert for a sober and just cause.

Perhaps as many as three hundred people surged along the street, singing and shouting before coming to a halt outside the Manse. Watching, from a very safe distance, was PC John Dewar. The highland bobbie chose not to intervene, but peered out instead from behind corners, licking at his pencil and keeping a very full log book of what happened, or rather what he claimed had taken place. At a later trial before Duns Sheriff Court, Dewar's precise catalogue of events seemed too comprehensive, too exhaustive for a single man to have noted.

Bell told the sheriff that the trouble came from 'parties behind the scenes', a clear reference to Dickson, Statham, Dougall and above all William Spears. But as even PC Dewar could not place any of them at the scene, the Sheriff chose to fine three others.

Events on that August night very nearly got out of control. But Spears could see there was real anger, if only it could be channelled in the right direction. He called the fishermen to a mass meeting in the Methodist Chapel in early December 1855. The venue is significant. After the revelry of August, Spears, Statham and the other leaders were desperate to be seen as intelligent and respectful. They might have preferred to convene in the church of John Turnbull, but the time was not yet right for the Free Kirk to associate with men who were attacking one of the principles of the establishment, an establishment which the new denomination still adhered strongly to.

William Dougall, whose father was the 'auld Barque' assumed the chair, allowing Spears the freedom to speak. The hall could not hold the crowd and it spewed out into the Square and to the twisting lanes beyond. More than eight hundred people listened intently as the squat little man stood on a bench to make his address. He had to shout to make himself heard, and even then those at the back could not make out what he was saying. The cheers told them it was popular, whatever it was. The Kingfisher cried out 'Tithe be no longer paid by the fishermen of Eyemouth'. He then held above him a prepared document which was unrolled and every man from the seagoing district was ordered to come forward and put his mark against it. As they did so, Spears continued,

> We can have no fear in refusing tithe payments. We can do so and yet have no ill feeling to Mr Bell, the minister of the established church here. We are only acting the part of conscientious individuals if, believing the tithe to be an injustice, we refuse its payment ... Away with such a monstrous injustice and prove tonight that we have both a sense of oppression and a disposition to resistance.

Spears' proclamation – some called it the Fisherman's Covenant – was a call to the barricades, the first salvo in open warfare which would involve a propaganda battle fought out firstly between the liberal *Berwick Advertiser* and the Tory *Berwick Warder*, then later in a series of partisan placards and printed pamphlets which would be distributed and read throughout the county and beyond.

As events spiralled from standoff to violent confrontation, dissenting clergy who used the plight of the fishermen as a lever towards disestablishment flocked to Eyemouth. The town was also the centre of a row over political abuse in the General Election of 1859, and was one of the most unlikely places to be hit by a religious revival that stormed across Scotland in the following year. And as all of this was going on, the men kept putting to sea in atrocious weather, beating home against all the odds to a harbour which remained cramped, tidal and dangerous.

Other places, like Fraserburgh, Peterhead, Buckie and Anstruther had no such excitement in the 1850s and early 1860s. They used the time to greater advantage and won huge grants and loans to remodel or completely renew their harbour facilities. Eyemouth, so well placed and so well thought of when Stephen Bell first sniffed its distinctive air fell behind, badly behind.

Of course, Stephen Bell could not have known this when he raised a legal action against William Spears and three other skippers in November 1855. Publicly the minister professed his hope that a civil action would finally and amicably decide the rights and wrongs of the tithe. If Spears was obliged to accept the judgement of the court, a continuation of the rebellion was unthinkable. But the proceedings, which opened at Duns Sheriff Court in early February 1856, were clearly not going to be 'amicable'. Nor was there likely to be an early settlement.

The fishermen's committee spent the winter months canvassing support from around the coast, and their defence fund was soon well endowed. Tim Statham also opened up a second front in the columns of the *Berwick Advertiser*. The Secretary of the Fishermen's Committee's acerbic prose and sarcastic poetry would do much to keep the issue to the fore, and to win public support. 'Should Bell win', wrote Statham, ' it would be the ruination of Eyemouth. The conviction is forced upon us that it is the fleece and not the flock that these worthies of the Kirk are interested in.'

Then the first of many satirical little poems was printed. The rhyming couplets would amuse and entertain the anti-tithe side in the row. They outraged David Milne-Home, appalled the Presbytery and thoroughly depressed Stephen Bell.

> This priest was very bold and gay
> Three quarters of the year
> But o' it grieved him very much
> When tything time drew near

The fishermen felt their case to be watertight, and drank heavily on stories of their grandfathers and great grandfathers who had fought and won previous court battles. It was up to the present generation to finish the tithe off for good. Another meeting in the Methodist Chapel was called on 30 April 1856 to let the men hear at first hand of the actions of their committee. Willie Dougall told them that almost £50 lay in the defence fund, and this did not include other sums being gathered by the folk of Coldingham and Burnmouth. When the Kingfisher was called to address them there were ringing cheers and thunderous applause. Spears spoke in a soft, almost lilting tone. 'I am at a loss to know why I have been selected to bear the brunt of the Rev Stephen Bell's new attack upon the fishermen here. Probably he may have supposed that I may be the victim most easily sacrificed, if so I wish him joy in his selection'. He milked his audience like a polished politician, and called for good order and restraint at all times. They must continue to show respect for authority, which they could do and 'still resist oppression'.

Spears proposed that some of the funds be spent on the purchase of a radical banner and a flag of liberty. 'These', he said 'would convey to the rising generation the nature of the glorious struggle their fathers were engaged in in order to get that liberty which has now become the birthright of Britons, and which is only withheld from the fishermen'.

The Kingfisher was then hoisted on to the shoulders of some of the callants, and to more ear splitting cheers the large crowd paraded down to the quay, back up the Long Entry, across the market and then up and down the lane outside the manse.

Poor Stephen Bell; and pity indeed ought to be given to this man of God who valued principles and the law above his own personal safety and comfort. How much easier it would have been to walk away, to seek another parish, or to cave in to the community pressure that he felt whenever he opened his front door. After all, John Murdoch, his immediate predecessor, managed to stomach the place for little more than eighteen months. Yet to cut and run would scarcely have occurred to Stephen Bell. He had never wanted conflict, but neither could he shirk the consequences of events which were fast unravelling out of control. The minister stood his ground.

Chapter Nine

Pay no Tithe!

Stephen Bell ought to remember the fable of the dog and the piece of meat.
That by grasping at too much he has lost what he had and will find it im-
possible to recover it again
        William Spears' address to the fishermen of Eyemouth, 30 April 1856

In June 1856 all twenty-eight Eyemouth skippers were served with notices
to appear at Ayton JP court to account for their failure to pay fish tithe.
Each man was also sent a letter in the name of Stephen Bell, which attacked
William Spears as the ringleader and 'instigator of certain riotous proceedings in Eyemouth'. A hastily convened meeting of the fishermen's
committee decided to continue to publicise their argument in printed
handbills, and through articles in the press. A clear majority favoured simply
ignoring Bell's summonses. But Spears and Statham disagreed. The day
they were due in court ought to be used as a celebration, showing all of
Scotland that while the law might favour the Kirk, justice was assuredly
with the people. The movement was now attracting support from fishing
communities as far apart as Cornwall and Peterhead. Their defence fund
was swollen with contributions, and even the annual gathering of teetotal-
lers in the district had held a collection for the fishermen. What better way
to show the strength of their cause than an orderly march to the courthouse
and back? Besides, the banner and the flag of liberty had just arrived from
Edinburgh. The colours should be tested.

Monday 1 August 1856 was the day set for twenty-eight contrite men to
appear. The skippers did in fact make their way to Ayton, but not to enter
the dock. From before dawn the streets of Eyemouth were alive with
unusual activity, with men being arrayed into ranks and the Market Place
gradually being filled to overflowing with folk dressed in their best rig-out.
At about ten o'clock the St Abbs brass band played the fishermen of
Coldingham Shore down the Halydown Hill and along the Street to the
Market, where the crowds parted like the Red Sea. This group then swung
around and to the amazement of onlookers the rabble magicked into an
organised battalion. Immediately behind the band, and in marshalled ranks
of four, went the fishermen's committee, with Spears at the head. They
were all immaculately dressed and displaying rosettes of red, white and
blue. Next came the sixty-four naval coast volunteers, all in uniform, then

the skippers summoned for tithe arrears, followed by the entire body of fishermen from Eyemouth and the rest of Berwickshire and the local fish merchants, coopers and tradesmen. Bringing up the rear was a substantial number of stranger crews from Buckhaven, Fisherrow, Yarmouth and Penzance. By half past ten the procession was ready, and at that moment four 'picked men' came forward. Swung between them were lengthy poles, which they gingerly unfurled.

A low mumble of anticipation was replaced with resounding cheers as the flag of liberty was revealed. It had a heavy green hue and was embossed with a full-length figure of a fisherman, his hand resting on a basket of herring and, above his head in bold letters of gold the words 'Pay no Tithe!' The callants charged with carrying the flag hoisted it high and turned it round to the four corners of the Market Place so that all could strain their necks to see. Each rotation brought a louder cry than the last. Yet even these shouts were drowned out when the banner was pulled apart. It was even more decorative than the flag, with rich ornamental wreaths of flowers highlighting the inscription:

> In Liberty's ennobling cause
> Our Fisher lads stand weal;
> And gloriously have won the right
> Of freedom to the creel.

Spears, getting up on to a chair that had been thoughtfully brought out, held up his hand to silence the throng, then very simply, and quite softly, slowly repeated the words on the banner. The noise erupted once more as the St Abbs brass band struck up 'Caller Herring', and the procession moved out of the Market Place. As the march, of at least two thousand strong, passed the gates of the Kirk, prolonged and ironic chanting was delivered up. But there was no stone throwing, no catcalling, no ugly scenes to distract from the primary purpose. This was to be a peaceful demonstration.

The snaking army increased to between three and four thousand by the time it reached the outskirts of Ayton, some two miles to the west. Landsmen joined in, showing an unusual solidarity with their seafaring neighbours and drawing no doubt on a long tradition of religious non-conformity in this part of the Merse. At the recently completed Ayton Castle three cheers were sounded for the proprietor Captain Mitchell Innes, whose liberality in the wake of the *Lively* disaster was well remembered. The band struck up '*Weel may the boatie row*' and as they passed Ayton courtroom all bowed or removed their hats but did not stop to enter. The ranks then swung round for home, arriving back at the market place in the early afternoon and dispersing after three times three cheers. The committee was not just overjoyed at the turnout, but greatly relieved at the conduct of all involved. Indeed the fishermen did not troop into the Ship or the Cross-Keys to celebrate the day's events. Instead they picked up their nets and got ready for a night's herring fishing. What a difference to past days, and what an advert for their cause. The tide of public opinion, as voiced by the *Berwick Advertiser* was running with the fishermen. 'The demonstration has been a noble assertion of sound and sterling principles, honest manly sentiments, and genuine old British vigour and determination,' it said. 'Marred by no demogogueism, no furious mob eloquence, depending upon nothing but the all prevailing might of moral strength.'

The defiant march came in the middle of yet another successful drave, with the stranger crews who had deserted the port in 1855 encouraged back in numbers by the cry of 'no tithe at Eyemouth'. From the evening of 1 August the boats which crossed the harbour bar passed the famous flag, now triumphantly attached to the pier head. Statham fired off another ditty to the newspapers.

> Our Flag to the Mast we have nailed,
> It floats out an emblem so blythe
> Of the Justice and Rights of the Fishers
> In ending for ever the tithe.

That summer season more than 37,000 barrels of fresh or lightly salted herring were sent to market from the Eyemouth district. This was in addition to 50,000 barrels that were cured. It all contrasted very favourably with a decade earlier when less than 2,000 barrels had been dispatched fresh and around 16,000 sent cured. More importantly to the crews was what this all meant to their pockets. John Sutherland's end of year report was ebullient. 'This has to be the best season ever in this district. It has been prosperous to all ... Fishermen have had large takes at high prices. The curers have done well and notwithstanding the utmost exertion on the part of the boatbuilders, they cannot keep pace with demand'.

Virtually every boat in the Eyemouth fleet was now either decked or half decked. Bigger vessels allowed them to sail further and stay out longer, and a few also struck out far beyond their home havens. They sailed to Lewis for the spring herring season, and to the more established grounds off Yarmouth in late summer.

In the midst of all this activity little thought was given to the tithe, which most assumed was either dead or dying. Of course, Stephen Bell could not take that view, and nor could the laird David Milne-Home. The Tory journal, the *Berwick Warder*, continued to remind its readers of the recent

Chartist unrest and made the point that the fishermen were little better
than those agitators. They were common criminals bent on social upheaval,
perhaps even political revolution. The editorials were more than a bit over
the top and were satirised by Timothy Statham, now a regular contributor
of verse to the *Berwick Advertiser*.

> A Warning note in the Warder sounds
> And wild and loud it's ringing;
> The Church, the state's endangered now,
> That croaking lady's singing.

But some of the mud stuck and the *Warder* persisted in its attacks. It
even linked the defiance on the coast to the shock of an electoral contest
for Berwickshire in the general election of 1857 – the first contested poll for
more than a quarter century.

Franchise reform meant that the landed gentry could no longer buy,
bully or intimidate the entire electorate. Nonetheless, with only 1103 men
who qualified for the vote in Berwickshire, families like the Wedderburns
could exert influence. In the election their favoured candidate, Francis Scott,
just managed to hold the seat, albeit with a majority of only 89 over David
Robertson of Ladykirk.

The Liberal candidate was feted in Eyemouth and at a public meeting
organised by Timothy Statham, Robertson was cheered to the rafters. To
the utter dismay of David Milne-Home, Eyemouth, nine-tenths of which
he owned and which should have been beholding to him as the feudal
superior, became a staunchly Liberal enclave. On the day of the poll the
dozen or so wealthy enough to vote marched along with hundreds of
supporters behind a brass band to the hustings at Ayton. To a man they
backed Robertson and though the result was greeted with dismay, the tight
margin was cheered. As the *Berwick Advertiser* put it 'The county of Berwick,
which has for some time been regarded as fully given over to Tory power
and despotism has manifested a spirit and desire for freedom in the irresistible popular will'.

It would not do to over-emphasise David Robertson's populist roots.
Both his father (1818–26) and his brother (1832–4) had represented Berwickshire in the Commons, and Robertson would eventually succeed to the
family peerage as Lord Marjoribanks in 1873. But his public stance on a
variety of issues was a degree more enlightened than that of either the
sitting Tory MP or the laird David Milne-Home. That made Robertson,
whose wife claimed descent from John Churchill, Baron of Eyemouth and
the First Duke of Marlborough, a target for the fishermen's committee.
They were fighting the minister in the courts; they were at the centre of

a newspaper war. Now they sought a political ally in their battle against the tithe and for the development of the port.

It was estimated that 'want of water' prevented the fishing fleet from sailing or returning for up to twenty days a year. A more telling statistic was the financial cost, put at £1,300 a year. In July 1857 the *Napier* was obliged to wait in the roadsteads after an exhausting journey home from Yarmouth. As would be the case in 1881, there was a horrible running sea, in spite of the low water. Fatigue and impatience led the crew to risk beating across the harbour bar, and *Napier* was overturned on a single wave. Onlookers from the shore saw the boat pulled under within seconds. All six crew were saved, and with them the money they had earned from Yarmouth. But their vessel, which had cost £180 and was not insured, was lost.

Later in the year, in mid-November, the entire fleet sailed in defiance of a barometer warning of impending bad weather. When the gale came down and the boats attempted to make home, many had to abandon gear and one sank after colliding with the *Myrtle* which itself sustained heavy damage. Further north, the storms wreaked havoc. More than forty men were drowned when a number of boats sank in the Moray Firth. The disaster concentrated the minds of fishermen and merchants in Buckie and else-where to improve and extend their harbour facilities. There was no such move at Eyemouth where attention and energy continued to be diverted by the trouble over the tithe.

In February 1858 a breakthrough at least seemed imminent. Sheriff-Substitute Alexander Wood declared in court that so long as the fishermen went full time to the sea they were exempt from paying anything at all to the minister except the modus of £1 13s. 4d. They could not be held liable for additional herring teind.

Stephen Bell and the Presbytery of Chirnside now had a choice. They could accept this ruling and settle for the modus payment, including the sums withheld since 1856, or they could appeal the judgement. In more sober times the former course might have been an option. The whole affair might have been defused with the minister still entitled to a fair sum from the white fish fleet. But points of principle, if not the tantalising amounts that could yet come the way of the Kirk, and solid legal advice of the prospects for pressing ahead, were more powerful motivators. In the spring of 1858 an appeal was duly lodged.

This was heard in Duns Sheriff Court in July 1858 before Sheriff Principal Bell. The fishermen's committee stirred things up in the town by suggesting that as procurator (he advised the Presbytery on legal matters) for the Church of Scotland he could scarcely be considered impartial. It was a charge which outraged David Milne-Home, but one which was widely believed in Eyemouth.

With the decision expected any day the fishermen's committee decided on a further show of strength. On 1 August 1858, exactly two years since the mass march to Ayton, a similar demonstration was carried off. Once again upwards of 2,000 people crowded into the Market Place before being led off through the town by a band of musicians from Edinburgh. Given the narrowness of the lanes and vennels the procession almost linked up in a loop, with those at the end being greeted by the fishermen's committee at the front. It was another carnival, but behind the rosettes and ribbons was an appreciation by the leaders that this time they were going to lose. Two days before the grand demonstration, Sheriff Principal Bell issued an interlocutor stating that Eyemouth fishermen had, in some instances in the past, paid herring teind over and above the modus. It was a clear indication of his ruling to come, and was based on an exhaustive reading of the Court of Session pronouncement in 1793; the litigation which took place during the ministry of Dr Smith; and, rather bizarrely, on the 1756 action of James Allan against a neighbouring parish for a tithe of corn.

A final ruling was delivered less than a week after the march. William Spears and three others were found wholly liable to pay herring teind of £15 each, plus legal expenses. The judgement applied to the amount they had made in the 1856 drave, and had it been accepted it might have opened the floodgates, or perhaps the money wallets, for the Kirk to insist on payment from dozens of others for each and every season.

To a community already convinced the tithe was dead this came as more than a bit of a shock. The mob needed little persuading that Sheriff Bell had been got at, probably by David Milne-Home and his Tory lackeys. Wild rumours filled the air as well as the columns in the Berwick newspapers. Stephen Bell would make a thousand pounds a year from the fishermen of Eyemouth, and that from only taking a tithe of their herring money. What if he then pressed on and used the now discredited courts to try and take a similar proportion of all their earnings? Stephen Bell would be after £4,000 a year. The Church might build a cathedral where once a dilapidated, roofless Kirk had called the faithful few to prayer.

Statham teased out prejudices and whipped up an already explosive mood. 'What a smart little man this priest would be if only he could get a tenth of their incomes' he wrote. It would be the end for fishing in Eyemouth.

In the circumstances it is a wonder that the fishermen's committee managed to prevent more violence, especially when the closing bell was rung in the pubs. A lid was kept on the black and angry mood partly because

Spears decided to follow the path trodden by his own grandfather. It was his turn to go to law. The Kingfisher lodged an appeal against the Sheriff's judgement and raised an action in the Court of Session against Stephen Bell and the Presbytery of Chirnside for 'troubling and molesting' him as he went about his daily business. In the week in which the lawsuit was agreed upon, and perhaps to make a point that he was a fisherman first and foremost, Spears went to sea and landed more than thirty-eight barrels of saithe in a single haul. The catch was another record one.

As the case entered the Court of Session, what they were fighting for and why was amply demonstrated with the loss of yet another boat. *Albion's Delight* sank fifteen miles off her home haven of Burnmouth. It was a substantial half-decked vessel, yet was dragged under as swiftly as any open cobble. Again none of the bodies were recovered. The seven who died were James Aitchison, an elderly man who was only at sea because his son, the skipper, was on exercise with the coastal volunteers on board HMS Edinburgh, Abraham Pauline, married with six young children, and the following who were all single: James Johnston, James Anderson, Robert Fairbairn, Mark Anderson, Arthur Johnson.

The Burnmouth boats had followed the Eyemouth fleet out that morning, once more in defiance of the pier-head barometer. The dead men had no insurance and their families no savings. Black-bordered subscription lists again appeared in the Berwick papers.

The Wedderburns sent money, as they usually did, but the stock of the Milne-Homes was plummeting to new depths on the coast. It reached rock bottom during the snap General Election campaign of 1859.

As expected, David Robertson announced his intention to stand on a Liberal ticket against a new Tory candidate, his own cousin Sir John Marjoribanks of the Lees. In a fatuous attempt to influence the Eyemouth electorate, Jean Milne-Home's brother-in-law, the Hon Charles St Clair, posted placards around the town strongly advising tenants to vote Tory. To do otherwise, when ballot casting was a very public affair, might have 'unwelcome consequences.' Far from distancing themselves from such an outrageous manoeuvre, Jean and David Milne-Home endorsed the sentiments. Indeed the Lady of Wedderburn made a bad situation much worse when she publicly urged her people to either back Marjoribanks or abstain. Her letter to the *Berwick Advertiser* was reprinted in papers across Britain, with many ridiculing it as a 'ukase' after the fashion of the most despotic of Russian Tsars. In an editorial the *Scotsman* proclaimed 'Berwickshire, how many eyes are upon her? This is not just an election, it is a contest against an arrogant and insulting social despotism, against a claim by the landowners of a feudal power over the tenants such as nowhere in Scotland is exercised to nearly the extent, and is nowhere at all so unblushingly and contemptuously displayed.'

The letter, the placards, the threats were all deeply damaging to the Tory cause. Liberal supporters gathered them together on a single broadsheet, which they gleefully distributed. Timothy Statham, the fishermen's spin doctor in chief, did not need to use much of his skill to suggest a venal web linking the laird, the Kirk and the judiciary. In spite of the best efforts of the *Warder* such a conspiracy was now plain for all to see.

Statham, who would be the Liberal agent in Eyemouth until his death in 1876, organised a number of public meetings during the election campaign. Invariably these took place in the United Presbyterian Church, some seventy yards or so from Stephen Bell's manse. Of all denominations the UP stood firmly against any Church-State link, and was virulently opposed to both the Annuity Tax in Edinburgh and the tithe in Eyemouth. Some of the more temperate fishermen as well as businessmen like Statham and Drysdale Aitchison had joined the church in the 1850s. In politics these people were avowed Liberals, in religion confirmed dissenters or, as they would have been called at the time, 'voluntaries.'

Polling day, 5 May 1859 provided another excuse for a community outing. The Eyemouth voters, with a large crowd in train, marched behind the St Abbs brass band to the hustings at Ayton. There, cocking a snoot to their supposed betters, they shouted loudly for the Liberal. The few Tories who turned up to vote were booed at, and late in the day when strong drink had taken its toll, fights broke out. The police who had been standing around all day were at last given leave to baton charge and five drunken individuals were lifted. Matters were more serious further inland at Duns where a mini riot erupted and several men and women were arrested. One, shoemaker Willie Aitchison, was later sentenced to nine months hard labour for his part in the fracas.

When the election result was eventually declared it was a sensation. For the first time since 1832 Berwickshire had turned its back on the Tories. Robertson had polled 461 votes to Marjoribank's 428. Statham fired off a letter of congratulations, along with an invitation to a victory parade in Eyemouth.

Colourful bunting brightened the drab lanes and vennels and when Robertson's gig entered the Market Place it went under a huge green banner which proclaimed 'Welcome to Eyemouth'. The new MP gave an impromptu speech from the steps of his carriage, before being carried shoulder high to a packed rally at the United Presbyterian Church.

Did he mention the fish tithe? The text of his speech has not survived, but even if he did not, events in Edinburgh over that other religious impost, the Annuity Tax, were becoming more and more heated, and parallels with the situation in Eyemouth more and more obvious.

At a demonstration on the Calton Hill a number of 'respectable citizens' had been arrested, creating martyrs for the cause. The Annuity Tax could not endure and as the clamour rose for its abolition, Robertson's demeanour towards the stance of the Eyemouth fishermen softened even further. The fish tithe, like the demand made in Edinburgh, would also have to go.

The 1859 drave was distinguished more by the success of the fishing rather than any excitement over tithe. Bell did nothing to antagonise the men. No toughs were contracted, he did not attempt to recruit a new tallyman and he avoided the quays when heavy landings were being made. But the minister had not given up, and nor had the legal team of the Kirk. All awaited news of Spears' appeal and of the judgement from the Court of Session.

In late September, with still no word from the court, the Eyemouth men prepared to return to their deep-sea winter boats. First, though, they needed to build up a store of mussels, which had now become established as the only form of bait worth using on their lines. Supplies from Lincolnshire that year were both expensive and difficult to procure. A Glasgow fish merchant who had spent the summer in the town had another, more interesting and cost effective proposal. He knew of several beds of mussels on the Clyde, which could be harvested at no cost at all. In previous years individual boats had sailed west in search of bait, now half the fleet decided to give it a try. Around twenty boats with almost a hundred men sailed through the Forth-Clyde canal and on to Port Glasgow in the first few days of October.

When they returned a week later the women and bairns clamoured for stories of the adventure, and for presents from the 'toon'. But along with news of the trip, some fine lengths of cloth and jars of sweeties, a number of the roughest, most profane and most violent men came home with what seemed like a fairly dramatic character change. Where before they had shouted and sworn, they were now apparently transfixed in thought. What had happened to them on the Clyde?

After pulling up the mussels the fleet had tied up at Port Dundas, allowing the men a chance to step out into Glasgow. The cheerful and swaggering army had not even reached the pleasure dens of the city when they were distracted by an outdoor religious service. They were drawn down to hear the preacher and transfixed by his words. This was revivalism at its most hypnotic: the first experience for Eyemouth folk of a movement that had spread like a tornado from America, through Ireland before finally settling on Scotland.

They returned home just as the Primitive Methodists were preparing their annual camp on Fort Point. To the jaw-dropping amazement of the PM minister a mob of fishermen dandered up to the Fort, joined the faithful on the old earthworks and closed their eyes in prayer. Even the Old Barque William Dougal wasn't entirely convinced that it was not a massive practical joke.

But the men were deadly serious. Former drunkards like George Collin, who had never before flirted with Christianity, took it upon himself to stand atop of the Methodist Chapel in St Ella's Place and hammer new boards into the roof, watched by his son, also called George. Auld Dod and Little Dod would first embrace Methodism and later switch to the United Presbyterians. Neither would lose his religious belief. It sustained both in troubled times. On a day far ahead when all hope seemed lost, it would be Little Dod's faith that helped a crew through the horrors of Black Friday.

John Turnbull, now of the Free Kirk, was so taken by the change which had come over the lewd and violent fishermen that he went to Ireland and then to Glasgow to see for himself what was going on. He returned convinced of the power of the revival but still sceptical about its application in Eyemouth, that most heathen of Scottish towns.

Like the Methodists at the Fort camp meeting, Turnbull did a double take when he entered his Church on 20 November 1859. The normally empty pews were not just filled, but people were sitting in the aisles and standing at the back of the hall. There was an overspill into the street. Turnbull cleared his throat and delivered his sermon. People clapped, they cheered, they wanted more! What was going on? But it was only the start. 'On the following Tuesday an individual was struck down at my ordinary prayer meeting. During the week, the report of what had happened got abroad; and on the following Tuesday, more than a hundred persons attended our prayer meeting.'

For six weeks, day and night, there were services held in churches and in private homes. John Turnbull recorded all that went on, thanking God but scarcely believing it to be true. 'In the dark and stormy nights of December our boys held prayer meetings in the boats which were laid up at the end of the town; in unoccupied houses where they had neither fire nor light.'

Those who had been strangers to religion were the ones who succumbed with a particular passion, and often with a fear that brought on convulsions. Ministers were sent for in the middle of the night as strong men wept, beat their bodies and cried out forgiveness for their sins.

The fervour of lay preaching and communal singing that distinguished the 1859–60 revival fitted in neatly with the fishing culture. Vast numbers were struck down in Eyemouth. The UP minister, Rev James Harrower was 'prostrated with over exertion and excitement' when more than one-hundred-and-fifty came forward to be saved. The Congregationalists tested the ground by sending a preacher from Kelso. It was the first time they had tried to establish a base in Eyemouth since the Rev Brotherstone had been cold shouldered in 1806. This time things were very different. Rev Thomas G Salmon's three day visit became a month long mission, and he was obliged, exhausted but happy, to call in help. A second preacher, Rev James Strachan arrived from Aberdour and along with Salmon held services on a daily basis in the Masons Hall and on the beach.

What went on in Eyemouth in the winter of 1859 can be likened to the collective hysteria that engulfed Britain on the death of Princess Diana. Like that emotional outpouring, the effect on the vast majority touched by religion in 1859 would be transient. Some of the conversions, as detailed by John Turnbull were nonetheless remarkable.

> The men have prayer meetings in their boats. 'B' worships God, attends our prayer meetings; he does all he can to bring the members of his family. He has left off swearing and drinking ... 'C'. was rude and intemperate. He has given himself to Christ and is now one of the gentlest and most loving of men ... ' F' said to me 'Satan never had a more active or willing servant. I used to sit at my fireside and plan mischief. I have torn every shred of my clothes off my back in fits of drunken madness. I once jumped from the top to the bottom of the stairs in the house where I live, and paid for it with the loss of half my teeth'. This man has said to me *'see those distant rocks in the bay. I would rather swim out to them than return to my drinking or my bad ways I love Jesus the Lord now'.*

If prayer houses were full, places previously treated with reverence were emptied. The pubs and inns had a dreadful few weeks as hundreds signed the pledge. As remarkable as the clamour for Jesus was the sight of erstwhile drunkards reverently emptying bottle after bottle of spirits 'doon the cundeys [drains]'.

Outside observers were equally impressed. James Bertram, who wrote thumbnail sketches of the small fishing communities along the Scottish coast said of the place 'Those rude, unlettered fishermen ceased to visit the public houses, refrained from the use of oaths and instead sang psalms and said prayers'.

For the first, and probably only time, New Year's Day 1860 was a wholly sober affair for Eyemouth. The inns remained empty and the churches, which advertised special services, were full. Had the world gone mad?

People came forward eager to confess their sins. Jane Mack, who had been the partner of James Purves for more than five years even went to the Church session of Stephen Bell to admit the crime of fornication. Purves was not swept away by the same sort of nonsense and let his woman go on her own. They already shared a bed and had children – the first, Maggie Purves, was born on 25 January 1856 – yet they would not marry until September 1862, and even then not in front of a minister. Purves and Mack exchanged their vows at Lamberton Toll and made a home in a lane that would become known as Commerce Street. Purves was a fine fisherman and in the year after his wedding, with three fellows, he applied to become a pilot for the Harbour Trust. Even in good time, additional income was welcome. Along with Purves, licences were given to Robert Collin, Peter Burgon and his brother Charles. All but one of the four would drown on Disaster Day.

The religious revival was not a convulsion exclusive to the coarse and the uncouth. More sensible and intelligent people were swept along too, such as Timothy Statham and John Dickson. Not so Willie Spears. The Kingfisher could not fathom what was going on, and was certainly not going to join in. For once the great man stood powerless on the sidelines. He had no great interest in religion, and no intention of giving up his pleasures. If, as was said at the time 'Eyemouth was born again' it was done without the participation of the community's leader. Spears was content enough if it brought respect to the town, but not if it sucked out the character, the strength, the renowned independence of Eyemouth. Not if it sapped their will to do away with the tithe.

He need not have worried. The revival had no impact on the established church where Stephen Bell saw no increase in his congregations. Only one fisherman in the entire town regularly attended, and he was the paid precentor.

Christian faith did not make the fishermen weak in any respect. If anything the commitment of the folk was strengthened by the new found power of their convictions. As the movement was taking hold the fishery officer John Sutherland was ordered to note all the names and ages of the men who went to sea for a new central registry. This information, which showed there were 314 full time fishermen in the town, was given with extreme reluctance some believing it might be used to compel them into military service. 'And', Sutherland said ' from the feeling displayed in the matter I would not consider it safe to be in Eyemouth were it used for that purpose'.

Apart from Spears all of the anti-tithe leaders joined one or other of the dissenting congregations. Robert Dougall, who sometimes chaired the fishermen's committee meetings, was one of the first to be admitted to the Evangelical Union. Other fishermen including Robert Scott, William

Maltman, George Craig and a fourteen-year-old youth, William Nisbet, joined him in services held under canvas tents. 'Nibby' was already marked out from the rest of the callants of the town. He was less mischievous, though not 'soft'. He read books, but could also stand his ground in any argument. William Nisbet was destined to take on Spears' mantle as the leader of the fishing folk and spokesman for the town. In 1860 his two concerns were winning a full-time berth on a boat and helping erect a permanent stone building for his church. Over the next three years the members themselves laboured to bringing loads from Spittal quarry, just south of Berwick, to build a neat two-storey place of worship.

In March 1860, with the revival just starting to tail off, good news of a more worldly nature reached Eyemouth. The Court of Session had decided that no herring teind could be demanded from full-time Eyemouth fishermen. Victory seemed assured when six weeks later Chirnside Presbytery and Stephen Bell decided to withdraw from any further action before the Supreme Court in Edinburgh.

All this was front page news for the *Berwick Advertiser*, which rejoiced 'Conclusion of the Eyemouth Fish Tithe Case – Glorious triumph for the fishermen'.

William Spears called a meeting of the fishermen's committee and, after a short prayer (which Spears was content to allow) he outlined his strategy to keep the pressure up. The Kirk had acknowledged that it could not force payment of *herring* money from the *Eyemouth* fishermen. It could still, and presumably would still, demand the modus tax from local boats and some sums of tithe from stranger boats during the summer drave. Now was the time to deny the authority for any of this. The Kingfisher, in spite of the religious goings on, still had power over *his* people. There would be no more tithe of any sort paid by any man to the Church in Eyemouth. It was over: except it was not.

The Court of Session had been silent on the legality of the modus, or lesser teind, but had been explicit in supporting the Church for all arrears of both white fish and herring teind, withheld since 1855. Faced with this new defiance from the fishermen, Chirnside Presbytery once again urged Stephen Bell to action. In May 1860, against his better judgement, and in the certain knowledge of what would follow, the minister issued tithe bills for modus dues and payment arrears on all of the skippers in the town. The sums demanded ranged from £30 to £60 per boat.

Poor John Sutherland again felt unable to do his duty. He told the Fishery Board in Edinburgh that he could not enforce their order to have all the Eyemouth boats registered with numbers painted on their sides. 'At the moment the fishermen are involved in litigation over teinds with Rev Bell

and Mr Milne-Home and matters at present seem to have come to a
deadlock. It would be unwise to provoke the volatile tempers of the
fishermen'.

Statham in particular was concerned that the fresh legal move might
prompt another popular outpouring. The last thing the anti-tithe committee
needed was a riot. What they desired was the continuing support of the
public, especially the respectable public. Contact was again made with David
Robertson, who not only restated his backing for their position – so long
as it remained within the law – but even sent £25 to the defence fund. No
more was heard from the courts until the following year, and this delay,
along with Bell's decision not to issue any further demands in the meantime,
once more created the impression that the whole saga had been settled.

Spears and the committee were now certain that, as with the Annuity
Tax, the Church wanted a permanent solution. But a solution on what
terms? The General Assembly of the Kirk appointed a committee of inquiry
to look at the way ahead in May 1861. This promoted excitable rumours
that the Church was about to make one last determined effort to grab
money from the fishermen to strengthen its hand in any subsequent
negotiations. William Spears was expected to be the target. If so, he wrote
to the newspapers, Stephen Bell had better hunker down for a long haul.
'Should the committee of the General Assembly even in the name and for
the support of religion distrain and publicly sell the effects of the fishermen'
he wrote, 'they will find no obstruction. Of one thing only they may be
certain, that they will require to renew the unseemly display year after
year, for the fishermen have in the most solemn manner bound themselves
to refuse payment of tithe forever.'

Spears' stout words that there would be no obstruction or violent conduct
were never realistic, if they were ever believed. The religious revival had
retained a hold over most of the fishermen, but by the autumn of 1861 the
pubs were again doing good business. Anger over the perceived persecution
of the Kingfisher brought a mob on to the quay at closing time on 16 June
1861. From the harbour the drunken crowd rolled barrels up to the market
and out in front of the Church and adjacent Manse of Stephen Bell. The
minister watched the events unfold from chinks in his window shutters,
his little stout frame holding back the two women who also lived in the
house – his own sister Isabella and his maid, Mary Watson.

The crowd swelled and as it marched back and forth along the street,
two makeshift effigies of the minister and the laird were brought forward.
The dummies, with badly spelt placards swinging from their straw limbs,
were spat upon, thumped and strung up on the lamppost immediately
across from Bell's home. Stones and bottles rained against his door and

shattered the Manse windows as the effigies were set on fire. It was a frightening scene, and one that the committee had no control over. Worse was to follow.

When the *Berwick Advertiser* excused the incident, almost suggesting that the Church was to blame for the mob action, Chirnside Presbytery decided that the time had come for the public to be told the truth. It went into print. In a *Statement on the Eyemouth Fish Teind Case* the blame for all that had gone on was put squarely with the fishermen, and even more particularly with William Spears. The demands of the Church had been both legitimate and mild. The minister had been patient, in spite of intolerable abuse. Any fair-minded individual would agree that the fishermen of Eyemouth were in the wrong.

Within a week of the publication of the Presbytery's position, the anti-tithe committee rushed out its version of events in a pamphlet. These so-called 'rude, unlettered fishermen' eloquently repudiated all the claims made by the Church, denied the existence of any similar tithe elsewhere and chided the minister for his greed. Their insistence on the poverty of their profession stretched credibility. The herring season of 1861 had been another record one, with just short of £100,000 worth of fish being landed in the district, the vast bulk of which was brought ashore in Eyemouth. Some crews grossed as much as £400 for the season. The *Berwick Warder* warned of anarchy should the fishermen be allowed to win, and stories abounded that units of the military were on their way to subdue Eyemouth, all of which was ridiculed in this articulate polemic. 'In reference to all the bombast about the law and gunboats and troops of cavalry being sent to cut us down ... and about organised rèsistance to the law being a crime, we will remind you that there is no more doing here than is doing just now in Edinburgh.' Of course the law did not recognise two wrongs making a right, and events now quickened.

In the first week of October 1861 Spears alone was formally served with a notice to pay £30 in tithe money arrears within fourteen days under penalty of imprisonment and the rouping of his goods. The former he was prepared to accept. Being made a martyr possibly appealed to a man who did not suffer from vanity, but neither was shy in taking a lead. What did anger Spears, and very greatly, was the prospect of sheriff's officers rifling through the home which he shared with his elderly, and now very frail mother, Ellen Dougall-Spears. She was as gutsy as her son could ever be, and as solidly behind his purpose. But the Kingfisher was uneasy of the consequences for her of his refusal to obey the law. He knew the time of reckoning was close.

In the half-light of a dirty-grey dawn on 28 November 1861 three sheriff's

officers, supported by sixteen policemen, including the chief constable of
Lothian and Berwickshire, slowly marched down the Ayton Road, past the
building site of the E.U, the Church of Stephen Bell, and on to Spears'
Place. They had orders to arrest the Kingfisher and impound his furniture
for non-payment of tithe arrears. They had come in numbers, though they
did not expect to encounter much resistance. The fleet ought to have sailed
a good hour before their carriages had even approached the village. The
bulk of the men would be far at sea by the time Spears, who was again ill
and not himself fishing, was seized. That was their intelligence.

The main body of police held back on the Street as sheriff's officers
William Molloy, his son John and George Henderson went up the wooden
staircase that led to Spears' apartment. They knocked loudly on the door,
shouted out who they were and demanded that Spears come to meet
them. The Kingfisher responded by banging on his floor, crying at the top
of his voice 'the blackguards have come.' Jean Cowe, the widow he had
taken in after the loss of the *Lively,* was immediately roused and raced
out from her flat, the door of which was under the staircase. In a pantomime
scene the sheriff's officers looked on in astonishment as Cowe ran from
under their feet. She passed the verbal baton on to another woman, Jean
Maltman who emerged from her house opposite on hearing the commotion. It was Maltman who rushed past the Market, through Chapel Street,
on to the Long Entry and down to the pier. This Paul Revere raised a
hue and cry for everyone to be up and race to save Willie Spears. The
noise was tremendous and won her the lifelong nickname of 'Jeannie
Drummer'.

Folk did indeed tumble from their beds, and as the crowd grew so the
police moved forward. They would probably have managed to take Spears
but for the fact that the fleet was not at sea. Not quite at any rate. For
once the poor state of the harbour, which was partly blocked by a sandbank,
was to the benefit of the fisherfolk. Jeannie Drummer shouted with all her
might from the pier head and within minutes an army of fishermen tumbled
over each grounded boat to the wharf and then raced to the centre of town.

William Molloy, still at the top of the stair, turned round to see 'a great
crowd going along the street, and there were cries to murder us.' Super-
intendent Henry List and his men drew a cordon around Spears' Place, but
were soon under sustained attack from rocks and other missiles. In his
evidence at the trial of those who would be arrested for what followed,
List said 'I was pushed out of the stair and got a severe blow on one of
my shoulders. A number of stones were thrown and my men were covered
with mud. Women were in front of the crowd and men behind. The men
threw stones and the women kept up the yelling ... I am certain that I saw

between 400 and 500 people at this time, but I was told that other streets, which I could not see were full of people.'

One young lad came forward with a length of rope, the other end of which he tossed to a colleague. Together they rushed the group of policemen, pinning them back to allow the stone throwers an easier target. Some of the women got hold of a pail of kutch (tar) and began lobbing it on to the police. Others raced home and brought back night-pails, which were likewise thrown over the officers. A few of the women then paraded in front of the dirty, demoralised and now stinking policemen, swinging their hips and asking if any of the lovely looking gentlemen would care to take a walk with them.

At the height of the riot, and to the cheers of the assembled throng, Spears opened his door and two stout fisher lads rushed to stand by his side. With this Praetorian Guard in place the police were 'daured to lift him'. Of course they could not, and by this time had lost the will to try. The aim of the raiding party now was how to engineer a safe retreat out of Eyemouth.

They made a dash first for the town police office, adjacent to Spears Place. Every window in the office was broken and the men huddled under chairs and tables. After more than four hours of this continual barrage of stones and bottles they emerged to make a run for it. Those who were not fleet enough of foot were punched and kicked by the fishermen. One policeman was dragged to the harbour side and on pain of being thrown in – a prospect, as a non swimmer, that terrified him – was made to sign a declaration stating there had been no trouble carried on in Eyemouth that day! Unsurprisingly the declaration was not produced at the subsequent trial.

Several of the policemen were badly hurt. Sergeant John Bain was knocked unconscious and police constables Thomas Hogg, William Wight, John Benzies and John Thomson were all badly bruised by stones, sticks and the fists of fishermen. As the running battle passed out towards Millbank paper mill the officers managed to regroup. They drew their batons and charged back down towards the town, taking the crowd by surprise. As the folk turned a few fell over and were grabbed. Henry Angus and James Windram were thumped on the head and pulled by the hair back towards the carriages. Angus spluttered as he was pushed into the van, 'there will be murder unless you leave us be'. A phrase he would have come to regret when it was later repeated at the trial. One other man, George Scott was also arrested, along with three of the women: Isabella Collin, Catherine Burgon and Elizabeth Grant. They all appeared at Duns Sheriff Court on Wednesday 11 December 1861 and were committed to stand before a jury at the High Court in Edinburgh. The alleged rioters might have sat in jail for several weeks until this opened, but the defence fund was flush enough to post the substantial bail, which had been set at almost £700.

Their trial in Edinburgh opened in early February 1862. The public galleries were packed with Eyemouth folk, who cheered and booed as the evidence was retold. Only Angus and Windram were convicted, and perhaps significantly and in spite of the attacks made on the police, the jury specifically asked the judge to be lenient. Three months hard labour, which is what each man received, was doubtless considered a light sentence. In Berwickshire it was received with shock. 'Auld Hen' and 'Babs' would spend three months away from their families in a strange place with strange people. And what would happen to their wives and their bairns in the meantime? The defence fund ensured that they were taken care of, but the riot was a shock to the committee, and especially to William Spears.

The Kingfisher argued with the committee that someone could have been killed. Someone *might* yet be killed if the cat-and-mouse game continued. He would not have that happen. As the prime legal target for the Church, and the *de facto* leader of the people, Spears took the only course of action he felt was now open to him. To the tears of his old mother, whose safety he entrusted to Jean Cowe, the Kingfisher walked down his shoogly wooden stairway to give himself up. Another crowd with an equally ugly mood gathered as Spears was handcuffed and put on a cart between two uncomfortable policemen to be taken to Greenlaw jail. The man stilled the people with little more than a rolling of his eyes. 'Gaun hame' was all he said as a switch was flicked over the horses and the little carriage trundled out of Eyemouth.

Chapter Ten

Pyrrhic Victory

The dangers of proceeding to sea in such weather and with such indications of
the barometer, may some day, if persisted in, end in something very serious
Berwick Advertiser, 12 January 1866 after the Eyemouth fleet
once again sailed in defiance of weather warnings

The riot of November 1861 was a defining moment. It persuaded the Lord
Advocate that he would have to intervene. Three months after the trouble
James Moncrieff duly invited the members of the General Assembly Committee to a meeting in Edinburgh. What exactly did the Church want?
Clearly the tithe could not continue in its present form. After seven years
of heated litigation and two centuries of sporadic unrest Scotland's senior
law officer made that fact crystal clear.

William Spears greeted the news of the Lord Advocate's attitude with
quiet satisfaction from the comfort of his own home. The Kingfisher's tithe
arrears and fine had been raised and paid within hours of his arrest, and
he had spent only a few days in jail. When he arrived back in Eyemouth
it was, of course, to a hero's welcome. His mother, eighty-three and the
matriarch of the town, clasped her only living son to her stooping frame,
while the crowds cheered the Kingfisher's return. Soon there were others
who waited on an audience with Spears. Dissenting clergy, especially
ministers from the United Presbyterians, arrived in numbers. They saw in
the refusal of the man to kow-tow to the Kirk the very essence of opposition
to a state church link. The U.P. magazine cheered on the cause in two
articles, one entitled 'The Eyemouth Fish Teind Dispute' and the other
'The state church promoting voluntaryism'.

Though there would be no fresh tithe demands in Berwickshire, the
dispute was very far from being settled. The row now passed from what
ought to be demanded on the pier, to what might be given in compensation
to the Kirk. It would have suited the Lord Advocate if these negotiations
had taken place in private. But the public quarrelling continued during the
arbitration process. The pamphlet war erupted once more with seven tracts
printed and distributed. It kept the kettle boiling and made difficult and
delicate negotiations much, much harder.

The fishermen were of course ecstatic. They had won. Their industry
was on the veritable crest of a wave, as evidenced by John Sutherland's

now almost predictable year-end reports: 'For the fishermen the season of 1861 has been the best they ever experienced'.

So great were the herring catches that the Berwickshire men introduced a crank and pulley system they had first seen at Yarmouth. Though costly, this innovation reduced the landing time and accelerated the process of getting the fish to market. Money was also being spent hand-over-fist on new nets, lines and boats. In the autumn of 1861 the biggest and most expensive vessel yet built in Eyemouth was launched from Weatherhead's yard. At fifty-five feet long, part decked, and triple masted, *Economy* cost more than £300. The boat had speed and deep holds for the shoals that Alexander Maltman and his crew were intent on taking.

The dark downside of the fishing was also evident in the year of the tithe victory. A brand new Burnmouth boat launched just days after *Economy* was swamped on the approaches to Eyemouth Bay. None of the five-man crew could be saved. Skipper Joseph Anderson left a widow and five children; bothers Robert and William Lauder were also married and had four and two children respectively; William Johnston and David Martin were single. It was more sad sorrow for the Martins of Burnmouth. David's father William had perished when the *Lively* sank in 1853.

With stouter boats the men should have been more confident when putting to sea. But if the tide was strong on the run home, the risks trying to make port safely were just as heavy. For those like Alexander Maltman, whose craft needed greater water depth to get over the bar, the difficulties and therefore the dangers were greater still. What could be done for old Eyemouth harbour? It was a question that had exercised David Milne-Home from the time in the 1830s when he had pressed for the implementation of the Mitchell-Jardine plan.

Cost had always been the problem. Where would the money come from to underwrite any substantial scheme, with the Trust all but insolvent and the main trade of the port – the fishing boats – exempt from dues because of their liability to pay Kirk tithe? At long last with this to be abolished, attention could be switched to building up port funds. Indeed the timing could not be better. In the same year as matters came to a head in Eyemouth the government passed legislation allowing local harbour boards to borrow large sums of money at low rates of interest. Those places with ambition and where there was already evidence of substantial trade would no longer be held back by the meagre funds at the disposal of the Fishery Board.

It sounded too good to be true, and for Eyemouth it was. The Harbour and Passing Tolls Act of 1861 stipulated that loans could only be made against the security of revenue from existing dues. In Eyemouth the annual income, still based on a schedule which excluded the fishing boats, was paltry. It had haemorrhaged when the rail network expanded in the 1840s, taking away much of its former commercial traffic. The place would not qualify unless the books were turned around, and quickly. But how? David Milne-Home saw a way. He came up with a notion that would revolutionise the port's finances and, at the same time, end the tithe trouble by providing a decent stipend for the minister.

Instead of attempting to buy out the Kirk, the fishermen ought to agree to pay a new harbour rate, which would include an element to be given to the church. A modified form of this already existed at Dunbar. From the number of vessels using Eyemouth, the harbour coffers would quickly fill up allowing the Trust to tap into state funds for development. All boats, and not just the Eyemouth ones, would indirectly pay for the end of the tithe. The minister's stipend would be enhanced and there would be no need to try and raise a capital sum, which Milne-Home felt was well beyond the means of the fishermen. It was a neat, satisfactory and workable solution for everyone. And it could be delivered almost immediately

As ever, things were not as simple as that. When news leaked out of Milne-Home's plan there was almost another riot. The continuation of fish tithe, even in a disguised form, was not an option. What may have made good sense to the laird had a caustic smell to the people, and anything that bore the thumbprint of Wedderburn was treated with suspicion, if not downright disdain.

Milne-Home nonetheless drew up a draft harbour bill. The fishermen had got their way and the tithe would go. But *he* was the laird and feudal superior and he, not they, knew how to chart a way ahead for the future. Under the proposals Eyemouth boats would have been charged £4 a year and stranger vessels £2. This would give the minister an annual sum of about £80, a far cry from the £4,000 a year Bell was alleged to be after and certainly not enough for the palace he was said to be intent on building in place of the Manse. More importantly, the schedule would provide a surplus for the port of at least £300, five times the existing revenue of the Trust.

But at a packed public meeting in April 1862 the bill was unanimously rejected. Three days later David Robertson took the initiative and invited the fishermen's leaders to his country estate. Willie Spears, Timothy Statham and Robert Dougall were very clear when they arrived at Ladykirk, about sixteen miles inland. If the tithe was not to be altogether abandoned, which was of course the preferred option, the only possible solution was to buy out the Kirk's rights. Over lunch their host asked what sum might be acceptable and how it could be raised. The figure of £1,000 was suggested by Spears, though everyone around the table knew that this would fall far short of what the Church would want. An independent arbiter would be needed, but one, if possible, who might be sympathetic to the fishermen. Robertson suggested Captain Alexander Mitchell Innes of Ayton Castle as a suitable candidate. He was the man who had taken the lead in raising money for the widows and orphans following the 1853 *Lively* tragedy and someone, despite his wealth and status, whom Spears and the others felt they could trust. After the trio had departed on their gig for the trip down the rutted lanes of Berwickshire, Robertson summed up the meeting in a letter to the Lord Advocate. 'You might as well attempt to turn the sun from its course' he wrote, 'as the fishermen of Eyemouth from their determined purpose.'

Without the support of the sitting MP, the Lord Advocate would not countenance Milne-Home's bill entering the Commons. It was dead before it had even started. But Wedderburn, angered and slighted, would not give up. He wrote his own version of events to the Lord Advocate, fired off alarmist letters to the local newspapers and put a spin on the whole saga in three widely circulated pamphlets.

The crux of his message was the impracticability of a buy-out. 'If the rich and energetic merchants and shopkeepers of Edinburgh tried to purchase up the Annuity Tax and failed' he wrote, 'it will be no slur on the fishermen of Eyemouth if they fail in a similar attempt'. Not £1,000 but at least £10,000 would be required before the church would enter into serious negotiations. And ominously, if the rights were sold on the cheap 'a precedent would be set, which may justly cause alarm, not only to all persons of property but to all good citizens and subjects.'

Spears, again incapacitated through illness, had no control over a hasty and ill-considered pamphlet reply. Milne-Home's hyperbole looked less of a diatribe when Robert Dougall and the committee's response hit the streets. The laird was castigated as 'not only not honourable ... but scarcely honest.' Disestablishment of the Church of Scotland, something far from the minds of the tithe rebels in 1855 was now, apparently, one of their aims. Come that day, Milne-Home was warned, the whole tithe system would be overturned. 'The land which is now charged with the support of the so-called national church, would, in justice, go back to the nation'. This was dangerous language and it irked the Lord Advocate. He now urged both sides to re-double their efforts in the negotiations and to keep a more respectable silence in public. By the spring of 1863, and with a conclusion in sight, David Milne-Home tried again to force his own proposals back on the agenda. He took a rare drive down to Eyemouth and frankly told anyone who would listen that the amount that was about to be awarded was well beyond their means, perhaps even more than £10,000. This hit home with at least some on the quay and Milne-Home hurried off another letter. The fishermen were ready to consider alternatives, he told the Lord Advocate, and perhaps they should look again at his ready-made harbour bill? Robertson was appalled at this perfidy. It was his turn to contact Scotland's most senior law officer. 'I have seen much to deprecate and surprise in the conduct of Mr Milne-Home ... Who has been the *sole cause* of the mischief from beginning to end and but for whom the church would have gladly settled it through me long ago.' It was the final throw of the dice for David Milne-Home and with it he lost the game. The rejection of his harbour bill was another opportunity missed for Eyemouth at a critical time in fisheries development.

Arbitration now proceeded with some speed and within a year a settlement had been arrived at. All elements of fish tithe in Eyemouth were to be abolished on payment to the Kirk of £1,625 and to Stephen Bell of £275 in lieu of nine years' arrears. The fishermen were called to another meeting after the deal was concluded. The UP Kirk was packed for what everyone assumed would be a victory rally, and then on to the Ship for refreshment and music. But there were no tub-thumping speeches or triumphal bravado. Instead they got an unexpected and shocking message. And the fishermen swiftly turned on the messenger.

Timothy Statham, the committee secretary, stood up and started to explain that almost £2,000 would have to be borrowed and then paid back in annual instalments to the Commercial Bank to pay for the tithe buy-out. One man in the front row loudly asked how this was to be done, where the money was to come from? To loud barracking and shouts of 'shame' and 'never' Statham stuttered that they had agreed – 'who was they?' – that the boats would pay an annual tariff of a few pounds until the debt was paid off. Each fisherman would also be obliged to give a shilling or two a week. Pandemonium broke out. This was the tithe by another name! Neither was the crowd calmed by an assurance that the fishing boats would remain exempt from quayside dues until the loan was paid off. Those with any sense grasped that this would mean the harbour would continue to be impoverished, and its board of management unable to improve the cramped and crumbling wharves.

Willie Spears, once more ill and in bed, was not at the meeting. Without his calming presence the insults came thick and fast and Statham was like a rabbit caught in the cross-fire. He was an incomer, an interloper, a rich Englishman who had no idea of what their lives were like. As Statham pleaded for silence, some of the fishermen roared that they had been sold out. Any money ought to go to the harbour and not to continue to feather bed Stephen Bell. What about that harbour rate idea? Had David Milne-Home been hiding in the hall that night he might have blasphemed or at least torn out his hair. It was all too late to change now. A bill to abolish the fish teind in Eyemouth was at that moment being drafted and would be introduced into the House of Commons on 30 June 1864.

After more than half the crowd had streamed out some semblance of order was restored and Statham got down to the real business of the evening: the nomination of a Tithe Redemption Committee to manage the loan. The five initial trustees chosen were Robert Renton, John Kerr, John Collin, Peter Nisbet and Leonard Dougal. They faced predictable problems. There were plenty who tried to duck out of paying what they owed, often using the same ploys and devices that had been used against Stephen Bell. Astonishingly this even led to the same legal actions and threatened roupings as had been attempted by the Kirk.

The fund ran until January 1878, after more than £4,000 – double the agreed compensation – had been paid in instalments, interest and fees. A dinner was held in the town to mark the occasion and the secretary of the fund, George Collin 'Auld Dod' was presented with a gold watch and chain for all of his efforts. The eight-man committee by then was made up of Collin, his son George ('Little Dod'), Robert Dougal, Joseph Dougal, Andrew Dougal, David Dougal, Andrew Cowe and James Paterson. They were all respectable individuals and most were regulars at the UP Kirk. Though Spears never joined this committee, he was kept closely informed of what went on. Andrew Cowe was his housekeeper's son. James Paterson had been one of his crew and had even lodged with him for a time.

For fourteen years, while money in Eyemouth went to pay off the Kirk, other places with arguably less potential tapped into the provisions of the Harbours and Passing Tolls Act. Massive amounts were poured into Wick, Peterhead, Fraserburgh, Aberdeen and, to a lesser extent, Stonehaven, Lossiemouth and Arbroath. Because of the tithe debt, Berwickshire's major port was not in a position even to apply for funds until the late 1870s. Eyemouth missed its chance.

Thoroughly fed up with the way in which he felt he had been treated, David Milne-Home withdrew his goodwill. Instead of playing the benevolent laird he spent more time attending to his own needs. From the early 1850s he had warned the Harbour Trust against removing sand and gravel from the beach for ballast. With nothing in the way of artificial defence beyond some wooden groinings, a row of houses imminent on the shore was clearly being undermined. But the process went on regardless and in November 1861 a massive midnight sea scooped the foundations away caving two houses on to the sands and partially submerging all the rest.

More than a thousand pounds worth of damage was done and almost all of it fell on the Wedderburn estate. The Trust was sent a final, sternly worded, warning. No more loads to be taken from the beach or legal action would follow. But even this was ignored. With an account book spattered in red the Trust needed the trade of coastal vessels, and where else would they get ballast? In any case it was by no means clear that the sand belonged to David Milne-Home.

But the laird had had enough. In February 1863 he obtained an interdict from the Court of Session to prevent any further quarrying. If it continued he would sue the individual members.

Whether from a sudden and uncharacteristic rush of blood to their heads, or perhaps buoyed by the fishermen's victory in the tithe row, the Trustees opted to contest the litigation. Milne-Home therefore found himself involved in a second legal war with Eyemouth. This time he was the prime mover and the targets were not the fishermen but the well-to-do officers of a harbour which the Wedderburns had owned or controlled for centuries.

Like the tithe row, the courtroom drama over who owned the beach was not played out with the speed of the rising and falling tides. It took five years of expensive argument before a final decision was delivered.

During this time, and despite its cramped state, Eyemouth continued to be favoured by large numbers of visiting boats and by a home fleet, which grew year on year. There were forty large white-fish vessels in the mid 1860s and more than a hundred used exclusively in the summer drave. Most of both the haddock and the herring went fresh to market. This insulated the local economy from the vagaries of the export trade such as the blockade imposed during the American Civil War when trade with the Confederate States, large purchasers of herring as slave food, all but ceased. Berwickshire suffered but only when workers in the Midlands were laid off from want of cotton and could no longer afford to buy fresh fish brought by rail from the Borders.

There was even talk in 1864 of building a branch link to the main East Coast rail line, which skirted the edge of the parish. Like so many other schemes it would take years to move from the gestation of an idea to a proper plan. The people involved were the same men who had led the Harbour Trust to ruin, who presided over the school board, the parochial board and the Police Commission, small town politicians who meant well but soon got out of their depth. A depressingly familiar picture.

In July of 1864 commissioners compiling an official report into the sea fisheries of the United Kingdom took evidence in Eyemouth. William Spears and his cousin William Dougall were prominent amongst the witnesses and told the same story. The fishing had never been better, there were always problems of bait, of getting their catch to market, of interference from foreign boats, especially the French, but the main issue was the poor state of the harbour. In his evidence Spears said, 'Eyemouth is a very poor harbour at low water. There is no water then at all'. The harbour master Peter Wilson, who had only just arrived from Fraserburgh drew parallels with what had been achieved there and told the commissioners that Eyemouth had even more potential. 'It is considered that nearly double the number of boats would fish from this harbour if it were improved. There is no point of land so accessible from the north and there would certainly be a great increase of boats coming to the harbour if it were improved so as to be capable of receiving them'.

It fell to David Milne-Home to explain just why so little had been done. He waited until the close of proceedings and insisted that his evidence be taken in private. Not disguising his own anger with the men who were defying his instructions and threatening his properties, the laird was candid. Nothing in the way of aid had ever been received from the Fishery Board or any other outside body. No application had ever even been made. 'And I think one reason is this. There is a harbour trust here, and one condition of the Fishery Board is that all harbour dues shall be given up in the event of any assistance being given by the Fishery Board in repairing the harbour.' Burnmouth and Coldingham Shore had both been awarded grants, and Dunbar and Anstruther were in the process of receiving huge sums from the public purse. But not Eyemouth. The Trustees would not surrender their position even for the greater good of the harbour.

Rather bizarrely, Milne-Home found that he was coming back into favour with the fishing folk. With his wife, he resumed regular drives down to the coast and in March 1864 arranged for Eyemouth to become a signal station, in communication with the Met office in London. People remembered that it was David Milne-Home who had financed the barometer on the pier head. Now that he had lost over the tithe, maybe it was time to look more kindly on the landlord. More than anything else though, it was his legal action against the Trust which restored his popularity. There was a great sense of *schadenfreude* about the community, a dubious quality that perhaps yet endures. People took joy from the misfortunes of others, especially those others who they felt looked down upon them. There had never been a fisherman member of the Harbour Trust: a ridiculous state of affairs.

In March 1865, after yet another boat was wrecked trying to get in to the harbour in a swelling tide, Willie Spears was mandated by the fishermen's committee to approach the Fishery Board direct to see what could be done for the harbour. They would bypass the Trust.

The Fishery Board replied in generous terms, complimenting the fishermen for their 'superior boats and capabilities.' But no money was offered.

The resources they had were already earmarked for other schemes. However, B F Primrose, the Secretary, tantalisingly advised that application could be made for a special parliamentary grant. This would also avoid the conditions laid down for a loan in the 1861 Harbours Act. It was the 1830s all over again, and as with the Mitchell-Jardine plan, the idea of memorialising the Treasury would fail.

It may have been that Primrose expected the fishermen to glow with his praise and do nothing with his suggestion. But the Eyemouth men, enthused by the success of the tithe fight, were deadly serious in their purpose. They paid for James Stevenson, an Edinburgh based civil engineer, to survey the bay and sought the support and financial help of David Robertson and, naturally, David Milne-Home of Wedderburn.

The rehabilitation of the laird was by this time all but complete. Under his direction the Eyemouth Games and Regatta was revived in 1864, with more than 4,000 spectators drawn to the Fort Point to watch boat races and athletics competitions. Prizes ranged from four pounds for the principal sailing competition to five shillings for the leaping contest, which was won by a fifteen-year-old Burnmouth youth, Peter Aitchison. As he jumped his way to success his brothers James, John and Robert were straining their arms down in the bay, pulling with all their might in the yacht race. Their sisters, including Agnes who had just married William Crawford Aitchison, cheered the boys on. William was the eldest son of Helen Spears and John Aitchison, who drowned when the *Lively* was lost. He was also a nephew of the great Kingfisher. Incidentally, he was also Agnes' cousin.

David Milne-Home paid tribute to Spears when opening the summer games on the Fort. 'It is with regret that I note William Spears' absence from illness' he told the crowd. 'I am sure he would join with me in acknowledging the differences which have existed here for some years are now, by common consent, buried in oblivion'.

The home of the Kingfisher was a sick place in the years 1864–66. Old Ellen tended to William who tried his best to look after her. More often than not both relied on the attention of their housekeeper Jean Cowe. For Ellen the end was a long time coming, but eventually on 26 April 1866, at the remarkable age of eighty-eight she breathed her last. The woman was a link to another century and a bygone era. A time before steam, before rail, a time when Eyemouth was still a byword for smuggling and lawlessness. When Ellen passed away part of the Kingfisher seemed to go with her. He began to slip from prominence in the town. To be sure, Spears remained one of the big men, but he was no longer *the* big man. The home he had shared for so long with his mother was not a place he wished to continue to live in, and Spears moved to one of Statham's houses on the

Yard Heads Road. He took with him one of his crew for company. James Paterson was a widower with a young son. The boy, born as his mother died in childbirth, was named William after the Kingfisher, and Spears doted on him.

With the consent of the landlord, David Milne-Home, Jean Cowe was now given the full run of Spears' Place. Wedderburn owned nine tenths of the properties in Eyemouth as well as being a member of the Harbour Trust. His relations with the other Trustees were as strained as they could be, both sides waiting for the judgement in the civil action over beach ballast. It is strange just how significant legal disputes could be in a town that was so famed for lawlessness and profanity.

The Court of Session finally delivered a ruling in the spring of 1869. The proprietor won on all counts with damages and expenses awarded. As the Trust was already insolvent most of the costs would have to fall on the personal liability of the board members. In blind panic they pleaded with the laird to consider three proposals. First that he waive the compensation and accept only payment of his legal fees, and that in annual instalments. Second that they borrow enough money from the bank to satisfy the lawyers without paying damages, and finally that they resign en masse and surrender the harbour back to the control of the feudal overlord.

Milne-Home was not inclined to accept either scenario, but he had no wish to take on responsibility for the port. He therefore agreed not to pursue damages. The trust managed to borrow £300 from the Commercial Bank to pay the baying lawyers whilst at the same time slashing the interest paid to the other creditors. The salaries paid to the harbour master William Wright and the clerk James Bowhill were also reduced, but still it was not enough. They had to think the unthinkable. For the first time ever, fishermen and fish curers were invited to join the board. There was a catch. To prove their commitment, and reduce that of existing members, the new trustees had to produce £250 and accept personal liability for a share of future debts.

When the money was handed over the following fishermen were sworn in – George Craig, George Collin senior (Auld Dod), George Collin junior (Little Dod), Archibald Gray, James Paterson senior and James Patterson, junior who now lodged with Spears. Also admitted were four fish curers: Robert Renton, Thomas Alexander, John Dickson and James Crawford. They represented the most enterprising of Eyemouth merchants. Crawford in particular was building up a business of some renown.

Some of the new Trustees also sat on the tithe redemption committee and had an energy that showed. Meetings, previously called on an *ad hoc* basis and rarely well attended, now became frequent and animated. The new men came armed with the report of the Fishery Board's own engineer James Stevenson C. E. who had prepared a £10,000 plan of improvement. His summary was another glowing advert. 'There is no place on the coast where so much could be accomplished with so little outlay. As a white fishing station Eyemouth is the most noted and important in the kingdom, situated on the very key of the coast.'

But Stevenson's plan, like all of the others, was put on ice. The new trustees signed up just as the ever-returning shoals of herring and haddock mysteriously scattered for the first time in more than twenty years. The fish seemed to swim around, not on, the Berwickshire banks and for four long years poverty returned.

In spite of being, as Peter Wilson the fishery officer reported, 'the first boats on the coast to commence fishing and the last to leave off' catches were short and quayside prices desperately low. Even the French ships, which had arrived to both fish and barter virtually every year since 1817 went elsewhere. In spite of the antipathy often shown towards them, these foreigners were sorely missed. Peter Wilson gloomily wrote, 'There is in consequence much destitution amongst the fishing population and others dependent upon it.' The disappearance of the shoals coincided with a collapse in the stock of mussels on both the Clyde and the Boston Deeps in Lincolnshire, and to cap it all there was seemingly never ending bad weather.

Predictably, the thin times prompted even more risk taking than usual from the men who went to sea. Time and again they sailed in defiance of both weather warnings and a plunging pier head 'gless'. Fate was being mocked; it would eventually take vengeance. The reporter who wrote this prophetic line could scarcely have imagined the horror he was foretelling. 'The danger of proceeding to sea in such weather and with such indications of the barometer may some day, if persisted in, end in something serious.'

Another rehearsal for Black Friday came in February 1868 when once again Eyemouth men sailed in the certain knowledge of an impending gale. When the hurricane came down the boats scattered for home, navigating by instinct rather than vision in the inky blackness. Like October 1881 the people were waiting for the fleet as the first vessels raced past the headland. The fishery officer was there with them. 'The beach and fort were crowded by hundreds anxious for the safety of those who were exposed to such a dreadful visitation.'

The newly formed volunteer rocket brigade stood ready to shoot lines of rope, as thirty-one of the thirty-nine deep-sea boats rolled safely past the Hurkur rocks. But what of the fate of the overdue vessels? It was a tortuous, sleepless night of worry for the families of those crews, many of whom stayed on the shore all through the dark hours, keeping covenant with the sea. How long would they have to wait? How many would come home? How tragic was that night?

Word reached Eyemouth by the middle of the following day that all of the boats had made safe landfall at other ports and were on their way back. It was no comfort to the wife, now widow, of Archibald Nisbet. Erchie was the only man lost from the fleet in the storm of February 1868, swept overboard from the *Thistle*.

The poor state of the fishing brought hard times to all. Soup kitchens appeared in the market place and Jean Milne-Home sent down blankets and shoes for the destitute. There was little appetite and no time to think about gay events like the Games and Regatta. That of 1866 was the last to take place until the Peace Picnic was founded after the First World War. Even the number of marriages tailed off. Just one couple took their vows in the third quarter of 1868, normally the busiest time for weddings. Only nine weddings took place in the whole of that year. 'The only reason that can be ascribed to this' lamented the *Berwick Advertiser* 'is the depressed state of the fishing trade.'

The parochial board was swamped with applications for temporary relief, but it too was in a parlous financial state after gambling with a lawsuit. Eyemouth was one of the smallest parishes in Scotland – one of the reasons for the importance of the fish tithe to the minister. The rateable value was less than a fifth of Coldingham to the north and a third of Ayton to the south and west. Yet the rich and substantial enclave of Highlaws Farm which was in the centre of the parish was, by an historic anomaly, claimed by Coldingham. In 1866, again perhaps because of the victory of the fishermen, the parochial board felt bold enough to attempt to annex the territory. Inevitably this dispute also ended up in the Court of Session and with equal predictability, Eyemouth lost. Costs were also awarded against the parish. Highlaws would have brought in around £60 a year in additional rates. The price of failure, in fees and expenses, came to more than £1,000.

It was hard to bear on an already stretched budget. The rates went up and poor relief was shaved to the minimum. New applications were rigorously, not to say harshly, vetted. Even women widowed when their husbands drowned at sea were denied anything more than a pittance. Yet that did not stop the folk from applying on virtually any pretext. As John Turnbull had despaired as far back as 1837, aliment was demanded as a right, and children were often dispatched to pick up the allowance.

Outsiders felt the system was badly managed in Eyemouth; that the 'undeserving poor' were taking advantage of lax controls. In May 1873 the visiting officer for the Board of Supervision reported there were 'at least fifteen cases of doubtful pauperism in the parish', and recommended that Eyemouth band together with the neighbouring parishes to finance a workhouse. Fortunately for the poor of the eastern Merse, the heritors were against it, largely because they would have had to meet the bulk of the capital costs.

The plight of old Peter Waddell is an example of how poor relief was abused. Born in the village in 1802 he worked first as a seaman, then a fisherman and by the 1850s had opened a cheap liquor room in one of the crowded vennels. His wife, Catherine Mack, sister to Jane who married James Purves, bore Waddell at least fourteen children. Ten were boys and all of them were left-handed. In 1863 the eldest, Robert, married Jessie Rosie, whose Gaelic speaking family had arrived as migrants from the north during the boom years of the mid 1850s. With a large extended family, Peter Waddell and Catherine Mack ought to have been well looked after in their dotage, even given the straightened circumstances of the late 1860s.

In fact when his parents started to fail Robert Waddell did very little to help. He stood by and allowed his father, who was in very poor health, to continue fishing until 1869, when the man was almost seventy. Peter only left the sea when the family boat *Victor* was wrecked off Shields in June of that year. By then Robert had taken over the family house in the Market Place. Peter, Catherine, their twelve-year-old son William and three of their girls, then in their early twenties, flitted first to the old soap works down Mason's Wynd, and then on to a one-windowed hovel near the shore.

The parochial board was indignant when it had to admit Peter to the poor roll. Yet with the old man now all but helpless, with Catherine suffering from 'palsy', and with the three girls, Jessie, Katie and Jane barely able to keep themselves, the authorities agreed to give three shillings a week. Robert was pressed to do more for his parents, but it was not until 1874, after the death of his mother, that Peter Waddell was finally removed from the poor roll. He would live out his twilight years being farmed around his four daughters, who were all by then married: Kate to Thomas Miller, Jessie with George Kearney, Margaret to James Lough, Elizabeth to Peter Craig. Each was a fisherman. All would sail on Disaster Day. Two would not return.

Chapter Eleven

An Assured Future?

The woman that cannae work for a man disnae deserve yin
Comment made by fisher-wife to writer James Bertram in 1869

Eyemouth had a postal office from 1845. If any fisherman had been sent a letter – unlikely since few could read, but possible, especially during the tithe dispute – it would have needed detective work in the manner of Conan Doyle to track him down. How many George Dougalls, how many William Maltmans, how many John Windrams were there in the town? Men in this close-knit world were known colloquially by their nicknames: Auld Tarry's Wull, Little Dod, Collie's Tam, Puts, Auld Penny Rowe. The women's tee names were just as colourful: Kinnies Meg, Carrots Lib and Jeannie Drummer, who won her fame on the day of the tithe riot. But even if you knew who you were looking for, tracking them down was another matter altogether. The maze of vennels and wynds, characteristic of all fishing villages, was even more pronounced in Eyemouth thanks to the legacy of eighteenth-century free trade. It was only after the town fathers adopted new local government powers in 1868 that these streets were named. Along with the mundane Church Street and High Street were the more pretentious George Street, George Square, Queen Street and Commerce Street. The folk were impressed. 'Until the naming was done we were comparatively ignorant of even half the amount of importance attached to us!' Road signs would have been as welcome as excisemen in the days of old: 'Nothing would have been regarded as more dangerous to the peace and security of the smugglers than naming the streets, thus exposing them.'

The decision to adopt the 1862 Police and General Improvement Act was an ambitious one for such a small burgh. Substantive local powers were aquired in an attempt to improve the health and habitability of the town. There was plenty to be done.

In spite of a vastly increased population housed in the same small area of land, there was only one public privy, and that was simply a hole in a plank of wood that sat over the edge of the harbour. Very few of the houses had water closets of their own and mussel shells, some fourteen tons of which were used on a daily basis in the winter season, blocked most of the public drains. The new Police Commissioners ordered an immediate increase in public conveniences. Eyemouth would now have three. Memories of the great cholera epidemic were still strong and some attempt was made to clear up some of the immense amount of 'fulzie' (the rotting guts and mussel shells) left over from the fish trade. The people were told to tidy the land outside their houses and wash their own stairs. Scavengers were employed to clean the streets and Timothy Statham contracted to put down new sewers along the High Street and the Salt Green's Quay. Steps were also taken to regulate some of the frenetic building activity that was going on.

David Milne-Home laid out a new line of houses to replace those washed away by the storm of 1867, which he called Milne's Row. Eyemouth folk preferred the "New Row". Other streets were thrown up at a prodigious rate. It was more work for Statham's men. Alexander Glen arranged for the builder-cum-plumber-cum-entrepreneur to build cottages along the northeastern flank of the Yard Head's Road for the influx of migrants. Glen, like Statham, had done well from the boom years in fishing. His family by then lived in a house with no fewer than seven windows and employed domestic servants. Yet when Glen moved to Eyemouth from Montrose in 1852 he barely had enough money to buy a haddock line. The dip of the late 1860s, he was certain, was an aberration.

Only want of house room prevented even greater numbers from settling in Eyemouth and as demand outstripped supply the common lodging houses were stretched to bursting point. One in the Long Entry, which was licensed to take a maximum of five people, was found to have fourteen living in a single room.

New yards were filling in the spaces down on the quay. As had been predicted when the Manse was built in the 1830s it was gradually being surounded by smokehouses and curing stations. George Walker, a fish merchant from Glasgow, expanded his business right back to the Manse wall and threw up some basic tenements for his workers which overlooked the garden. Almost immediately Stephen Bell complained of the smell and the way in which his property was regularly invaded by children. This plea was ignored and the minister promptly took matters up with both the Police Commissioners and the heritors of the parish. 'I went in to the garden on Saturday last for a little fresh air', he told the latter, 'but was immediately driven into the house again by the stench. The garden wall is becoming more dilapidated on account of the children climbing and walking upon it. I beg to request that the wall be repaired and raised so as to secure some degree of privacy to the inmates of the Manse, a matter I believe faithfully attended to in every parish in Scotland with the exception of Eyemouth.'

To placate Bell, Walker even erected a wooden fulzie box. But the garden was never again a pleasant place to walk in, at least not when the wind was blowing from the harbour. The fishermen who lived and worked behind the Manse took perverse delight in mischievously leaving barrel loads of offal packed close to the wall for days on end. In high summer, with flies in abundance, the smell could knock you down at ten paces.

If the expansion of fish yards was personally distressing to Mr Bell, it did at least signal a recovery from the depression of the late 1860s. Another positive sign came in the reappearance of foreign drifters, though they continued to cause problems to the local men by sailing over and damaging the herring nets. It was back to the happy days of ramming and being rammed, of chucking anything that came to hand at the 'enemy' boats, and of ambushing any Frenchman stupid enough to wander away from his comrades when on shore.

Berwickshire fishermen were themselves partly itinerant. Crews fell into the habit of chasing the herring shoals as far north as Caithness in the spring and then as far south as Yarmouth in the early summer. In May 1869 with the local haddock fishing still light, a small flotilla left the home ground for better prospects on the Tyne. The season there was short, and the boats braved bracing storms to make the most of the time they had. Inevitably the men were caught unawares when a squall blew up.

Three Eyemouth boats got into difficulties and became separated from the rest when they cut loose for the shore. Two of these belonged wholly or in part to Robert Waddell. He was skipper on the *Victor* and along with the rest of his crew, including his old father, was pitched into the sea when the vessel tipped up. All six men managed to scramble on the broken timbers and were later rescued. From their vantagepoints they watched, as Waddell's other boat, *Ten Brothers* was also turned over by the seas. Two men failed to surface. James Aitchison, whose brother Peter had won the leaping contest in the Summer Games of 1864, and Alex White, a native of Cockenzie were never seen again. Peter and his other brother John nearly lost their own lives as they swam around the sinking craft in a vain search for the lost men. While this was going on another boat, the *Wanderer* from Coldingham turned over after being hit by one mighty lump of water. All five of its crew were trapped and drowned under the upturned hull. James and Hugh Rae, brothers and owners of the boat were lost along with three hired men whose names were not recorded.

The dire news was communicated home via the new telegraph station, which had been functioning in Eyemouth for less than a month. What would have caused greater trauma to the wives and children of those cruelly taken by the sea that was their benefactor? The shamefaced looks of the other crews as they avoided eye contact when they sailed through the bay and past the pier where the women stood? Or the hollow knock at the door from the postmaster?

Special prayer meetings were held on the day of the fleet's return. These triggered a second, albeit much smaller, more localised and much less dramatic Christian revival in Eyemouth. Some of those who had been touched by religion in 1860 but had then lapsed back into bad habits returned to the pews. Jane Mack, who had even gone so far as to confess the sin of fornication before the Kirk session of Stephen Bell, now walked into the more welcoming hall of the United Presbyterians. This time her man James Purves went with her. Purves did not totally recant all of his past weaknesses. He might have his own bench at the UP, but his backside was much more comfortable on the barstools of the Ship Inn.

Shaken by the losses he had sustained off Shields, Robert Waddell opted to spend more time on shore building up a smoke yard opposite the Home Arms Hotel. When his younger brother William was drowned in September 1871 Robert cut all ties with the sea and sold his share in the *Ten Brothers* to James and Peter Aitchison. With William Waddell dead the boat would obviously have to be renamed. The Aitchisons kept faith with the theme and repainted the hull with the legend *Two Brothers*. This might have seemed appropriate but it tempted fate in a most tragic way.

Almost three years to the day after their brother James had been lost, Peter and John steered their boat to virtually the same fishing spot off Tyneside. Another oppressive storm blew up, spinning the little boat around like a dish on a stick. As it did so a flash of lightning struck the foremast, bringing the beam crashing downwards. The biggest lump pinioned John Aitchison to the boards, breaking his neck and killing him instantly. Two other men were badly injured and though the boat appeared lost, Peter Aitchison somehow managed to steer it to land. *Two Brothers* or *Ten Brothers*, the vessel seemed jinxed.

Once more the telegraph was used to relay tragedy to Berwickshire, to inform Jane Dougal that she was now a widow. Jane had two children to keep: one a baby of just three months who had been named after his dead Uncle James, the other a girl, Ann, aged just three. She moved to Burnmouth where her sister-in-law Agnes Aitchison gave her shelter. Aggie's man, William Crawford Aitchison, son of Helen Spears and nephew to the Kingfisher, could share Jane's pain. His father John had drowned in the *Lively* back in 1853.

The Kingfisher occasionally went down to Burnmouth and as was his habit, regularly pushed coins into Jane's hand and tossed sweeties to the bairns, including Agnes's two-year-old infant Mary. Sometimes Spears' lodger James Patterson drove the Kingfisher down the coast in a cart. It was as much for his own pleasure however, and it wasn't long before the widower Paterson was courting the widow Jane. When they eventually married Spears generously got out of the house he shared with James and his son William on the Yard Heads and moved back to his old apartment in the centre of the town. There was room there. Jean Cowe's son Andrew had recently moved out.

This ought to have been a time when Spears was settling down to a peaceful and relatively comfortable retirement. But from a combination of generosity to others and a drouth for strong drink, the fortune he had once enjoyed was largely frittered away. The Kingfisher was 'aye ready' to give to others, especially those who had suffered from the sea, and there were many that fell into that category.

A few weeks after *Two Brothers* was swamped, another shipwreck occurred off Berwickshire. *Morning Cloud* was an old undecked vessel, which the skipper and owner William Craig had already decided to lay up after the drave of 1872. Ill fortune ensured that what should have been one of the boat's last trips ended in disaster for the crew. The boat was sighted by the rest of the herring fleet shipping water in a gale of only moderate intensity. By the time they had beat up to the foundering craft, it was gone and there was no sign of any of the five men on board. William Craig left a widow and seven children, George Crombie a widow and six children, James Collin was newly wed and had no bairns. Two single men, George Dougal and Robert Paterson, also drowned.

Craig's wife, Margaret Aitchison, was another relative of the Kingfisher, another of his sister's children. Spears again dug money from his own pocket to help sustain his niece and her large brood of bairns. Margaret needed her uncle. The most the parish ever gave her was three shillings a week.

Snagged nets, tangled lines, wrecked boats, lost lives: the precariousness of the fishing was never clearer. Incidents and near disasters, were still played out in an almost annual drama both on the high seas and nearer to home on Eyemouth shore where local people gathered with ominous regularity.

Everything came back to the harbour, to the urgent need for improvements before a tragedy became a cataclysm. The stumbling block was, as it always had been, who would pay to provide safe, deep water in the tidal approaches? Regardless of their continuing obligation to pay tithe redemption rates, a move was at last made to start charging harbour rates from the fishing boats. But would crews be far-sighted enough to agree to being double-taxed?

It fell to John Dickson, son of the famous merchant and now chairman of the Harbour Trust, to put this question to the test. Ignoring grumbling he pressed ahead with a new harbour order and set up a separate fund for port improvements. Those outside the town who had an interest in the place were not slow to contribute. Money came from Glasgow traders, Birmingham fish salesmen and a variety of other businesses from Edinburgh and London. Willie Spears, who acted as the local agent for a firm of Musselburgh net manufacturers, handed in a cheque for £3 which had been sent to him.

The Kingfisher no longer made any pretence of fishing and scraped a living from this and other irregular work. He was also involved in burgh affairs, though perhaps more as a figurehead than anything else. It was on his suggestion that a frieze of a fishing boat was placed over the mantel of the Town Hall when it was topped out in 1874. The *Supreme* was the name of the Kingfisher's old boat, but had now been passed on for the new, sleek, decked structure of Robert Craig, brother of the drowned skipper from the *Morning Cloud*.

At the public unveiling of the neo-gothic building Spears acknowledged the cheers of the folk, but made no speech when he was called to stand up. The man was now pushing sixty, a good age even for someone who had been fit and well all his days, which of course Spears had not been. To a whole generation of fishermen and migrants to the town the Kingfisher was simply one of the old salts, albeit someone who was still given massive, universal respect.

More heed was paid to men like Little Dod, to Spears' nephew William Crawford Aitchison and especially to William 'Nibby' Nisbet. His daring at sea was as pronounced as that of Spears in his younger days, and folk often waited for Nibby's view before giving their own. The man did not lack courage. In October 1869 while on a mussel-gathering expedition to the Clyde, he had dived into the river in pursuit of one of his comrades who had slipped overboard during a boozy late-night session. George Dougal could not be saved and Nibby nearly drowned himself, diving time and again after the falling body. His efforts were praised to high heaven by the crews when they returned to Eyemouth, as was Nisbet's determination to help Dougal's family get through the first days and weeks of the bereavement.

Shortly after this he was invited to enter the brotherhood of the Freemasons, one of a select few fishermen admitted to the order. Nisbet had arrived. In 1876, when a lifeboat was finally stationed in Eyemouth, he was the obvious choice as coxswain. By then this quiet-spoken, wiry man had taken charge of the fishermen's committee. But he lacked the steel of Spears and found it hard to restrain the more volatile skippers, such as when the laird tried to hijack the tithe redemption fund.

It was almost twenty years since David Milne-Home's harbour rate had been rejected, something he still considered to have been a grave error of judgement. But Wedderburn was happy to help when the Harbour Trust asked him to approach the Public Works Loan Board on their behalf. It was supposed to be only a speculative inquiry, but Milne-Home opened discussions to secure a loan for port improvement based on the only collateral available in Eyemouth: the weekly sums collected through the tithe redemption fund. When this became public knowledge it was as if the clock had been turned back to 1861. The men, who had very nearly paid off that debt, would have none of it. It is unlikely the Loan Board would have accepted the fund as security in any case, but, snubbed again, Milne-Home ceased negotiating with London. Consequently the public purse once more remained closed to Eyemouth. A further few years were wasted.

With remarkable stoicism the fishermen's committee merely shrugged its shoulders. You could often walk over the berthed boats from the Salt Greens to the Gunsgreen side without touching water. A new harbour was bound to come eventually: it was only a matter of time, and good luck. Other projects were going on which provided even more tangible encouragement to this optimism. The railway extension group had been in existence since the 1860s, but the big push was now on to get a branch line from Burnmouth. A survey was commissioned, which suggested that it could be built for around £15,000. They could approach a body like the North British Railway Company to finance the scheme, but that would involve handing over control. No, far better to try and raise the cash locally. Who better to turn to for help than David Milne-Home! And who better to smooth the path to the laird than his old friend, William Spears.

The Kingfisher duly arranged a meeting, which unusually took place at Wedderburn's magnificent home of Paxton House. It was a grand jaunt reminiscent of the day a delegation, which also included Spears, had traipsed the lanes of Berwickshire a decade earlier to thrash out a settlement in the tithe dispute with David Robertson. This trip was much less successful and though Milne-Home wished them well he kept his cash box locked. The tenants of Eyemouth who were so quick to shout him down and publicly decry his ideas were never slow at holding out their hands for his money.

The railway committee slouched back home and did relatively little. Perhaps they should contact the North British Railway Company? Or perhaps they should just consider matters for a while? As with the harbour there was an expectation that rail would come ... eventually, by some miraculous means. The prosperity of the town made it almost certain.

The fishing industry had rarely been more productive. Around £100,000 worth was landed in Eyemouth District in 1870, and this increased every year in the decade which followed. But wealth was not assured and nor was the future.

A good proportion of the earnings went on new boats and gear, which kept the Brownsbank carpenters and shipwrights constantly busy. But a lot of the excess income was still squandered in the quayside bars where bottles and barrels were emptied in Olympian fashion. The writer James Bertram confirmed the reputation of hard-drinking, hard-working Eyemouth. The fishermen, he wrote, 'are a rough, uncultivated people and more drunken in their habits than those of neighbouring villages.'

All attempts to moralise and sober up the bulk of the people ended in ignominious failure. The local Lodge of teetotal do-gooders did manage to have the licenses of three whisky shops revoked, but that left fourteen inns untouched.

When they were not drinking some of the men took to playing games. Though there was no repeat of the summer athletics and regatta, Fort Point continued to be used as a rudimentary golf course and cricket pitch. In August 1874 after a crowd of several hundred had dispersed, part of the ground they had been standing on gave way and slipped into the sea. Had the landslip occurred an hour earlier, dozens would have fallen to their deaths.

Leisure time ashore was also spent at meetings and concerts in the various churches, the Masonic Lodge Rooms and, after its completion in 1874, in the Town Hall. Companies of actors and musicians provided regular entertainment and on one occasion a troop of Negroes spent several days performing black spiritual songs in the town. Who got the biggest cultural shock, the locals or the African-American visitors?

The local halls also echoed to the sound of political meetings. The growing wealth of the burgh meant that fishermen as well as merchants now qualified for the vote. When David Robertson was elevated to the peerage on the death of his father in June 1873 the importance of this block was put to the test. Both the Tory, Lord Dunglass, and the experienced Liberal, William Miller of Manderston, needed the support of Eyemouth. One hundred and thirty men in the town had the franchise, out of a total county roll of no more than sixteen hundred.

Miller, thanks to the efforts of the now very elderly Timothy Statham, was assured of a large gathering when he came down to the coast to speak. As the former MP for Leith Burgh he made the kind of bland assurances familiar to politicians of today. What did they want? A new harbour? Railway extension? Better prices for fish, lower mussel costs? Why, so did he! At the end of the night, and with nobody at all interested in questioning the man (what was the point?) the chairman, John Dickson junior, moved a resolution that 'William Miller is a fit man to represent Berwickshire'. After a unanimous show of hands Miller was cheered to the rafters.

Two days later Lord Dunglass and his entourage came down the Ayton road for a similar rally. Again the attendance was good, but the reception Dunglass received was markedly different. There were no cheers when he came into the room, and only muted applause at the end of his speech. Unlike Miller, the Tory was then questioned for some considerable time: on the Game Laws, the Permissive Bill, the Tweed Fishery Act, the Irish Church and above all, on fisheries and harbours. Eventually the chairman John Johnston drew the meeting to a close but when he called for the endorsement of the Conservative candidate only a few hands were raised in stony silence. Dunglass stormed out of the hall and out of Eyemouth.

On polling day both candidates went to quite extraordinary lengths to get their vote out. The days of Tory influence and intimidation might have passed, but the age of electoral expenses was yet to dawn. Dunglass and his allies, including the Milne-Homes, commandeered almost every available carriage and ferried their supporters to and from the public voting stations. As well as the lucky few electors, hundreds of hangers-on were likewise brought forward to cheer or boo, depending on which way a ballot was cast.

Impressive though these efforts were, they could not match the enterprise of William Miller. He used his position as a director of the North British Railway Company to lay on special trains, which traversed the Berwickshire line all day long, picking up Liberal voters and supporters. But to get the Eyemouth men to the Ayton hustings Miller had to be even more ingenious. With most of the fishermen who qualified away fishing off Shields, he chartered a steam tug to bring them home for the day. *Pearl* arrived at the quay to the sound of a brass band and the cheers of a big crowd. Like politicians themselves, the fishermen waved to the people before boarding waiting carts which were whipped up to Ayton. To a man they polled for Miller and were treated to a slap-up meal and a bottle or two to keep out the chill for their return journey to Tyneside.

It was an expensive bit of electioneering but it paid off. The Eyemouth vote made all the difference to the Liberals, who held Berwickshire with a majority of just fourteen.

Like the practised politician that he was, William Miller hastened to downplay his manifesto promises. He received proposals for a branch railway with good grace, yet sent back a bland and decidedly circumspect reply. Of course he would do what he could, but the fishermen had to be aware of the financial situation of the country, the already extensive commitments of the North British Railway Company, and his own very limited influence.

Miraculously, that influence returned to its previous strength when, in January 1874, just seven months after his victory, a general election was called. Miller quickly ensured that Burnmouth station was enlarged, something the fishing interest had been agitating for since 1866. It was a very welcome development, but what about the branch line connection with Eyemouth? Miller shuffled his feet, but did not say it could not be achieved and this was enough again to buy a bunch of votes. The fish-curers sent a memorial confirming that the fisherfolk of Berwickshire would again do their duty.

Only one other candidate came forward to offer a challenge, and it was neither Dunglass nor even an official Conservative. Major R. Baillie Hamilton of Langton styled himself as an Independent, beholding to no party. He did not bother to canvass much in the solidly Liberal east of the county, in contrast to Miller who was received with adulation in Eyemouth. He was careful not to repeat previous promises, but Miller did say that actions, like the enlargement of Burnmouth station, spoke louder than words. He could also announce that the Fishery Board had agreed to part pay for improvements to Burnmouth harbour, and he would use all his influence to do even more for Eyemouth.

It was a concern to Milne-Home that his coastal tenants, unlike those from the inland estates, doggedly refused to accept good political advice. He strongly favoured Major Hamilton and authorised the distribution of posters and pamphlets warning voters to beware of 'specious promises'. The placards were not as nakedly abusive as those exhibited by Charles St Clair in 1859, but they did ask whether William Miller could be trusted. In Eyemouth the question related to the crucial issue of the harbour. Hadn't Miller been MP for Leith for nine years, and didn't he give frequent assurances that a breakwater would be built there? Weren't the good folk of Leith still waiting?

It is impossible to say what effect, if any, these posters had on voting intentions. The Eyemouth men did not waver in their support for Miller, but others must have switched their allegiance and Hamilton swept Berwickshire with a majority of seventy-four. The *Berwick Advertiser* put the result down to the action of Wedderburn and his cohorts in the shire. 'There is reason to fear' ran an editorial 'that acts of intimidation and coercion on the part of the landlords were more numerous than was first supposed.'

In spite of the political hue of Eyemouth, Major Hamilton was surprisingly active on its behalf. In the year of his election the new Harbour Order Act, which charged dues on fishing boats for the first time, came into force. It would still take years for the exiting debt on the port to be paid off and

Hamilton took it upon himself to convince the bondholders to accept just a third of what they were due. He then gave £400 from his own purse to help cover the remaining liability. When this was added to a £200 contribution from the fishermen and to £400 raised from the merchants of the town the harbour was declared solvent for the first time in thirty years. At last attention could be turned to the infrastructure of the town's principal asset.

Not only was the harbour entrance tidal and often dangerous, the quays themselves were unsafe and uneven. People still slipped into the water, or cracked their bones as they tumbled on to the boats. Henry Angus just managed to save his eight-year-old son William from drowning when the lad lost his footing on a crumbling part of the wharf. Henry plunged in to the water and dragged William out. He then carried the almost still body home to the care of his wife Jane Ovens.

Jane feared she would lose a son. But most days she worried that she might never see her husband again. Henry Angus, like all of the fishermen, reaped the rewards of fine catches and rocketing fish-auction prices. The winter haddock fishing off Berwickshire in 1875–76 was the best ever with most crews grossing more than £30 a week between them. Some made more than £50. These were the wages of middle-class artisans, not common seamen. Whatever the weather, regardless of the barometer warnings, at least one boat was bound to be enticed out; and when one sailed the whole fleet went. Community dashes to the beach to wait on the return of the fleet when the weather turned were now regular, heart-stopping events. On 14 October 1875 the men tarried too long at their haddock lines when a squall thumped down on the ocean and three were caught in the hurricane. It was late in the afternoon when *White Star*, with Little Dod at the helm, bore through the roadsteads. The boat seemed imminent on the rocks when a towering sea swooped over and shot the craft like an arrow on to the beach.

White Star's deliverance when all had seemed lost suggested a bleaker fate for the remaining two boats which were still out. It was mid-morning on the following day before word swept through the vennels that a telegram had arrived signalling the safe arrival of both boats at Leith. Safe, but for one man. Joseph Hastie had been washed overboard almost on the first tidal wave that smashed the timbers of the *Heroine*. He left a wife and five young children. His body, minus the head, a foot and one arm was later washed up at the Killiedraughts, to the north of Fort Point.

Six weeks after this, the *Progress* was dashed to bits on the Hurkur rocks, the crew saved only through the prompt action of the rocket brigade and the bravery of men prepared to dive in and risk their own lives. A special thanksgiving service was held that night in the Town Hall. But God could only do so much. The salvation of the fishermen would only be assured by safer facilities.

A lot of work though was going on behind the scenes. William Nisbet and James Paterson had managed to persuade the fishermen to start contributing a small weekly amount to a harbour fund: this in spite of the new port dues they had to pay and their continuing obligation to the tithe debt. They were following the lead of Burnmouth where the crews had been levying an additional charge for many years. This partly convinced the Fishery Board to pay three-quarters of the cost of improvements. Work began in October 1877 to strengthen the quay and extend the wharves.

Collections for the Eyemouth account had barely started when a winter sea poured into the bay and over the lower part of the town. When the tide retreated it took with it part of Smeaton's pier.

It is ironic, not to say tragic, that the first state funds ever advanced to Eyemouth went on repairs rather than expansion. The Public Works Loan Commissioners agreed to a loan of £2,000, on security of the new harbour rates, to restore an infrastructure that was so obviously deficient. However, the very fact that government money had now been given to Eyemouth boded well for the future. The cash was followed by the appearance in the town of another government committee charged with investigating the state of the fisheries in Scotland. Like previous commissions, the members were impressed with the energy and activity and amazed that such a business was carried out apparently in spite of the cramped and inadequate facilities. 'At Eyemouth where the fishing boats are perhaps the largest and finest in Scotland the harbour is inconveniently small, the boats are all aground at low water, and cannot enter or leave the harbour before half tide. It would cost about £10,000 to enlarge and deepen the harbour.'

With this endorsement the fishermen's committee at long last joined forces with the harbour trust and the railway group to co-ordinate their disparate efforts. But what should have been a pooling of ideas and resources became a contest to see who could shout loudest and demand the most. Ambition knew no bounds.

Thomas Meik and Company, the Edinburgh firm of civil engineers who had surveyed a possible railway link to Burnmouth, now looked at the harbour. They were given a blank sheet of paper and proceeded to offer a vision of the future. The existing basin could be deepened and new piers flung out into the bay at a cost of not £10,000 but £60,000.

Unfortunately, but predictably, the assumption of success was not matched in a professional submission. Both the Board of Trade and the Public Works Loan Commission declined the advance. Failure this time around was not well received. It led to some petty squabbling between the harbour trust and the fishermen's committee who walked out of the joint negotiations. Petulant infighting continued for a further three years. The fishermen, led by William Nisbet, not only stopped their voluntary contributions for port improvements but many also refused to pay burgh rates, water dues and harbour fees. 'It is a trick far too common in Eyemouth' reported the clerk to the Police Commisioners 'to insinuate that their rates are paid. They pay some and then tell neighbours they have paid all so that when Donaldson [the rate collector] returns to collect it, he appears to be charging double. With them any scheme by which they can get clear of paying rates they consider right.'

The same names crop up over and again … Paul Patterson, John Broomfield, Robert Lough and Archibald Nisbet. And it wasn't just the poor and the dissolute that played games with authority. Some of the wealthiest merchants and fish curers also held back their assessed dues for as long as they felt they could get away with it. Even Little Dod was threatened with a court summons.

The ultimate sanction available was the seizure of goods and property, but though this was often threatened it was never carried through. Such an act would have been a provocation too far, reminiscent of the persecution of William Spears. In cases when the burgh commissioners discussed poindings they thought it highly unlikely that anyone could be persuaded to carry them through.

Eyemouth people had always shown disdain for authority, but the lawlessness of the 1870s was a product, rather bizarrely, of an extension of services and amenities. The vastly increased population meant that a new public school was needed. An improved water supply was piped into the burgh, gas lamps extended, new streets laid out, sewers put down, street cleaners employed. All of these were applauded as good things; but all of these had to be paid for. Yet as a parish Eyemouth was woefully small and even a slight increase in public spending meant a marked leap in the rates. Was it fair, the folk asked, that they should pay so much more than those in Coldingham or Ayton did?

In any case knuckling down to authority went against the grain. Nowhere was this clearer than in the reaction to compulsory schooling. Objections were raised to the cost of lessons but more than that, the children were all too often needed at home to bait lines and otherwise assist in the real business of life. In 1871, the year before the Education Act, more than a third of all pupils were absent for virtually an entire term.

Again it was as much the well-to-do as the paupers who tried it on with the system. In December 1877 Robert Waddell, now a prosperous fish curer, was ordered before the School Board for refusing to pay fees in advance and for attempting to withhold a percentage for the days on which his children were needed in the fish yards. Waddell did not care for the school, and when some of his bairns complained of being whacked by their teacher, Archibald Mclean, he took matters into his own hands. With his wife Jessie Rosie trotting along behind him, Waddell strode into the classroom, gripped Mclean by the collar and growled in his face. The next time, if Mclean was stupid enough to try it again, he would bring his shotgun with him. It was grand sport for the schoolchildren, got Waddell a written warning from the Board and persuaded Mclean that it was time to quit Eyemouth.

Every attempt was made to convince or to cajole children to better school attendance. In the years after 1872 state school grants were largely based on numbers in class and on examination results. But this did not matter much to some parents who either ignored the demands or simply refused to appear when called to account. Again the same names crop up. Paul Patterson, skipper of the *Star of Hope* until an affliction with rheumatics and an affection for the bottle lost him his berth; James Windram, crewman of *Six Brothers;* Thomas Collin from the *Myrtle;* William Crombie of *Florida;* William Angus from the *Harmony;* Robert Lough of *Lily of the Valley* and Robert Johnston, who crewed on the *Wave*.

The rates rebellion, the drunkenness and profanity of so many of the families, the disdain for education and disregard for religion confounded those on the Police Commision and the School Board. Morality was a stranger in the town. Like the Wild West, street fighting was a regular nightly entertainment and pre-nuptial fornication hardly brought shame. What was to be done?

At least matters were again moving along for the harbour. In the winter of 1880 the fishermen's committee, at the urging of William Nisbet, resumed their weekly payments into the harbour fund. No further proof was needed of the urgency of improvements, but Mother Nature provided it in any case. On Christmas Eve 1880, and with the fleet many miles out on the ocean, townsfolk made the familiar rush to the shore when the sky erupted. All had known a storm was in the offing from the clear warning of the pier-head barometer, yet the men had sailed regardless. It was not just bravado this time, but want and hunger that drove them to their boats. The winter haddock fishing had not been as slack for many years. Those who had saved nothing from the boom years felt hard times: and that was a large proportion of the seafaring families.

One after another the forty-two deep-sea boats were sighted rounding Fort Point or at the roadsteads to the bay. The blinding snowstorm and the terror of the events that unfolded froze both the bodies and the nerves of those on shore. The first craft to attempt the harbour entrance was caught on the bar, tumbling the men about inside. Other boats in like fashion crashed on to the beach or were driven at breakneck speed up the passage of the river Eye. Three boats were forced to stay out all night, but by noon on Christmas Day all had returned and every man had survived. Another near miss, and one which again concentrated minds.

In the spring of 1881 the fishermen's committee and the Harbour Trust repaired their relationship after three years of sulking at each other. Robert Allan, on behalf of the Trust, was made chairman of the new joint body with John Dickson speaking for the curers and Little Dod, George Collin junior, elected by the fishermen.

At long last there was unanimity of purpose in the town, and with a general election in the offing another chance to make the harbour a political issue. Major Ballie Hamilton, now unashamedly on a Conservative ticket, and regardless of all that he had done, was not well backed in the town. Eyemouth remained loyal to the Liberals. Their candidate was Edward Marjoribanks, cousin of David Robertson who had helped the fishermen during the tithe dispute. In a speech to a capacity audience in the Town Hall Marjoribanks even called upon William Spears, 'the old King of the town' to rise from his chair and speak. But Spears, now a shadow of his former self, was only able to wave an acknowledgement. Sitting next to him, and there to help, were William Nisbet, James Paterson and Little Dod.

The Liberals recaptured the seat and Marjoribanks gave generous thanks to the Eyemouth voters in a victory speech in the town. He also vowed to do all that he could to advance the cause of the harbour, which was music to the ears of the joint committee, especially since they had just re-engaged the services of Thomas Meik.

In June 1881 a new plan was unveiled, and it was one which eclipsed even that proposed in 1878. The cost was greater too. Meik now envisaged extending the harbour back up the Eye as well as into deep water in the bay. It would be a harbour of refuge for not just fishing boats but even small ships. It would come in at a cool £80,000.

The plans were pasted outside the fishery office, now occupied by a new man called John Doull. Men took time to study the papers and marvelled at the detail. They then blindly walked past the barometer and jumped down to their flimsy boats. Meik's scheme was a beacon for brighter days. It appeared at a time when the lashing storms seemed to have no end. In July at the burgh picnic John Doull spoke of the future. 'Building is going on in the town and when the harbour is enlarged which it will be in the course of two or three years, Eyemouth will take its place as one of the leading fishing stations of Scotland.' In August the proposals were given the unanimous approval of the joint committee and rubber stamped at separate meetings of the harbour trust and the general body of fishermen.

The support of the government, as ever, was widely expected. But perhaps there truly never was a better chance for Eyemouth. Another piece in the jigsaw slotted into place when the North British Railway Company confirmed it would, after all, build and run a branch line to the main network as soon as the harbour scheme was up and running. The port plan was already on its way to Whitehall and the waiting had begun. In the meantime the fishermen could do nothing more than sail and fish and take risks: just as they had been doing for many years.

But idling, not risk taking was the lot of the crews as the dirty weather of summer extended into the autumn. Even the hardy men of Eyemouth often found it impossible to cast off in conditions unknown for a generation. Ten consecutive days were spent ashore in September, and things were equally grim in the first week of October. The Kingfisher, his mind now starting to wander, was noticed shuffling round the town babbling about an earthquake to come. If he wasn't senile he was drunk. *Willie Spears aye liked a glass!*

On Sunday 9 October 1881 those who had religion put on their best clothes and made for the Kirk of their choice. Like the bars which dished out a different kind of intoxication, there was plenty of variety. The pious made their way up through the wynds and vennels, the vast majority walking past the door of Stephen Bell's Church. They headed instead for the Methodists in St Ella's Place or up the aptly named Church Street to the Evangelical Union or the United Presbyterians or further still to the recently built Free Kirk at the top of the Smiddy Brae.

Two of the leading skippers of the town were on Sunday-school duty. George Collin (Little Dod) at the UP and William Nisbet, who was super-intendent at the EU. Dod read a lesson for the bairns and then led the signing of a hymn, the words of which would return to his mind on a long night of terror which fate was preparing for him.

> But yet the Lord who is on high,
> Is more of might by far
> Than noise of many waters is
> Or great sea billows are.

Across the street William Nisbet closed his meeting with a final hymn which the children later said had brought tears to his eyes.

Here we suffer grief and pain
Here we meet to part again:
In heaven we part no more.

Early on Monday Nibby's wife Effie, like the rest of the women, was up before dawn preparing her husband's haddock lines. A couple of thousand mussels were shelled, the flesh attached to the hooks and the yarn expertly interlaced with grass and coiled into a skull-basket. But Willie did not sail that day. Nobody did. The heaving seas set an impenetrable water wall against them. It was the same story the next day, and the following, and the one after that. There was relief when on Thursday night the winds dropped and the incessant rain slackened off to no more than a pelt. The portents for Friday were good.

It was almost midnight on Thursday 13 October 1881 when Kate Maltman roused her son James Lough from his bed. Mathew Crawford was at the door. He had come to check that Laffy had not forgotten about the wedding in the morning. In truth after a week on shore the best man designate was reluctant to commit any more time to leisure. But his father, the skipper of the *Lily of the Valley,* told him not to be so soft, and the die was cast. The boat would sail a man short, and Crawford's insistence save the neck of young James Lough.

Kate went back to bed, but was up within four hours. The air was still and the morning likely to dawn clear and fair. 'Whit a gran' day' would be the regular refrain from the fisher-women. Kate hurried to get her chores completed. Her young bairns played around her: John, Effie, Helen, Mary and the one-year-old baby, Jane. Kate tarried a while before shaking her husband and eldest son awake: one for the sea, the other for a wedding jaunt. They both needed their rest. It was going to be quite a day.

Chapter Twelve

The Pickit Men

Ye wad juist think that they had been pickit
>   Often repeated comment on those lost in the Disaster

Here are the names of those lost in the great East Coast Fishing Disaster of 1881 and many of the dependants they left. The list of the children and dependants is as complete as has been possible from the existing records. In total 93 widows and 267 children were left in the wake of Black Friday.*

Eyemouth Boats and Men

HARMONY
6 men lost in East Entrance to Eyemouth bay.
PETER ANGUS, aged 31. Left a widow and daughter Helen.
WILLIAM ANGUS, Brother of Peter, aged 32. His pregnant widow Mary Craig gave birth to Margaret on 16 July 1882. Other dependent children, William, Matilda, Helen, George, Mary and James.
HENRY ANGUS, uncle of above men, aged 53. Left widow Jane Ovens and son James.
JAMES WARD, aged 29. Left a widow Mary Angus and daughter Sarah.
GEORGE CRIBBES, aged 55. Left a widow and son George.
Two of his other sons died in the Disaster – Alexander, aged 31 in *Forget-Me-Not* and James, aged 25 in the *Good Intent*.
ALEXANDER CRAIG, aged 37. No noted dependants.

RADIANT
7 men lost in East Entrance to Eyemouth Bay.
JOHN WINDRAM, aged 57. Left a widow Alison Renton and children Andrew, Margaret and Alexander.
JAMES CROMBIE, aged 37. Left a widow Alison Fairbairn and children John and Agnes.
WILLIAM GRAY, aged 36. Left a widow Mary Wilks and children John, Alice, Isabella and Mary.
JOHN BURGON, aged 30. No dependants noted.
DAVID FAIRBAIRN, aged 37. No dependants noted.

* Only the names of children on the relief roll are noted. Boys aged fourteen and over and girls over the age of fifteen are not included

JOHN FAIRBAIRN, aged 35. Left a widow Mary Crombie and children John, James, Alexander and Jane.

ALEXANDER FAIRBAIRN, aged 28. No dependants noted.

The three men above were brothers. Their elderly parents, James Fairbairn and Agnes Burgon watched them all fail and drown from their vantage point on the shore when the boat was wrecked in the bay. In April 1884 James made an application for help from the relief fund which was turned down. 'He is too old for the fishing, his wife too frail. He lost three sons – two of them unmarried and living with him – at his own door he saw two of them perish. Now another son Paul has left to be married and his final son may soon do likewise'. Old James Fairbairn was forced back to the sea.

PRESS HOME
Six men lost in the east entrance to Eyemouth Bay.

ANDREW COLLIN, aged 36. Left a widow Elizabeth Stott, sister to the three brothers drowned on the boat. Andrew was also the brother of Joseph Collin, drowned on *Fiery Cross*.

LEONARD DOUGAL, aged 18. No noted dependants. His brother James Dougal was lost on the *Lily-of-the-Valley*.

GEORGE WINDRAM, aged 25. No noted dependants. Two of his brothers John and James died on the *Six Brothers*.

ROBERT STOTT, aged 26. Left widow Ann Ready who gave birth to a girl, Bridget, on 17 February 1882.

JOHN STOTT, aged 22. No noted dependants.

JAMES STOTT, aged 20. No noted dependants.

The three above were brothers. Their father William Stott sailed and survived the Disaster. None of the bodies of the Stott brothers were ever found.

JANET
Six men lost at Burnmouth

JOHN MALTMAN, aged 45. His wife, Janet Burgon or Windram was already dead. His younger children, William and Jane were rendered orphans.

ALEXANDER MALTMAN, son of above, aged 22. Left a widow Ann Paterson who gave birth to Alexandrina on 13 February 1882. Also has another child, John.

ROBERT MALTMAN Brother of Alex and son of John. Aged 20. No noted dependants.

GEORGE MALTMAN Cousin of Alex and Robert. Aged 17. No noted dependants.

HENRY BOLTON, aged 47. Left a widow Rosina Borthwick who gave birth to Johnston Borthwick Young on 7 July 1882. Their other children were Henry, Elizabeth, David and John. Rosina Borthwick's brother Johnston Borthwick died on the *Margaret and Catherine*.

THOMAS SWANSTON, aged 19. No noted dependants. His father William Swanston sailed and survived.

LILY OF THE VALLEY
Six men lost at Burnmouth.

THOMAS MILLER, aged 37. Left a widow Catherine Waddell who gave birth to Thomas on 14 March 1882. Their other children were Catherine, James, Jane, and Maggie. When their mother died in 1891 the eldest daughter took charge of the family and received an allowance from the relief committee.

JAMES LOUGH, aged 40. Left a widow and John aged 12, Euphemia, who died on 19 January 1884, Helen aged 9, Mary 7, Jane one year. James was the father of Laffy, who did not sail on Disaster Day though he wanted to.

ROBERT LOUGH, aged 38. Left a widow Agnes Cribbes or Lough who gave birth to Robert on March 26 1882. Their other dependent child was Alice Lough who died on 4 November 1887.

DAVID RITCHIE, aged 34. Left a widow who gave birth to Helen Ritchie on 30 July 1896, the last posthumous baby to be born. Their other dependent children were David aged 10 and Mary 3.

JAMES DOUGAL, aged 23. Left a widow Margaret Collins who gave birth to Jamesina Dougal on 16 December 1881. James's brother Leonard died on the *Press Home*.

ALEXANDER SWANSTON, aged 19. No noted dependants.

FORGET-ME-NOT
Seven men lost near Berwick.

WILLIAM NISBET, aged 35. Left a widow Effie Dougal.

ALEXANDER NISBET, aged 37. Left a widow Ann Nisbet, children Alexander aged 12, Robert aged 11, William 9 and Jessie who was born on October 3 1881, the last child to be born before the Disaster.

ROBERT COLLIN, aged 41. No noted dependants.

JAMES SIMPSON, aged 17. No noted dependants.

ANDREW DOUGAL, aged 33. Left a widow Isabella Paterson and children John and Ann.

ALEXANDER CRIBBES, aged 31. Left a widow Elizabeth Robertson. His father George Cribbes drowned on the *Harmony*, his brother James died on the *Good Intent*.

WILLIAM SCOTT, aged 28. Left a widow, Isabella Cowe. She gave birth to a son William Nisbet Scott on May 16 1882. The boy subseqently died on 15 February 1884.

WAVE
Six men lost near Berwick.

PETER PATERSON, aged 49. His wife, Isabella Young was already dead, rendering their children – Ann, Robert, Hugh and James – orphans.

JOHN PATERSON, son of the above, aged 17. No noted dependants.

PETER BURGON, aged 42. No noted dependants.

ROBERT JOHNSTON, aged 40. Left a widow and children Janet, Margaret and Georgina. Also an adult dependant, Alex Johnston.

DAVID JOHNSTON, son of the above, aged 19. No noted dependants.

JOHN HASTIE, aged 34. Left a widow and children James, Grace, Alexander and Josephine.

BLOSSOM

Five men lost in Goswick Bay.

GEORGE DOUGAL, aged 40. Left a widow and son Andrew.

WILLIAM YOUNG, aged 51. Left a widow Euphemia Collins and children Christina and Ann. His son James was lost on *Fiery Cross*

JOHN BURGON, aged 44. No noted dependants.

WILLIAM CROMBIE, aged 26. Left a widow Mary Waters who gave birth to Thomas on 23 June 1882.

ROBERT YOUNG, aged 20. No noted dependants.

David Stevenson is the sole crewman who survives. He was dragged ashore at Goswick. Stevenson had celebrated his daughter's wedding on the morning of Black Friday.

BEAUTIFUL STAR

Seven men lost at sea.

GEORGE SCOTT, aged 54. His three sons drowned with him. Widow Effie Scott.

JOHN SCOTT, son of George Scott, aged 26. No noted dependants.

GEORGE SCOTT, son of George Scott, aged 23. No noted dependants.

WILLIAM SCOTT, son of George Scott, aged 21. Left widow and children Jane, Alexander and Margaret.

ROBERT COLLIN, aged 28. Left a widow Isabella Windram who gave birth to Robert George Collin on 1 December 1881. He was brother to Thomas and James who died on *Myrtle* and to Alexander who died on *Sunshine*. Four brothers killed.

JAMES BROOMFIELD, aged 28. Left a widow, and children John, William and Robert. His brother, John was lost on *Sunshine*.

EDWARD FISHER, aged 24. No noted dependants.

INDUSTRY

Seven men lost at sea.

ANDREW COWE, aged 52. Left a widow and children Robert and Catherine.

JAMES PATERSON, aged 47. Left a widow Jane Aitchison (formerly Dougal) who gave birth to Margaret Patterson on 14 December 1881. Their other children were Ann Aitchison and James Aitchison aged 11 (from previous marriage to John Aitchison who drowned off Shields in 1872), and John Paterson.

WILLIAM PATERSON, Son of James Paterson, aged 17. No noted dependants.

THOMAS SCOTT, aged 21. No noted dependants.

ANDREW CRAIG, aged 52. Left a widow Agnes Hair and children Peter, Jane, Agnes, Mary and Joan.

JAMES DOUGAL, aged 43. Left a widow who gave birth to Jamesina Dougal on 16 December 1881 (two days after Margaret Paterson, wife of fellow crewman James Paterson, gave birth to Margaret). Their other dependent child was Mary-Ann.

THOMAS SPOUSE, aged 40. Left a widow.

FIERY CROSS

Seven men lost at sea.

ROBERT COLLIN, aged 45. Left a widow Helen Windram who gave birth to Robertina after the Disaster. Other dependent children Ann, Helen, James and William. He is the brother-in-law of James Windram, drowned in *Enterprise*.

WILLIAM COLLIN, brother of Robert, above, aged 43. Left a widow and daughter Ann.

JOHN COWE, aged 41. Left a widow Euphemia Nisbet who gave birth to William after the Disaster. The boy died on 12 June 1882. Their other dependent children were Euphemia, Peter and John.

JAMES YOUNG, aged 24. Left a widow Margaret Stewart. His father William Young died on the *Blossom*.

JOSEPH COLLIN, aged 41. Left a widow Elizabeth Cormack and nine dependent children, more than any other of those lost in the Disaster. They were James, Mary, John, Elizabeth, Joseph, Euphemia, Thomas, Margaret and Andrew. Joseph's brother Andrew was drowned on the *Press Home*.

HUGH GRANT, aged 38. Leaves widow Mary Robertson who gives birth to James on 7 May 1882. Their other dependent children were Mary, Hugh, John, George and Joseph.

ROBERT WILSON, aged 34. No noted dependants.

MYRTLE

Seven men lost at sea.

WILLIAM HOOD, aged 43. His wife, Alison Carson was already dead, leaving his son William as an orphan.

JOHN HOOD, aged 19, son of William Hood, above. No noted dependants.

GEORGE BONE, aged 41. Left a widow Margaret Storey and children Thomas and Isabella.

GEORGE BONE, aged 17, son of George Bone, above. No noted dependants.

JAMES PURVES, aged 51. Left a widow Jane Mack.

THOMAS COLLIN, aged 24. Left a widow Helen Colston who gave birth to Isabella on 20 February 1882. Their other dependent children were Helen Hastie, Margaret Hastie and Alex Collin. (Helen Colston's first husband Joseph Hastie was drowned in 1875.)

JAMES COLLIN, aged 21. Brother of Thomas Collin, above. No noted dependants. Another brother, ALEXANDER died on *Sunshine* while Robert was killed on *Beautiful Star*.

GUIDING STAR

Seven men lost at sea.

HENRY DOUGAL, aged 38. Left a widow and children George, Alexander, Margaret, Mary-Ann and Henry.

JOHN DOUGAL, aged 28. Brother of Henry Dougal, above. Left a widow Jessie Purves who gave birth to Jessie Hood Dougal on November 9 1881. Jessie's father James Purves drowned on the *Myrtle*.

WILLIAM MALTMAN, aged 35. Left a widow who gave birth to Johnsena Maltman on 25 July 1882. Their other dependent children were Janet, David and Maggie.

GEORGE DOUGAL, aged 25. Left a widow and children Jane and Mary.

GEORGE WHILLIS, aged 39. Left a widow and children Josephn and John.

THOMAS FISHER, aged 30. Left a widow who gave birth to Thomasina Fisher on 16 December 1881. Their other dependent children were William, Alice, Janet, Elizabeth and Ann.

JAMES DOUGAL, aged 30. No noted dependants.

FLORIDA
Seven men lost at sea.

JOHN PATERSON, aged 44. Left a widow and son, William.

PAUL PATERSON, aged 37. Left a widow Ellen Young and children Ann, John, William and Thomas.

JOHN PATERSON-FAIRBAIRN, aged 36. Left a widow Jane Dougal and children Elizabeth, Joan and Margaret.

THOMAS FAIRBAIRN, aged 19. Half-brother to John Paterson-Fairbairn, above. No noted dependants.

THOMAS DOUGAL, aged 33. Left a widow Ellen Crombie His brother John drowned in the *Invincible*.

WILLIAM CROMBIE, aged 41. Left a widow Margaret Dougal who gave birth to Williamina on 13 February 1882. Their other dependent child was Isabella.

JOHN CRAIG, aged 18. No noted dependants.

LASS O' GOWRIE
Seven men lost at sea.

George Windram, aged 60. Left a widow and children Robina and Margaret.

DAVID WINDRAM, son of George Windram, above, aged 37. Left a widow and Jane, Alice, Helen, David and Elizabeth.

WILLIAM WINDRAM, son of George Windram, above, aged 25. No noted dependants.

PETER COLLIN, aged 21. No noted dependants.

JAMES WINDRAM, aged 33. No noted dependants.

ROBERT KEARNEY, aged 30. Left a widow who gave birth to Robert on 1 December 1881. Their other dependent children were Gregory, Jane, Hannah and Elizabeth.

CHARLES BURGON, aged 25. No noted dependants.

SIX BROTHERS
Six men lost at sea.

ROBERT COLLIN, aged 46. Left a widow Helen Windram and children Robert, Elizabeth, Agnes, George and another unnamed.

JAMES COLLIN, son of Robert Collin, above, aged 21. No noted dependants.

GEORGE COLLIN, aged 41. Left a widow and children Agnes, William and Robert.

JAMES COLLIN, son of George Collin, above, aged 18. No noted dependants.

JAMES WINDRAM, aged 40. Left a widow Margaret and children Margaret, John, James and William.

JOHN WINDRAM, brother of James Windram, above, aged 28. Left a widow Margaret Aitchison.

Another brother GEORGE was lost on *Press Home*.

SUNSHINE

Six men lost at sea – with an average age of 24 this was the youngest crew lost.

GEORGE GRANT, aged 28. Left a widow Elizabeth Dalglish who gave birth to the first posthumous Disaster baby, Georgina at 8am on 4 November 1881. They also had an infant son, Hugh.

ROBERT SCOTT, aged 28. Left a widow Ann Swanston who gave birth to Margaret Scott on 15 November 1881.

JOHN BROOMFIELD, aged 22. No noted dependants. His brother James died on *Beautiful Star*.

RICHARD WINDRAM, aged 28. Left a widow and children Mary, Isabella and Robert.

ALEXANDER COLLIN, aged 17. No noted dependants. He was the brother of Robert who drowned on *Beautiful Star* and also of James and Thomas who died on the *Myrtle*.

ROBERT LOUGH, aged 19. No noted dependants.

MARGARET AND MARY

Five men lost at sea.

JOHN MALTMAN, aged 28. No noted dependants.

JAMES MALTMAN, cousin of John Maltman, above, aged 22. No noted dependants. His father, Alexander was the only man lost from the *Economy*.

WILLIAM COLLIN, aged 30. Left widow who gave birth to Isabella sometime after the Disaster. The baby died on 18 April 1882. Their other dependent child was Jessie.

ROBERT GILLIE, aged 23. No noted dependants.

JOHN GILLIE, cousin of Robert Gillie, above, aged 22. Leaves widow Ann Lindores and son John.

MARGARET AND CATHERINE

Six men lost at sea.

JAMES LOUGH, aged 23. No noted dependants.

PETER LOUGH, brother of James Dougal, above, aged 21. No noted dependants. James and Peter Lough had another brother, John who drowned on *Good Intent*.

PETER CRAIG, aged 32. Left a widow Elizabeth Waddell who gave birth to Peter Craig on 17 February 1882.

ALEXANDER STOREY, aged 25. Left a widow and daughter Janet.

HENRY PATERSON, aged 24. No noted dependants.

JOHNSTON BORTHWICK, aged 17. No noted dependants. His brother-in-law Henry

Bolton Young died in the *Janet*. His sister Elizabeth named the child she gave
birth to after the Disaster Johnston Borthwick Young.

GOOD INTENT
Two men lost at Spittal.

JOHN LOUGH, aged 32. Left a widow and children Robert, William, James, John
and Richard. His brothers Peter and James died on the *Margaret and Catherine*.

JAMES CRIBBES, aged 25. No noted dependants.

ECONOMY
One man lost.

ALEXANDER MALTMAN, aged 48. Left a widow Margaret Adams and children
Alexander and Robert. His son James drowned from the *Margaret and Mary*.

ENTERPRISE
One man lost.

JAMES WINDRAM, aged 28. Left a Widow Margaret Wilks, who gave birth to
Jamesena on 1 April 1882. Their other dependent children were Margaret and
William. His brother-in-law Robert Collin was one of the dead from *Fiery Cross*.

INVINCIBLE
One man lost.

JOHN DOUGAL, aged 52. Left a widow Jane Maltman and children John, Helen,
Catherine and Ann. His brother Thomas Dougal was lost in the *Florida*.

ONWARD
One man lost.

ALEXANDER DOUGAL, aged 21. No noted dependants.

JAMES AND ROBERT
One man lost.

ANDREW JAMES HARROWER DOUGAL, aged 24. He married Euphemia Lough
on 8 October 1881, just six days before the Disaster. She was heavily pregnant
and gave birth to Andrew Harrower Dougal on 31 January 1882.

FISHER LASSES
One man lost.

WILLIAM YOUNG, aged 58. Left a widow, Margaret Lough and children Christina
and Ann.

Burnmouth Boats and Men

TRANSCENDENT
Seven men lost at sea.

THOMAS KERR, aged 32. Left a widow Maria Kerr.

GEORGE MARTIN, aged 48. No noted dependants.

JAMES ANDERSON, aged 24. Left a widow Janet Anderson who had a child, Jemima, sometime after the Disaster. Their other dependent child was Agnes.

JAMES LINDORES, aged 27. Left a widow Elizabeth who gave birth to Jemima Lindores on 25 March 1882. Their other dependent child was William.

JOHN ANDERSON WOOD, aged 25. No noted dependants.

GEORGE WILSON, aged 32. No noted dependants.

JAMES LINDORES, aged 25. No noted dependants.

GUIDING STAR
Seven men lost at Holy Island.

MARK ANDERSON, aged 51. No noted dependants.

JAMES JOHNSTON, aged 28. Left a widow Helen Johnston who gave birth to Helen sometime after the Disaster. Their other dependent children were Janet and Joan.

ROBERT ANDERSON, aged 53. Left a widow Janet Anderson and children Elizabeth and Robert.

THOMAS AITCHISON, aged 30. Left a widow Jessie Aitchison. She remarried on 15 December 1883, the first Disaster widow to do so.

WILLIAM JOHNSTON, aged 30. Left a widow Janet Johnston and children William, Isabella and Jane.

GEORGE ANDERSON, aged 30. No noted dependants.

ALEXANDER ANDERSON, aged 30. No noted dependants.

EXCELLENT
Two men lost off Goswick.

ALEXANDER AFFLECK, aged 22. No noted dependants.

THOMAS MARTIN, aged 24. No Noted dependants.

CHRISTINA
Four men swamped from small cobble.

ROBERT LINDORES, aged 51. His son James Lindores was drowned on the *Alice*. No noted dependants.

JOHN MARTIN, aged 18. No noted dependants.

WILLIAM MARTIN, aged 20. No noted dependants.

JOHN AITCHISON, aged 17. No noted dependants.

ALICE
Four men swamped from small cobble.

JAMES LINDORES, aged 24. His father Robert Lindores is drowned on *Christina*. No noted dependants.

WILLIAM LINDORES, aged 21. No noted dependants.

THOMAS MACKAY, aged 18. Left his father William as an adult dependant. He died on 18 January 1889.

WILLIAM STRUTHERS, aged 18. No noted dependants.

Coldingham Shore (St Abbs) Boats and Men

TWO SISTERS
Three men and the boat lost at sea.
CHARLES PURVES, aged 55. Left a widow.
JAMES THORBURN, aged 42. Left a widow and children Isabella and Wilhelmina.
WILLIAM THORBURN, brother of James Thorburn, above, aged 38. Left a widow
Isa Thorburn and children Christina, Elizabeth and Isabella.

Cove Boats and Men

From Cove, near Cockburnspath, eleven men were drowned leaving four widows
and fourteen children.

RENOWN
Three men lost at sea.
RICHARD GORDON, aged 33.
THOMAS FAIRBAIRN, aged 19.
JOHN FAIRBAIRN, aged 31.

SNOWDON
Six men and the boat lost at sea.
DAVID FAIRBAIRN, aged 34.
JOHN FAIRBAIRN, aged 24.
THOMAS FAIRBAIRN, aged 24.
DAVID FAIRBAIRN, aged 17.
ROBERT GRIEVE, aged 24.
JAMES GORDON, aged 18.

VELOX
One man swept overboard.
ANDREW HENDERSON, aged 23.

PEARL
One man lost at sea.
JOHN FAIRBAIRN, aged 32.

Fisherrow Boats and Men

From Fisherrow seven men were drownd leaving two widows and nine children.

ALICE
Seven men and the boat lost at sea.
ALEXANDER HAMILTON, aged 23.
WILLIAM WALKER, aged 39.
ROBERT HALLEY, aged 21.

WILLIAM CAIRD, aged 27.

JOHN CUNNIGHAM, aged 22.

THOMAS LANGLANDS, aged 19.

GEORGE LANGLANDS, brother of Thomas Langlands, above, aged 21.

Newhaven Boats and Men

Newhaven gave up fifteen men, leaving two widows and nine children.

PERSEVERANCE
Seven men and boat lost near May Island.

JOHN CARNIE, aged 32.

WILLIAM INGLIS, aged 30.

JOHNSTON WILSON, aged 21.

DAVID LYLIE, aged 25.

BOREAS HALL, aged 31.

PETER INGLIS, aged 18.

WILLIAM LISTON (RUTHERFORD), aged 37.

STORMY PETREL
Three men lost at sea.

DAVID STEVENSON, aged 58.

HUGH STEVENSON, son of David Stevenson, above, aged 32.

PHILIP STEVENSON, son of David Stevenson, above, aged 30.

CONCORD
Three brothers swamped off Dunbar.

JOHN JOHNSTON, aged 37.

JAMES JOHNSTON, aged 30.

WILLIAM JOHNSTON, aged 23.

ROBINAS
Two men lost at sea.

WILLIAM LISTON, aged 20.

ALEXANDER NOBLE, aged 42.

Chapter Thirteen

Draped in Mourning

Much of the Disaster would have been prevented and many lives saved had there been a deep water harbour at Eyemouth

Peter Wilson, former fishery officer at Eyemouth

Men stayed at their watch on Fort Point for a whole week after the Disaster. In the immediate aftermath no news was taken as a positive sign, that the overdue boats had sailed out the storm and were yet heading back to shore. But mixed in with the hope that waned on every hour and with every tide was the cold reality of death. Going to do their duty on the Fort was an escape for the men: an escape from the emotional out-pouring in the town below, an excuse to join a camaraderie of survivors. The duty for the women was to comfort the certain widows and help look after their bairns. But those who held hands and spoke soft words all too often had their own heavy sorrow. When might the knock come at their door?

Though the death toll would be highest at Eyemouth, every life lost was a tragedy that threw families to the verge of manic despair. At Coldingham Shore three men had drowned on the *Two Sisters*, while eleven souls were taken from Cove when *Renown* and *Snowdon* sank. The sea also claimed fifteen men from Newhaven, leaving ten widows and fifty children, while the loss of the *Alice* from Fisherrow meant another seven deaths, two more widows and another nine fatherless bairns.

Twenty-four men from five boats were taken from the villages of Burn-mouth and Ross. Like the crowds who stood transfixed in terror on the Eyemouth shore, those down the coast saw men and boats go down before their very eyes. Aggie Aitchison, who thought she would never hold her husband alive again, was one of the fortunate ones. William's boat breasted the waves and heaved into the harbour late on the afternoon of Black Friday. All hands were safe.

So many other boats remained unaccounted for, so many men were still posted missing. Hours passed before news came through that the Burn-mouth boat *Excellent* had come ashore at Goswick, south of Berwick. What little sun there had been that day had long disappeared by the time the crew arrived home. Two of their number did not walk down the Brae with them. Alexander Affleck and Thomas Martin had been thrown overboard when the gale was at its height and the survivors of the *Excellent* had more bad news to give besides.

They had seen the *Transcendent* go down with all hands. Gone too, almost certainly, was the *Guiding Star* sighted in serious trouble heading towards Holy Island. The men also told of seeing some of the Eyemouth boats swamped nearby, and of watching as *Blossom* had been driven on to rocks near where they had made landfall. Coastguards had battled to get to the wreck, but all seemed hopeless.

In fact the rescue party did manage to get on board the *Blossom* just before it disintegrated. Two seemingly lifeless bodies were dragged from the surf to the beach. David Stevenson, whose daughter had married Matthew Crawford that very morning, lived. Peter Burgon, brought ashore with him, did not. The other four men from the boat were nowhere to be seen.

This melancholy news reached Eyemouth at about the same time as the men of the *Excellent* were telling their tales at Burnmouth. Darkness did not deter those on deathwatch. The beach and the Gunsgreen shore remained crowded with the anxious and the hopeful. A second tide was due around midnight – enough water again to carry the boats across the bar. But no vessels appeared in the late and early hours. Few would ever now return.

When light came up on Saturday morning Effie Scott, who had kept spirits cheered before men were flung to watery graves before the collective eyes of Eyemouth, retired to her house down Chapel Street. Where was *Beautiful Star*? When would her husband George and her sons John, George and William come bounding up the road? Effie had held on to her neighbour Agnes Burgon when the *Radiant* sank yards from shore, and had wept with her as Aggie's boys David, John and Alexander Fairbairn were dragged almost from the fingertips of their mother. At least Aggie had the certainty of their deaths; Effie would never know for sure what happened. After a week of waiting at the door and watching at the quay Effie Scott stopped eating, hardly spoke and seemed to be permanently in a daze. She died in February 1882, but her soul had long since gone to join her menfolk.

The last surviving witness to the Disaster was Effie's great-niece Jane Swanston. She watched as the old woman lost the will to live. 'They bided in a tiled house down Chapel Street, and she aye said, '*is George no coming in yet?*' And the pair woman broke her hirt and she never cam' ower the bed. Ither weemin saw their men droon and they couldnae dae a thing.'

The first remains of the dead were recovered the morning after the Disaster. Screams again echoed along the Salt Greens when two bodies suddenly bobbed up from the depths of the harbour. They floated around in an eddy stirred by the sluggish waters of the river. Hooks were stretched out, but like some macabre funfair attraction the corpses kept moving away or slipping under the water only to reappear elsewhere. It took some time for them to be captured, and when they were finally landed the hooks had done gruesome damage. George Cribbes and Alexander Craig had been amongst the six man crew of the *Harmony* which had been the first known loss, sinking in the east roadsteads. Later on that Saturday, Cribbes' widow Agnes Bird was brought another body, that of her thirty-one year old son Alexander who had died on the *Forget-Me-Not*. The remains of another of her boys, James from the *Good Intent*, were never found.

Saturday was exactly a week since Effie Lough had married Andrew Dougal. It was the only anniversary she would ever have. His boat *James and Robert* had returned without him. Andrew had been knocked overboard miles from home and was the only one of the six-man crew to lose his life. The child that kicked inside Effie's belly would be a living reminder of a seven-day husband. Andrew James Harrower Dougal junior was born on 31 January 1882.

Other boats that were made fast at their regular moorings also encouraged the belief of the salvation of a whole crew only to register the truth of a single man taken. Margaret Adams, who's son James Maltman was feared drowned on the *Margaret and Mary* was waiting on the pier when *Economy* washed through the harbour. The crew just shook their heads and looked forlorn when they saw her gaze. Her husband Alexander Maltman, the man who had told the Kingfisher 'many a tear will be shed for the Eyemouth fishermen going to sea this day', was dead, washed overboard just as the gale hammered down. His body was never recovered and neither was that of James.

William Spears walked the shore and wandered to the house he had once shared with James Paterson on the Yard Heads; a house that Paterson had made a home with Jane Aitchison, who he married after her first husband drowned off Shields. It was Saturday afternoon when Jane was told she was a widow for second time. She had four young children, two of whom had already lost one father in 1872. Drowned too was James's son and her stepson, seventeen-year-old William. Jane was also heavily pregnant and would give birth to Margaret on 14 December 1881.

All the deaths on Disaster Day touched Spears, but those lost from *Industry* surely numbed him more than any others. James Paterson had lodged with him. Spears had watched as the boy William grew and developed into a fisherman. Nobody was happier than the Kingfisher when a match was made with Jane Aitchison and he even moved back to his old rooms off the High Street to give them space. Jean Cowe his former housekeeper was happy enough to have Spears back. He had taken Jean and her family in when her husband John had gone down with the *Lively* in 1853. Jean's son Andrew had taken a berth with Patterson on the *Industry* and he was now dead as well. All seven of the crew perished, the others being Andrew Craig, James Dougal, Thomas Spouse and Thomas Scott.

Across Eyemouth the bonds which linked families together and which drew folk to live in the same houses and tenements brought the same story of morose despair. Truth and rumour merged but the overall picture was clear to the fishery officer John Doull. He walked the sad path to the heights of the Fort, listened to the survivors and drew his own conclusions. The *Janet* had gone down with all hands off Burnmouth. The *Margaret and Catherine* had been seen shipping water nearby and had then disappeared from sight. The *Lass O Gowrie* was on the bottom, taking with it sixty-year-old George 'Seabreeze' Windram, the oldest fisherman to have sailed. Drowned with him were two of his sons and a nephew. *Sunshine* was gone as well. The six crewmen had an average age of just twenty-three. They left three widows, two of whom were in the latter stages of pregnancy. All but one of the seven men drowned on the *Fiery Cross* left a widow, and three of the five women were pregnant. Between them they already had twenty-five children. Elizabeth Cormack, the wife of Joseph Collin, had nine bairns under the age of twelve to look after. Doull wrote in his logbook, 'Eyemouth cannot recover from this sad disaster for many years to come.'

And so the tales were retold, and so the weeping increased and so the terrible scale of the Disaster emerged. Then on Sunday morning, back from the dead, the *Ariel Gazelle* limped past the Hurkurs and up the harbour. This miracle of men alive after more than two days on the cruel sea surely proved that all was not lost.

It was said that a naval gunship had seen boats sheltering behind the Isle of May. The men were probably heading for Fife and might be home within hours. Maybe they had stopped off for a jaunt in Edinburgh, and were lying blind drunk in a Rose Street tavern. Timid laughter and thin jokes, but hearts were heavy and shoulders stooped.

A few hours after the sea reprieved the seven men of the *Ariel Gazelle*, the crews of four boats which had managed to make Shields arrived back in Eyemouth. They were sighted at the outskirts of the parish, having walked down from Burnmouth railway station. A large crowd awaited them in the Market Place: women hoping to see their husbands or their sons, children convinced their dad was coming back. The prayers of many were answered. For the majority, though, the significance of seeing the crews of the *White Star, Success, Economy* and *Enterprise* was the sad story which their eyes alone told.

Jane Mack learned of the loss of Auld Pur'es from the lips of Little Dod. The *White Star's* skipper had seen the *Myrtle* turn over with James lashed to the beams. The old wifey knew he was gone when Dod grasped her arm and pulled her head to his breast. Jane was another who died in spirit on Disaster Day. Even the love and care of her daughter Maggie Purves and the support of her son-in-law James Lough, who had survived the storm, could not bring Janey round. She took to drinking heavily and was later refused a communion card by an elder of the UP Kirk on the grounds of intoxication. The minister, the Rev. D. K. Miller, was saddened by this. He told the session that poor Jane had gone mad from her sorrow.

Drowned with Pur'es were Thomas Collin, who left a widow and four children, and also his brother James. Their parents had already been told of the loss of two other sons. Robert, who left a pregnant widow and an infant, died on the *Beautiful Star* while seventeen-year-old Alexander was one of six men carried to the deep on the *Sunshine*. In all thirteen members of the Collins family were taken on Black Friday.

The returning crews also spoke of the sinking of the *Florida*. Another seven fishermen dead, five widows created and ten children orphaned. Four of the bodies were eventually found. The three which the sea would not yield up included Paul Patterson, who had been given a 'lucky berth' after spending weeks on shore with a bad back. His wife Ellen Young, with four infants at her hand, thought she already knew poverty. The years ahead would show what real struggle was.

Janet Johnston waited at home rather than on the pier for news of the *Wave*. Perhaps instinct told her there was no hope for her husband Robert and eldest son David. Or perhaps there was nobody about who was willing or able to look out for her other eight children. From the steps to her door Janet watched as Stephen Bell made a slow, halting path down the Long Entry. He stopped in front of her and in his gaze she was doomed. There was no hope for the *Wave*. All aboard were certainly dead. Janet was inconsolable. She wept for days and weeks. Then one morning in late November the woman was nowhere to be found. A search around Eyemouth proved fruitless and was extended to other villages. Eventually Janet was located wandering behind the pier at Berwick, dressed only in thin undergarments and in an agitated and violent state. Some wanted to put the widow away in an asylum, but her neighbours would not hear of it. Janet was nursed back to some semblance of sanity; her children looked after by the very poorest of the poor.

It is indeed a wonder that mass madness did not break out in the wake of the Disaster. Even the bearers of good news brought with them the shadow of death.

At midnight on Sunday 16 October the crew of *Fisher Lasses* crept into Eyemouth, tapping their familiar tap on the windows of their homes. They were all assumed to be drowned. No word had been heard from or about them since the boat was seen to lunge out to sea when the storm erupted. Arriving in Shields after more than fifty hours on the ocean the men had gone straight to the railway station without thinking to wire news of their deliverance. But they were not all safe. One of their number, fifty-eight-year-old William Young, had been knocked overboard and swept away before his fellows could throw out a line. Margaret Lough was now a widow with two young children to feed.

James 'Laffy' Lough owed his life to chance. He ought to have been on the *Lily of the Valley* when it sank at Burnmouth instead of on a wedding excursion to Edinburgh. Laffy signed his father's death certificate and did all he could to help the widows and sixteen children left from the loss of the boat. Three of the five women who lost husbands were also pregnant.

Laffy had never taken much of an interest in religion before, but he was now drawn to services in the Evangelical Union chapel. In time he would become a respected elder. Mathew Crawford also joined the Church, and his brother John later became a respected minister. As much as any Church could ever be, the E.U. was a fisherman's Kirk. Thirty-two of the one-hundred-and-twenty-nine Eyemouth men who died were members. They left behind sixteen widows and seventy-six children. But of all the men drowned, William Nisbet was the one who everyone felt grief over.

His body was found on Goswick sands. Four of the five other crewmen from *Forget-me-Not* were also there, but unlike Nibby they were all wearing simple life aids. Did he have no time to grab one or was he, as people thought, too busy helping his callants put theirs on to bother about himself? The bruised and battered remains were washed and coffined by Nibby's wife Effie Dougal and the women of the E.U. The laying to rest of William Nisbet was almost too hard for the community to bear. Men uncharacteristically wept in public as the crowds reverently gathered outside his house, spilling down Home Street, up to the Yard Heads and back towards the Market Place.

Yet a more unlikely leader for the fisherfolk would have been hard to conjure up. Nisbet had been a teetotal vegetarian who went to night classes to learn how to read. He was regarded by all as the pick of the pickit men, and his casket was carried shoulder high to the cemetery by eight freemasons. There William Nisbet, son of Eyemouth and a child of the sea, was buried with all the honour and dignity that Lodge St Ebbe could bestow.

On Wednesday 19 October, the day after the funeral, Nisbet's pet parrot, who had been struck dumb by the gloom of what was normally a happy home began to chirp away for the first time since his master had left five days before. Over and again the bird pathetically repeated 'Effie, Willie's awa' noo ... Willie's awa noo.'

On that day the last crew to have survived the storm finally made it home. William Spouse, skipper of the *Progress*, had telegraphed the Burnmouth boat's safe arrival at Bridlington on Saturday evening. But they could not persuade the local Shipwrecked Mariners Office to loan them their rail fares and with less than eight shillings between them they had no option but to sail back to Berwickshire. Spouse held the tiller for thirty-four-and-a-half consecutive hours. When *Progress* finally reached Burnmouth he had to be carried bodily from the boat. It was his duty, he told villagers, to get the boys back. He would allow nobody else to steer.

Funerals seemed to be never ending in the first week after the storm. But the ocean was loathe to give up what it had taken and yielded just thirty-one recognisable bodies. The last to be recovered was the decomposed remains of John Hastie from the Wave, washed up at Lamberton Shields in March 1882. Bits of clothing continued to find their way to the shore for many months after that. Robert Wilson's oilskin from *Fiery Cross* appeared on Eyemouth beach almost a year after the Disaster.

Few of the boats and hardly any of the men were properly insured. But their story touched the nation and money began to pour in. Separate relief funds were launched in Berwickshire, in Edinburgh and by stockbrokers in the City of London. Collections were taken at church doors, charity concerts were held and special football matches involving clubs like Heart of Midlothian, Brechin and Arbroath organised. Even the Tay Bridge Disaster Committee sent a substantial donation. Within three weeks twenty thousand pounds had been raised in an outpouring of public generosity. By Christmas the total exceeded fifty thousand pounds.

The Berwickshire MP Edward Marjoribanks pledged £200, Queen Victoria sent a widely publicised 'anonymous donation' of £100 and similar sums were given by the Earl of Home, the Earl of Lauderdale and the Earl of Wemyss. Colonel David Milne-Home who had succeeded to the Wedderburn titles on the death of his mother in 1876 also sent £100. His father, the old laird, wrote a cheque for £50 and even the servants at Milne Graden raised £3. More poignant were the tiny amounts pledged by folk from all walks of life and all parts of the country: like the widow from Mid-Lothian who sent a shilling along with a note, which simply read 'I wish it could be more'.

Yet in spite of this generosity and the huge sums raised, care was taken from the outset to ensure that the money would be sufficient for the numbers who would draw upon the fund. Two committees were established: a central one in Edinburgh and a more active body in Eyemouth to manage the day-to-day operation of the account. This was headed by the Chief Magistrate Robert Allan and had as its secretary John Donaldson, the Inspector of the Poor. They decided who qualified and who did not, and had the discretion to alter and even halt payments. It would prove to be a powerful tool, which was deliberately used to try and change the dissolute social habits of those now pauperised.

The well-established predilection of the people to ask for whatever they thought they stood a chance of getting, persuaded Messrs Allan and Donaldson to take a tough line. 'We have an idea here that the distribution of so much charity in the district may tend to weaken a spirit of self reliance among the people,' wrote Donaldson in the Relief Committee Minute Book. 'We are anxious to show that whenever there are good grounds for withholding relief that will be done.' Quite so, but did the application of these Victorian values have to be so harsh and at times so apparently arbitrary?

An application for help from the widow of George Nisbet was rejected on the grounds that he had not been at sea as a fisherman when he drowned. Technically the decision was the correct one, but Nisbet had given his life when wading into a whirlpool of death at the Gunsgreen rocks in a desperate attempt to shoot a line to men stranded on the Hurkurs. Was there morality in now denying his dependants bread?

The Board of Trade did recognise George Nisbet's bravery and sent a posthumous award of £35 to his widow. But Robert Allan insisted that the Disaster Committee be given control of the money which it would dole out to her 'as and when we think she requires it'. Without even asking the widow's opinion, a knitting machine was purchased on her behalf. Even a 'respectable woman', which was the description given to her by John Donaldson, was deemed unable to manage her own affairs.

The committee also blocked the application of James Fairbairn and Agnes Burgon. Donaldson was prepared to look kindly on the elderly couple who lost three sons when the *Radiant* went down in the Bay, yet who struggled on until 1884 before pleading for relief. In the week in which Robert Allan made this decision, on the grounds that it might open the flood door to others, another Eyemouth fishing boat, the *Welfare*, was wrecked at the roadsteads and three married men killed. Allan was again unmoved by overtures to admit the widows and their eleven children for that very reason.

There can be no doubting the pure motives of those who served on the Disaster Relief Committee. They certainly saved countless families from starvation and their canny approach to the fund has to be put in the context of the massive numbers they had to care for. Robert Allan, John Donaldson, Colonel David Milne-Home and the others deserve more credit that criticism. Yet at times the hard-nosed reality of the task in hand perhaps obscured the need for greater compassion.

The relief committee established a system of fixed weekly allowances. Each widow received five shillings, along with an additional two shillings and sixpence for every boy until he reached the age of fourteen and every girl until her fifteenth birthday. In the years leading up to the Disaster some fishermen had been used to bringing home as much as £5 a week in the winter, and much more than this in a very good herring drave. The poorest paid men in the town, like the street cleaners and the school janitor, earned at least a pound.

Where in the past the school board had struggled against a tide of truancy, now the relief committee was able to insist on regular attendance by the children of the drowned. Yet the trouble James Cox had experienced in filling his classrooms before the Disaster was as nothing in its aftermath. All the boys over the age of nine or ten wanted to be at sea and most of the girls were needed at home to shell mussels, bait lines and watch younger siblings while their mothers went to the gutting yards. There was no time for school and no need for book learning. But the rub was this. If the orphans did not attend, the committee cut off their allowances. Some families, like that of Paul Patterson and Robert Johnston, had a history of disdain towards education. It is not surprising that their children continued to play truant or that the women railed against this attempt at social control.

There were some comical excuses dreamed up to try and persuade Robert Allan not to strike down some of their aliment. 'Agnes Simpson has a sore head but will come to school if she can wear a hat'; 'Anne is being kept from school as she is very tall for her age'.

But in the main the reasons given were pathetically honest. Thirteen year old Effie Gillie would not come to school again because 'The family are in starving condition and she is needed at home.' 'Robert is required at home to look after the younger members of the family while the widow hawks fish for a living'; 'the children cannot come to school . . . (The widow) cannot clothe them'.

It was all too often catch–22. Those children who were kept away were genuinely needed to help keep the family alive and together. But absence from class meant a certain reduction in the household income by the dictates of the relief committee.

If the education question was troublesome, that of the conduct of some of the widows caused even more debate. Again it was catch–22. Young women with small children to keep needed both the company and the support of a husband. Yet widows even seen just walking-out with a man risked losing their entire aliment for 'misconduct', and it was gone for good if they remarried. An attempt to counter this by offering dowries of £19 had only a minimal effect and half a dozen widows gave birth to illegitimate children. Paul Patterson's wife Ellen Young was one of these. Throughout the 1880s money was constantly deducted from her allowance for alleged misconduct, for not sending her children to school and for public drunkenness. She was by no means the worst 'offender'. Helen Johnston, whose husband James drowned on the Burnmouth boat *Guiding Star* had four illegitimate children before marrying again in 1896.

It was soon obvious even to Robert Allan that the strict rules were having little effect on the morals of the women and were instead causing harm to the children. 'It may not be judicious to stop the whole of a widow's allowance when she has an illegitimate child', he said. 'The children of the drowned men are being made to suffer from the misconduct of the mother.'

As the relief committee did its work, the fishermen looked to their own for the way ahead. Shortly after they buried William Nisbet, Little Dod called the seafaring men to a meeting. They would take all the help that was presented to them from whatever source but they would not allow a single child to leave the town. An offer from Quarrier's Childrens Home in Bridge of Weir was politely declined. The bairns would stay; they were the future.

The crews that had survived would re-form with some of the youngsters. Little Dod spoke for all when he said they had now to get on with things. Eyemouth had endured much in its past, there were those alive who remembered the visitation of the cholera which took away almost as many people. They *would* overcome this calamity.

On Monday 31 October, Little Dod threw his sea boots over his shoulder and strolled from his door down the Salt Greens quay to where *White Star* was moored. The boat, like the rest of the fleet, had been tethered there since returning from the storm. Others walked behind him, including boys released from their mother's aprons. Dod glanced at the barometer, which was set fair. He handed his line-skull to one of the crew and jumped down on to the boards. It was time to sail.

The *Ariel Gazelle* led the way out past the Hurkurs, beyond the Gunsgreen Shore and to the fishing grounds again. The women watched as they always did. What were their feelings that morning? Fear? Pride? Defiance?

Where before the men of Eyemouth had struck out further and stayed out longer, now they were timid and careful. Light winds all too often kept them back from sea, and when they did venture beyond the roadsteads it was to creep along the margins of the coast like their great-grandfathers had done. Rarely would they strike out en masse to the deep water where the heavy shoals swam. They did not sail on a Friday out of respect for the lost.

Four days after the first trip and exactly three weeks after the Disaster the first posthumous baby was born. Georgina Grant's father George had been taken at the age of twenty-eight when the *Sunshine* sank. She came into the world a little after eight in the morning, the very time that the boats had left Eyemouth on Black Friday. Over the next few weeks and months a further twenty-three 'tragic little ones' arrived. There were undoubtedly others: bairns born to women who had not married their lovers.

Boats' crews habitually lived close together, the womenfolk often as thrang a group as the men who sailed. That support was needed, and delivered, in good measure especially to those confined in childbirth: three pregnant women from the *Fiery Cross*, the *Guiding Star* and the *Lily-of-the-Valley*, and two each from *Sunshine*, *Janet* and *Industry*. The children, whether girls or boys, were handed the names of the dead as an act of remembrance and a source of pride: John, George, Thomas, James, and William. Johnsina, Georgina, Thomasina, Jamesina, Wilhelmina, Alexandrina. What sort of a future would these children have? What sort of a future could there now be for Eyemouth?

There was one polar star of hope in all this misery. The storm, which might have been a tragedy with some lives lost, had become a Disaster of unparalleled magnitude because there was no place for the boats to run to. The choice on offer to men caught in a hurricane out on the deep was remain where they were and take a chance with the elements, or play Russian roulette with the razor rocks of home; gamble on being taken forward on a flowing tide, but risk the waters ebbing against you. Here is the real reason for the carnage on the coast. Those who tried for the harbour were all too often wrecked when running towards it. Others preferred the chance offered on the high seas. What chance on that day of all days?

Influential voices were raised in high dudgeon to demand a port where the fishermen of the southern Forth could find refuge whatever the weather and regardless of tides. There seemed a moral obligation to build it at Eyemouth, but there were other well-rehearsed reasons too. Meik's plan was already trundling through the corridors of Whitehall, surely it would now be rubber-stamped?

But with half the local fleet gone and a third of the men dead, was Eyemouth a viable proposition? It was not the only possible site for a harbour of refuge. An asylum port for the whole east coast had been talked about for several years and Peterhead had established itself as the clear favourite. Economic arguments were quickly marshalled to bolster

Berwickshire's bid. Fraserburgh, for example, had once been a much poorer fishery station than Eyemouth, but after £200,000 had been expended on improvements, the number of boats using the place had multiplied many times over. 'What Fraserburgh now is, Eyemouth with proper harbour accommodation would certainly become,' Peter Wilson, former fishery officer in both places wrote to the *Scotsman*. 'And from its more favourable situation, being near to the great centres of population, the value of its fisheries would immensely exceed anything in the Kingdom.'

But there was a problem. And it was an old one for Eyemouth. 'With a fishing fleet diminished by one half, and consequently a diminished revenue, the Trustees are in an inevitably weakened position for offering the government the requisite security, but these unfortunate and unforeseen circumstances ought to lead the government to consider the claims of Eyemouth as exceptional and treat them accordingly.' But would it?

Fishermen put *their* faith in the place. Those spared by the hurricane stayed, and over the next three years others arrived to settle. There was an expectation that Eyemouth would recover and that the much discussed new harbour would at last be delivered. At the burgh picnic in July 1882 John Doull spoke of the effects of the Disaster but repeated his belief, made at the same event twelve months before, that Eyemouth would prosper.

This belief in the future of the town went beyond words. The boatyard was again operating at full capacity. The nineteen sunken boats along with the lost gear and lines were worth close on £7,000. The twelve new craft launched in the twelve months after the Disaster could not be paid for immediately. James Weatherhead was sanguine, though. All would be fine when the deep-water harbour was built, as it must now be.

A final submission to the Loan Board on the basis of Thomas Meik's £80,000 scheme was drawn up in the autumn of 1882. A model of the works had been displayed at the International Fisheries Exhibition in Edinburgh the preceeding March, drawing widespread approval. Two dozen survivors of the Disaster were specially invited to attended the event, though few would have been aware of their presence. On the insistence of Little Dod they declined a request to come wearing their sea attire. The Eyemouth men would not make a show of themselves, and instead dressed anonymously in their best clothes for the day out.

When the application was dispatched to London it was unusually bulky. Attached to the application from the harbour trust were petitions and memorials of support from twenty-seven other ports – solidarity from fishermen who sailed from St Ives to Peterhead. Submissions also came from town councils, chambers of trade and even the Mayor of Birmingham.

Like those from the fishermen they all urged that Eyemouth be treated as a special case. The Lord Provost of Edinburgh summed it up thus.

> The Disastrous calamity has rendered imperative the construction of a safe harbour of refuge ... Had such a harbour existed no such appalling loss of life would have resulted ... Eyemouth, situated in a deep and capacious bay, already partially protected by rocks, is the most suitable port for such a harbour.

A welter of statistics and projections was also forwarded, demonstrating the potential of the place and the economic benefit that a refuge harbour would bring.

Table One: Fishermen, boats and gear in Eyemouth 1859–1882. *Eyemouth Fishery Office letters and reports*

Year	No. of resident fishermen	No. of boats of all classes	Value of boats
1860	230	134	£6,902
1865	265	187	£10,145
1870	329	200	£12,380
1875	350	166	£16,080
1880	370	149	£23,264
1881	365	151	£23,648
1882	238	111	£14,888

Table Two: The progressive increase in trade at Eyemouth port. *Eyemouth harbour Trust memorial to Public Works Loan Board, 1882*

Year	No. of boats belonging to Eyemouth	Fish landed in Eyemouth (tonnes)	Harbour revenue
1847	55 (40 herring; 15 winter)		
1860	100 (68 herring; 32 winter)	3614	£147 5 10
1870	147 (102 herring; 45 winter)	4690	£66 5 3
1879	127 (82 herring; 45 winter)	6073	£497 15 6
1880	141 (93 herring; 48 winter)	5636	£433 4 5
1881	141 (93 herring; 48 winter)	6192	£521 6 11

To this was added the confident prediction that revenue would increase to at least £2400 per annum within three years of the completion of the works.

The Public Works Loan Board did not spend a lot of time on the application and was certainly not swayed by the emotion of the memorials.

The petition could not be considered because the conditions for security as laid down in the Parliamentary Act of 1861 – that of existing harbour dues – were not satisfied. They would not advance funds on speculative, perhaps spurious projections of possible increased revenues. The PWLB had bad experiences of similar promises elsewhere.

Instead of cutting their cloth accordingly and scaling down the size of the scheme, perhaps to the level envisaged by Stevenson in 1866 when a £10,000 plan was mooted, the Trust went for broke. Encouraged by all the talk of a harbour of refuge for the East Coast, Thomas Meik was invited to revise his scheme upwards once again. The new plan, unveiled in November 1882, was not to cost £10,000 or even £80,000. Meik proposed enclosing the entire bay. Piers would be thrust outwards from the cliffs at the Fort and from the Gunsgreen shore and a huge breakwater crafted on to the Hurkur skerries. It would catch the mood of the moment and supply a much-felt need. Once again the issue was finance, because Meik's third plan for Eyemouth harbour was priced at close on £200,000.

It was another gamble by the Trustees, but what had they to lose? The application for a grant from state funds rather than a Public Works Loan was not necessarily pie-in-the-sky. The government had signalled its acceptance of the genuine need for at least one deep-water fishery haven on the Scottish east coast. A reasonable argument could be made for two: Peterhead to serve the north and Eyemouth to meet the needs of ports from Leith to the Tyne. In mid-November 1882 John Doull wrote to the Fishery Board in Edinburgh asking if they would support a bid for a Treasury grant.

> Knowing as I do the greater portion of the eastern seaboard of Scotland it is very questionable whether in any other locality there exists a spot so directly facing the storms of the German Ocean which could be so cheaply made into a harbour of refuge as Eyemouth bay ... there is not in the least doubt but that the extensive and rich fishing grounds lying in close proximity to this coast would attract a very large fleet ... It is quite certain that that several crews who were lost in the Disaster of October 14 last year would have been saved had there been a proper harbour of refuge here.

The local MP Edward Marjoribanks pledged his backing and just before Christmas 1882 a delegation from Eyemouth met with the Under Secretary of State for Scotland, Lord Rosebery. Included in the group was George Collin. Little Dod had spent a lot of time addressing public meetings across Scotland, raising funds for the widows and dependants and he repeated the events of Black Friday to Rosebery. But the government minister had already showed his hand in backing Peterhead and he urged the Eyemouth committee to radically scale down their scheme. They might well get something less. They would not get the harbour of refuge.

Instead of taking Rosebery's advice the Trustees of Eyemouth harbour preferred that of Lady Macbeth. They screwed their courage to the sticking place and had an audacious stab at the Chancellor. Public feeling was with them, as evidenced by the support of newspapers like the *Scotsman*. 'A harbour of refuge at Peterhead would be of no use to boats running for shelter south of the Tay. It is to be hoped that the government will see their way to construct a harbour accessible to the Berwickshire fishing fleet at all tides and having railway communication with every centre of population at all hours.' The pace was kept up by the Eyemouth railway committee, who were reassured by the North British Railway Company that it would 'look sympathetically' at a branch line as soon as the harbour scheme was started. All was energy, all was expectation. All would be dashed.

In March 1883 Robert Allan called a special meeting of the Harbour Trust. Sitting around him were fish curers John Dickson, James Crawford and Robert Alexander and the laird of Gunsgreen, James Gibson. Proceedings did not begin until the MP Edward Marjoribanks joined them. The eagerly anticipated responses from the Treasury and the Fishery Board had arrived, and the news was bleak. Robert Allan's words were minuted. 'The former declining a grant as the proposed works would not be sufficient improvement to warrant a grant of public money, and the latter intimating that the proposed works would be of too great magnitude for the board to undertake.'

As had been the case in the 1830s and the 1840s the Eyemouth scheme looked as though it would fall between two stools.

The trust could accept the rejections, do nothing and let possibly the best chance the harbour had ever had go to waste. They could apply to the fishery board for a small grant of around £10,000 to improve the piers along the lines of Stevenson's plan of 1866. Or they could try and persuade the Loan Commission to advance as much as was possible based on their present revenue and implement Thomas Meik's blueprint in stages. There was little debate that night. By whatever means possible, they would press ahead with Meik's scheme.

Further negotiations went on with the PWLC and at last a loan was agreed. Not £200,000, nor £80,000 nor even £40,000, which was the bare minimum the trustees actually required to carry out the first stage of the works. The Loan Commissioners would give just £25,000, and the conditions attached were stringent. As there was insufficient collateral from the port revenues the burgh rates would be required as additional security. The

Public Works Board considered the advance a generous one since the scant extent of Eyemouth parish could not, in all honesty, provide the guarantee which, strictly speaking, they needed.

Robert Allan, wearing his Chief Magistrate's hat, took the proposal to his fellows on the Police Commission. They at once gave their consent to mortgage the rates, though the prospect of implementing that clause in the agreement seemed remote in the extreme, unthinkable even.

What was lost on most people was the true significance of the tranche of money that was on its way to Eyemouth. The £25,000 would only *start* the process. It was to be used to dredge the harbour back up towards the confluence of the river Eye, providing additional berthing spots and space on the quay for curing stations and the anticipated rail halt. More boats would then be able to use the port, increasing the revenue and allowing for a second stage loan to widen and deepen the access channel. When this was done a final phase would be undertaken, with the enclosure of the entire bay and the construction of new internal piers.

Given past traffic and fish landings there was no reason to doubt the projections. The Public Works Commissioners were bound to advance further and much greater sums. It might take longer than they would like, but the trustees, indeed everyone in the town, were convinced that once started, the works would have an unstoppable momentum.

At the burgh summer picnic of 1884 a happier John Doull spoke of new streets being laid out and of families arriving to take the place of those lost in the Disaster. The town was, of course, looking forward not back. Eyemouth was even becoming a notable tourist resort and the rail link so much talked about now appeared a certainty. As to the habour loan, which had just arrived, another of the speakers John Doughty said. 'It is a small affair compared with what is to come ... They would have ample accommodation for thousands of boats ... Ayton would yet become a suburb of Eyemouth, and about the year 1900 Eyemouth would have claim to its own voice in the [Parliamentary] legislature.'

The £25,000 was seen as a down payment on the future. It would pump prime the works to create the Grimsby of the north. Never mind Peterhead and the harbour of refuge, which it had secured, Eyemouth would yet win through.

Work on the harbour began in the late autumn of 1884 at the close of the drave. As winter drew on, the activity of squads of Irish labourers was a busy contrast to the sluggish nature of the sea. Where had the white fish gone? Catches were the lowest in living memory. The boats searched far and wide for the lost shoals, even employing steam tugs to tow them more than seventy miles out and back again. It cost over the odds since few trawlers were keen to risk coming to Eyemouth. What would they do if a squall blew up? Where would they find refuge? The £4,000 the local fleet paid in 1884–85 could ill be afforded, and it was not repaid in their landings.

The sour mood of the fishermen darkened further when they saw what was taking shape on the quays. The drive to extend back *up* the river would not improve the draft at the entrance. They needed deep water. They needed a harbour that could be used by all sizes of boat at all states of the tide. And they needed it quickly.

The official laying of a foundation stone for the works in October 1885 was supposed to be a carnival event. The showers that lashed down all day might have been an omen. Nonetheles Wedderburn and his entire family were feted, with a special cheer reserved for the old laird David Milne-Home. William Spears was not there to greet him or to savour the moment. He had died two months before on 10 August. As the poor roll records state 'this old fisherman was brought to poverty through drink'. Spears' Place, which had once hosted dinner parties for lords and parliamentarians as well as for fish curers and gutters, was cleared out. What Stephen Bell had failed to do, the parish achieved. It seized and sold the Kingfisher's furniture and effects to recover the few pounds in relief Eyemouth's forgotten hero had been allowed. His body was then put in a cheap board coffin and buried in an unmarked grave. If there was little fuss made of William Spears' death in his home, some from the Eyemouth diaspora remembered him in a very public way. This tribute, composed by an anonymous Birmingham man, almost certainly a fish salesman called Robert Scott, appeared in the *Fisherman* magazine.

> In Memory of William Spears,
> Who lived to be seventy-four years,
> And died on August tenth,
> Eighteen hundred an eighty five,
> He ceased to plod the sea alive,
> And lifeless lay at length.
>
> He died at Eyemouth, where for long
> His spear was aye in battle strong,
> But fought not he for strife,
> But for a point he thought was higher
> Than the summit of the auld Kirk spire -
> A spark of heavenly life.

As part of the stone-laying event, a new boat was launched for William Aitchison (namesake and cousin of the Burnmouth fisherman, William

Crawford Aitchison) from Weatherhead's yard. Colonel Milne-Home's daughter had the honour of naming the vessel, which was called *The Janey* after her own grandmother Lady Jean. That night a hundred and fifty sat down to dinner in the Town Hall and to the shouts of 'Let Eyemouth Flourish' toasts were made to the harbour, to the continued prosperity of the fishermen and to the future of the town.

Aitchison must soon have regretted his outlay on the *Janey*. The poor winter haddock fishing of 1884–85 was just the start of a long and progressive decline. Steam trawlers scooped immature fish from the waters and ruined some of the most productive spawning grounds. Year on year things got progressively worse for the Berwickshire men. Between 1884 and the close of the century the value of haddock landed in Eyemouth, the kernel of the port's trade, slid from £54,000 to less than £2,000.

At the same time as the haddock crash, earnings from the summer herring drave also slumped. Enormous catches off Shetland and the north coast depressed auction sale prices to such an extent that boats often could not afford to sail. Harbour revenue, which according to the Trust's confident projections ought to have been soaring, evaporated. Not one single repayment on the loan was possible.

To compound matters, unexpected geological problems delayed the first part of the development and the entire £25,000 was spent long before the works were complete. When the Loan Commissioners refused to advance any more money – not unreasonably – the contractor George Lawson withdrew his men, leaving the inner basin only half finished. The harbour was now in a worse state than it had been before the Disaster. Boats still had to pitch and roll in the bay, waiting on tides to allow them past the entrance. Once through, their access to a large part of the Salt Greens quay was blocked by a partially finished replacement for the old middle pier. Even if the crews did manage to find a secure spot they might not be able to offload their catch for the piles of earth and debris left abandoned by Lawson's navvies. It was imperative to get more public funds as quickly as possible, but the Loan Board would not entertain any further application until at least some of the original amount had been repaid.

Robert Allan turned to the clause that allowed for the levying of an additional burgh rate for harbour purposes, but in this he was unexpectedly frustrated by others on the Police Commission. The Chief Magistrate could neither persuade nor cajole his fellow members. The poverty of the fishing had started to strike with a vengeance and paying the regular rates was hard enough for the vast majority. Two hundred were struck off the municipal electoral roll for non-payment: a telling statistic given the past importance men in the town had placed on the franchise. What was the

point in asking for more? It would simply increase the notional debt that
Eyemouth already had.

Eventually the forceful Robert Allan got his way and an additional levy
of a shilling and a penny in the pound was imposed. As predicted, little
extra money was raised, and for a time there was both a rates strike and
a boycott by the fishermen of their landing dues. Why, they asked, should

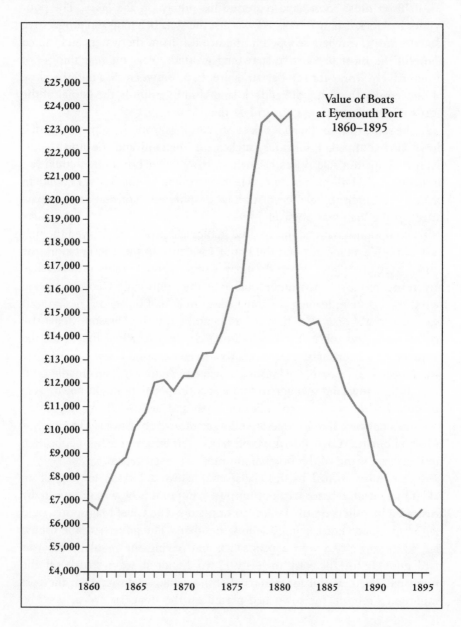

**Value of Boats
at Eyemouth Port
1860–1895**

they pay money they did not have for the upkeep of a harbour they could scarcely use?

The Trustees, who should have known better but were now desperate enough to try anything, employed debt collectors from Haddington to make a proper reckoning of what was owed to them. Like previous men brought down from Edinburgh during the tithe row, they were beaten up on their first day at the pier. They did not return for more.

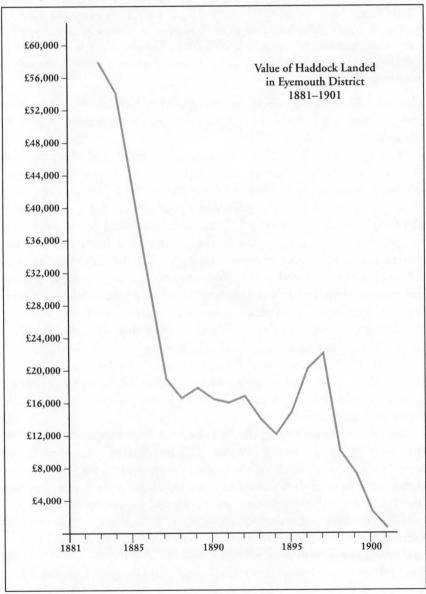

Value of Haddock Landed
in Eyemouth District
1881–1901

With earnings at an all-time low, new boats and equipment could not be bought. Weatherhead's yard, which had worked at full stretch and had employed upwards of thirty carpenters for more than forty years was mothballed, the business heavily in debt. Other operations closed down, and the inward tide of people was reversed. Eyemouth was not, after all, on the verge of greatness; it was instead at the edge of despair.

> One cannot but notice the dull, stagnant state of trade at this once thriving little burgh. Men may be observed standing at the corners of the streets out of work. The high harbour rate to the fishermen as well as the assessment upon the households cannot be borne ... The harbour which was to be the harbinger of brighter and better days, has only given an increased taxation. All is desolation.

Alexander Glen, that go-ahead merchant who had arrived from Montrose with nothing in the 1850s to build up a thriving curing station, moved to Glasgow. Others followed.

The torpor of the fishing, which accounted for more than eighty per cent of local employment, impacted on all aspects of life. Crime levels soared, making Eyemouth the black spot of the Borders. Her Majesty's Inspector of Schools reported that 'Attendance at Eyemouth School is the worst in all of my experience in Scotland.' Education, which had never really been valued, was now a luxury. The bairns could earn a few pennies at the whelks, from baiting lines or even caddying for wealthy visitors on the new golf links, when it opened in 1891. Vigorous attempts were made to address the truancy issue, but it was senseless to try to fine parents for keeping their children off school in such circumstances. In any case the poorer ones who did appear were all too often turned away from class because they did not have shoes or were infested with lice.

Starvation stalked the streets. A visiting inspector of the poor was moved to say, 'there never was a more poverty stricken place than Eyemouth'. Another commentator observed, 'All that the people can get is thin kale and scant bread.'

The Disaster Relief Committee had from the very start tried to improve the moral habits of those on the roll. This interference was resented and some widows instinctively rebelled against directives to stop drinking, to attend Kirk, to send their children to school, to live a clean and Christian life. Yet in the late 1880s dozens were prepared to sign up for this social control if it meant a few shillings a week of additional help. Almost twenty years after the tragedy, with the fishing more depressed than at any time in living memory, a fresh wave of applications flooded the fund. The widows and orphans were now seen as having some good fortune. They were paid a regular amount, however small. School fees and doctors' charges were met directly and clothes and blankets were given to them as a matter of course.

The new applicants included women who claimed to have been betrothed to men who drowned. Others even said they had given birth to children and were only now willing to admit the father was one of the lost. Parents of the dead clamoured for help, and even the fish curers, now in straightened circumstances, made a claim for more than £1,200. This, they said, was only part of the money they had lost when the boats went to the bottom of the sea.

Almost every claim was turned down by a committee paranoid that the fund, which had not been well invested, would run out of money. One exceptional case was admitted. The widow of George Nisbet, who had been denied help despite his heroism on Black Friday, was allowed on to the roll in April 1891. 'The committee gave her a knitting machine at the time of Disaster, believing that she could make a living with it but owing to the miserable condition of the trade of Eyemouth she can get no work for it.' She was allowed five shillings a week to support both herself and her two children.

There was a pitiable scramble for help, for any kind of handout going. The churches did what they could, setting up soup kitchens in the Market Place which sustained more than two hundred individuals through the winter of 1892–3. With the rates years in arrears little could be expected from parish relief. Only those in the very direst of need were admitted to the poor roll: like the seventy year old spinster whose earnings from a mangle barely reached a shilling a week, or the eighty-one year old man who had been forced back to the sea.

Eyemouth folk had never been too proud to take what was offered. Their inclination to demand charity was often remarked. But people still looked after their own. In the very darkest days after the Disaster not one child was allowed to leave the town. Women who went mad from grief, like Janet Johnston and Jane Mack, were watched over and helped by those who were themselves in torment. In spite of the concerns of the Disaster Committee, Eyemouth did not go soft because of the relief fund pledged to help the widows and orphans; rather folk took what they could get and then got on with their work and their lives.

But the crisis of the late 1880s and 1890s was a deadly affair. The desertion of the fish caused a second Eyemouth disaster.

The community ideal of caring for all increasingly could not survive. For the first time ever poorhouse accommodation was organised for the destitute and asylum places for the insane. Troublesome boys were sent away to industrial schools, training ships or worse still, to jail. People lost faith

and began to leave in droves. Some went to the shipyards on the Tyne and
the Clyde, promising to return but rarely doing so. Others cut all ties and
left for America, South Africa, Australia and even Argentina and Chile.

Marriages, traditionally celebrated at the end of the herring drave in
October, became rare events. The birth rate fell dramatically – by as much
as a third in 1892 – and more than a hundred houses were left vacant. The
population of the burgh, which had increased every decade since records
began, showed the largest fall in the county in 1891. It would go on tumbling
well into the twentieth century.

Just as the despair seemed deepest, a crumb of comfort was tossed
Eyemouth's way. The Public Works Loan Board, which was loath to throw
good money after bad, agreed to advance a further £10,000. This allowed
the moderate works started in 1884 to be completed. By then too, a rail
link with Burnmouth was under construction. But this would not run on
to the new piers in the bay. There *were* no piers in the bay, and poor
financial planning meant that the halt had to be built several hundreds yards
even from the existing quay. Fishermen, who thought they would be
swinging their loads straight on to railway bogies, would have to trundle
them in carts up the Smiddy Brae.

By the time the station was opened the massive tonnage of fish which
had once been heaped on the Salt Greens was but a memory. The very
nature of the industry had changed. Men forgot the haddock fishing and
took to travelling-the-herring. They had long experience of chasing the
silver darlings from Caithness to Norfolk, but in the past this was as a
supplement to their main winter business at home. After 1890 almost all
of the crews became itinerant, trailing with them gangs of their own fisher
lasses and spending more time at Yarmouth, in Shetland and at Ardglass
in Ireland than in Berwickshire. It is another irony that for long periods of
the year the new harbour at Eyemouth lay deserted. Civil servants at the
Loan Board had forecast that the place would be a bad risk and this view
was vindicated when the whole debt had to be written off in 1901. The
port's file was underlined in black. Future advances should not be made
without careful and detailed consideration.

Many small fishing communities gave up the ghost at the turn of the
twentieth century as fleets increasingly congregated in regional centres,
particularly along the northeast coast. It would have been a foolish man
indeed to bet that Eyemouth would survive as anything more than a shadow
of its former self. But survive it did. Enough people decided to stay put
rather than risk everything for the unknown of the cities or the New World.
Some like James Lough who had married Jane Mack's daughter Maggie
Purves emigrated to America only to come back within five years. The

family faced a clutch of bills, which they had left unpaid when they raced for the steamship, but they were glad to be *hame!* Glad to be back beside the same families, who had lived in the town when it was a village, who had been Haimoothers for hundreds of years. The bad times were endured and by the eve of the First World War the fishermen were again starting to make money, and dream up plans of expansion and development.

Had there been the decent harbour which the port deserved then the carnage of 14 October 1881 would have been far less. It might never have happened at all. Those facilities could have been delivered in the 1830s and 1840s. But for the mid-Victorian outbreak of tithe madness they would have been built in the 1850s or 1860s. Had the hurricane not come down in 1881 the fishermen might well have been given the deep water they craved at that time. And had the haddock crash been delayed for a decade then, perhaps, the grand scheme of Thomas Meik would have been successfully implemented in stages.

In any of those events, Eyemouth would have been a different place and perhaps none the better for it. But the generations robbed of life by the consequences of Black Friday would have been born to enrich and further the town and a unique community.

Fishing is still the dominant industry in Eyemouth. The problems, which get an airing in the bars and as the men mend their nets on the quay, are the same ones that consumed Little Dod, William Nisbet, the Kingfisher and the rest more than a century ago. The harbour is too small, more deep water is needed. The shoals are being ruined by modern technology and by foreign fleets. The politicians have no idea of what their lives are like, and would not care if they did. And the men still risk everything each time they leap onto their boats and edge out past the Hurkur rocks on the way down to the sea.

Epilogue

Children of the Sea

It is a sheer waste of money to prepare harbour schemes costing about
£100,000 on the basis of state advances meeting the bulk of this, especially for
places like Eyemouth which has small resources and is in the black books of
the Public Works Loan Board
Internal Scottish Office memo, 10 December 1925

The Disaster Relief Fund continued until December 1921, when just £3 15s. 5d. remained from a total that had once exceeded £54,000. In spite of the dire situation that enveloped Eyemouth in the 1890s the community somehow managed to keep going. While other fishing villages regressed into mere coastal creeks, sheltering a handful of little boats, the Eyemouth fleet remained. Slowly but steadily it grew again and slowly but steadily the numbers of fishermen increased. Almost with each passing decade plans were brought forward to enlarge, deepen and expand the harbour. Without fail these were returned from the various bodies to which application was made. Eventually the Holy Grail of deep water was achieved when piers were driven into the bay in the 1960s creating what local people call 'the canyon'. Other improvements followed and a large berthing basin was chiselled out of the Gunsgreen rocks in the late 1990s. The benefits of these schemes have been considerable, but they are a far cry from what the fishermen of Eyemouth thought they were on the verge of getting when the wind came down on that dreadful day in October 1881.

It took a century for the population of the town to recover. The same families living in Eyemouth then are predominant today: the Loughs, Dougals, Craigs, Maltmans, Patersons, Aitchisons, Collins and Windrams; the Nisbets, Crombies, Burgons and Dicksons.

Strangely, though, there is nobody who bears the surname Spears. This was a big family in more ways than one for many decades in the late eighteenth and nineteenth centuries. Ellen Spears had five boys, but three died in infancy and Andrew was drowned with his father when their fishing boat sank in 1828. The only surviving son was William and he neither married nor had children: an odd thing, given his warmth towards bairns.

The name survived in one form though. As a child I was intrigued as to why my father was often referred to as 'Spears.' It had been his father's (my grandfather's) middle name, but nobody knew where it had come from. Perhaps, I thought, it had something to do with 'Spears' Place', a little lane that led off from the High Street.

In 1981 on the centenary of the Disaster a book written by the local EU minister twenty-five years after the event was reprinted. There, in the pages of *'An old-time fishing town: Eyemouth'* was not just the story of Black Friday but reference to the strange episode of the tithe dispute and the importance of a character called William Spears, the Kingfisher. I was intrigued even further.

From my earliest waking moments I had been told tales of my ancestors: of how James Purves had drowned while strapped to the tiller of the *Myrtle*, of how his daughter Maggie and her husband James Lough had done a moonlight flit to America in the desperate poverty-stricken days after the Disaster. Maggie took one look at the New World and was so unimpressed that the family saved for another five years to come home – and then to a mountain of bills they had left unpaid when they emigrated.

The interest I showed brought dramatic and colourful stories from my granny, Peggy Dale and my papa Peter Waddell. Other old-timers like Teeny Matt, Campbell Muir and Robbie Nisbet also delighted in sharing their part of an oral history tradition.

Did I know, my grandmother asked me one day, that my father's paint store in St Ella's Place used to be the original Methodist Chapel? Only later did I learn that this was the venue for Spears' 'Anti-tithe' speech in 1855. It was where ranks of fishermen queued up to sign their own Covenant against the Kirk. Had I heard of William Nisbet, asked old Robbie, one of his direct descendants? Never was a town robbed of so much as when Nibby was drowned. What tales Teeny Matt spun of Lamberton weddings, the life of fisher-lassies and the bravery of old salts like 'Tarry' Maltman, 'he couldnae see a man droon'. But sometimes Teeny told more morose accounts. 'They sailed on Black Friday' she said, her eyes bleak and stony and sad, 'because the bairns had nae bread'. The former burgh clerk Campbell Muir spoke of the reality of people in despair. Eyemouth was in such desperate straits after the Disaster that a penny on the rates was too much for some people to bear 'Can you imagine, Peter, can you imagine that?'

Walking around the town brought its own fascinations. The odd architecture, the mounds of earth on Fort Point . . . Why was it called Fort Point? The strange Mansion House across the harbour, the odd names used for certain areas. From the age of seven I worked as a bottle boy at the Ship hotel. The deep, cavernous cellars were used, it was rumoured, during the smuggling days. When was that? What had happened?

Eyemouth positively reeked of history, yet it was all taken for granted, not much spoken about and certainly not taught in the school. My teacher

George Kinghorn drove me to find out more: to search, and above all to question. The only available source to me at that time was Daniel McIvor's book. But *why* had the boats been out at all on 14 October 1881 when, as he said, the fishermen knew a hurricane was on its way, a fact that kept almost every other east-coast fleet at their moorings? Were they stupid or just greedy?

These questions were uppermost in my mind when I stood on the pier one hundred years to the day after the carnage of the Disaster in a commemoration ceremony celebrated by some of my friends because it won us a half-day holiday from school. Other thoughts occurred to me as I stared out past the Hurkurs. *Why* had the boats been wrecked on the rocks and why did others not even try to come into the harbour that day?

Daniel McIvor's book, excellent as it was, seemed to accept facts without probing for reasons or causes, in the same way as the people of Eyemouth blindly accepted the oddities of the town. The local Museum, also established in 1981, helped illuminate some of the stories but again did not answer the basic point of *why* Eyemouth had suffered so disproportionately in the storm.

These questions gnawed away at me. It was by chance (or was it?) that one day on the train to Edinburgh I met John Home-Robertson MP, Eyemouth's feudal superior. What on earth did that mean? We got chatting and he mentioned that his family had a mass of old documents relating to Eyemouth, most of which had been gifted to the National Archives of Scotland.

Years later, encouraged by my University tutor Donald Withrington, I began to do some serious study into the history of the fishing industry. By then I was also puzzled as to why the losses of Black Friday had gone virtully unnoticed. Did one hundred and eighty-nine deaths count for so little? If it had happened today it would get blanket media coverage for months, there would be countless inquiries and investigations, and massive support for both the families and the communities affected. On its own the story was surely worth telling. But McIvor's book had been forgotten. The Disaster was an 'unfact' of history waiting to be rediscovered.

Perhaps there were no records, no detail, insufficient information? Far from it. There was a mass of material, too much in some cases. Minute books of the Relief Committees, archives from the parochial board, the school authorities, the Fishery Office and the Harbour Trust; newspaper accounts, government reports, Kirk records; and above all, the papers and documents of the Homes of Wedderburn.

This was no freak accident caused by a chance hurricane. The poor state of Eyemouth harbour had been responsible for many other deaths and on countless occasions prior to 14 October 1881 the shore had been crowded with anxious townsfolk, praying for the safe return of their boats and their men.

Amazement mixed with disbelief at the scale of the port development plans from the 1750s onwards, and the often cack-handed reasons for their failure, and then there was the tithe, and the great stand-off between Willie Spears, Stephen Bell and David Milne-Home.

The minister had not been an Eyemouth man, but there was a smattering of detail about Mr Bell's background in Lanarkshire, his marriage in 1865 and his death, without issue, in December 1881. A lot more was known of David Milne-Home, the mighty Wedderburn family and their links with Eyemouth, past and present.

But who exactly was Spears, where had he come from and why had the family disappeared? It was another roller-coaster ride of discovery. The sources were remarkably extant, so much so that it almost seemed the voices of the past were shouting out to me. The Spears had been forced from rural parts during the Lowland Clearances of the eighteenth century and had made their way to the coast where they first became smugglers and then fishermen. The family intermingled with the people of the sea and was touched more than once by shipwreck and tragedy. Only William was left after Ellen Dougal-Spears' husband and eldest son Andrew paid their dues to the deep. When William died so did the name and so did the story of the tithe.

Then one day while leafing through some documents, I noticed a single reference to Helen Spears. Not the Kingfisher's mother, but a sister I had no idea existed. She had married John Aitchison in 1837, moved to Burnmouth, had many children and had lived a very long life. Helen Spears-Aitchison was my own great-great-great grandmother. It was a jaw-dropping moment. *There* was the link to Spears. Others soon followed as I unravelled my family tree. It was the ancestry of many who still live on the Berwickshire coast.

How sad, though, that beyond a tee-name that was somehow bequeathed through the ages to my father and a street sign in an insignificant lane, nothing existed as a legacy to William Spears. Not even a marked burial plot for a man who led a twenty-year community fight against the civil and religious establishments ... and had won.

In May 1998 his contribution was finally recognised when the local authority erected a bronze statue of the Kingfisher in Eyemouth's Market Place. It would look out over the square where almost a century and a half before he had rallied the people in marches, demonstrations and dramatic defiance. I was proud to be present at the unveiling, prouder that the cloth over the figure was tugged down by my infant son Jack, Spears' great-great-great-grand nephew. He had been christened just three months before in the former Evangelical Union – now Trinity – Church in the town. Gillian and I gave him the middle name *Spears*. The name had returned to one of the children of the sea.

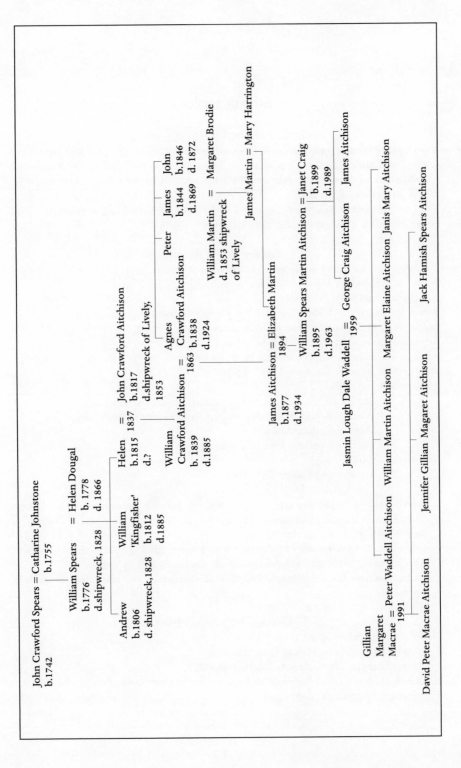

John Crawford Spears = Catharine Johnstone
b.1742   b.1755

William Spears = Helen Dougal
b.1776   b. 1778
d.shipwreck, 1828 d. 1866

William 'Kingfisher'
b.1812
d.1885

Andrew
b.1806
d. shipwreck,1828

Helen = John Crawford Aitchison
b.1815 1837 b.1817
d.?   d.shipwreck of Lively,
                    1853

William Crawford Aitchison = Agnes Crawford Aitchison
b. 1839   1863 b.1838
d.1885   d.1924

Peter   James   John
         b.1844   b.1846
         d.1869   d. 1872

William Martin = Margaret Brodie
d. 1853 shipwreck
of Lively

James Martin = Mary Harrington

James Aitchison = Elizabeth Martin
b.1877   1894
d.1934

William Spears Martin Aitchison = Janet Craig
b.1895   b.1899
d.1963   d.1989

George Craig Aitchison   James Aitchison

Gillian Margaret Macrae = Peter Waddell Aitchison   William Martin Aitchison   Margaret Elaine Aitchison   Janis Mary Aitchison
                    1991

Jasmin Lough Dale Waddell = George Craig Aitchison
                        1959

David Peter Macrae Aitchison   Jennifer Gillian Magaret Aitchison   Jack Hamish Spears Aitchison

Bibliography

I MANUSCRIPT AND ORIGINAL SOURCES

The Home of Wedderburn Mss which is housed in the National Archives of Scotland under the classification GD/267 is a treasure trove of material on Berwickshire and Eyemouth dating back to the sixteenth century. I have used this source extensively in the research and preparation of the book.

The Lord Advocate's Papers are also stored in the NRA. Those relating to Eyemouth and the fish tithes dispute are under classification AD/156/38.

Fishery Board Records

The papers used are housed in the National Archives of Scotland:
Fishery Board Annual Reports 1882–1885
Parliamentary questions 1898–1903
Report by the Fishery Board committee on Scottish harbour accommodation
Report by G Balfour on Dunbar and Anstruther harbours
Report on harbours in Eyemouth Fishery District
Applications made for aid to construct piers and harbour 1882–83
Miscellaneous harbour accommodation papers 1894
Eyemouth Fishery Office:
> Letters and Reports 1817–1890 Letters Dispatched 1891–1905
> Weekly Report of Herring Fishing in Eyemouth District 1854–1931
> Means of capture 1899–1915
> Totals of Vessels, men and gear 1899–1926

Eyemouth Harbour:
> Reports and Papers 1837–1896
> Development Fund 1911–1931

Memorials relating to the development of Eyemouth harbour consequent to the fishing disaster. These include memorials and petitions to the Treasury, the Board of Trade and the Public Works Loan Board from Eyemouth Harbour Trust, the Eyemouth Fishermen's Committee, the Committee of Fishermen from Burnmouth and from twenty-four other ports including Peterhead, Fraserburgh, Wick, Penzance, St Ives and Mousehole. Also similar petitions from Edinburgh Chamber of Commerce and the Lord Provost of Edinburgh.

Eyemouth Harbour Trust

The archives are retained by the Trust.
Eyemouth Harbour Trust Minute books 1797–1923
Eyemouth Harbour Trust accounts ledgers 1797–1882
Eyemouth Harbour Trust: Proposed harbour Extension Cost benefit Analysis by PIEDA consultants (Edinburgh, 1987)

Heritors Records

These are housed in the National Archive of Scotland.
Eyemouth Heritors: Minute Books 1843–1928
Cash Book 1847–1929

Municipal Records for Eyemouth

The following are housed in Eyemouth Museum.
Eyemouth Police Commissioners: Letter Books 1866–1887
Eyemouth Burgh Commissioners: Minute Books 1899–1905
Eyemouth Town Council: Minute Books 1905–1919 Letter Books 1889–1924
The following are housed in the archives of Scottish Borders Council
Eyemouth Parochial Board: Minute Books 1863–1899
Eyemouth Parish Council: Minute Books 1895–1899
Eyemouth School Board: Minute Books 1873–1919
Ledger Letter Books 1878–1886

Church Records

All of the following are housed in the National Archives of Scotland unless otherwise stated.
Eyemouth Kirk Session: Records 1826–1900
Marriage Proclamation register 1881–82
Records of United Secession, United Presbyterian, East United Free Churches in Eyemouth
  – minute books, members registers and baptismal records 1842–1917
Chirnside Presbytery Records 1734–1896
North Leith Kirk Session papers anent fish tithe
Evangelical Union Church: Communicants Roll Book 1861–1907 (Eyemouth Museum)
Minute Book 1897–1900 (Eyemouth Museum)

Eyemouth Disaster Records

Held in Eyemouth Museum
Disaster Relief Committee: Minute Books 1881–1901
Letter Books 1881–1922
Alterations on roll 1882–1897

Records of Lodge St Ebbe No. 70

Held in Lodge St Ebbe Number 70
Minute books, entry books and sundry papers from the founding of the Lodge on 5 March
  1757

Court and Legal papers

The following records are held in the National Archives of Scotland.
Records of Duns Sheriff Court diet books, register of extract decreets, record of inerlocutor
  books, processes and warrants
Court of Session Records
High Court of Justiciary Records
*Record in Declarator of William Speirs (sic) Fisherman, residing in Eyemouth against the Reverend
  Stephen Bell, Minister of the Parish of Eyemouth and residing there. 27 June 1859*

Customs and Excise Papers

Records of the Scottish Customs Board

Dunbar District Outport records–Letter Books Board to Collector 1754–1829–Miscellaneous Excise Records

Other sources

Census records 1841–1891

Births, Marriages and Deaths Registers (New Register House, Edinburgh)

Letter from R V Innes, Inspector of the Poor, Eyemouth, to the General Board of Health, London, 1 December 1849. This detailed the dramatic spread of cholera in Eyemouth.

Log book of Robert Aitchison, skipper of the Gratitude, which survived the storm of 1881. The log book covers the period 1880–1890.

The Book of Eyemouth: Compiled 1944–45 (unpublished, Eyemouth Museum collection)

Transcript of *Round Scotland by Radio Express–Number One: Berwickshire* transmitted by the BBC from Edinburgh on 2 April 1937.

Waddell, Margaret '*Eyemouth better known as Haimouthe: The names of the wynds, vennels and the nicknames of the folk who lived there in the good old days*' (Unpublished pamphlet, December 1972, Eyemouth Museum collection)

Souvenier Booklet of Eyemouth Methodist Church (Eyemouth Museum collection)

Valuation rolls of Eyemouth Parish 1859–1890 (Scottish Borders Council collection)

Oral recollections of Margaret (Peggy) Dale-Waddell, Peter Waddell, Christina Aitchison (Teeny Matt), Jane Swanston, Campbell Muir, Robbie Nisbet.

2. NEWSPAPERS, PERIODICALS AND PAMPHLETS

Berwick Advertiser 1807–1923
Berwick Warder (previously *Berwick and Kelso Warder*)
Berwick Journal
Proceedings of Berwickshire Naturalists Club
Berwickshire News 1870–1923
Blackwood's Edinburgh Magazine
Border Magazine
Chambers Edinburgh Journal
Christian News
Evangelical Repository Magazine
Fish Trades Gazette
Life and Work
Primitive Methodist Magazine
Quarterly Maritime Magazine
Scotsman
Scots Magazine
Scottish Economic and Social History
Scottish Church History Society Records
Scottish Jurist
Scottish Local History Forum
Timber Trades Journal
United Presbyterian Magazine
Witness

3. PAMPHLETS AND PAPERS RELATING TO THE EYEMOUTH
FISH TITHES DISPUTE

Statement By the Presbytery of Chirnside and Minute of the Committee of the General Assembly in the Eyemouth Fish Teind Case (Edinburgh, 1861)

Reply of the Eyemouth fishermen to the Pamphlet of the Presbytery of Chirnside (Berwick, 1861)

Letter of David Milne-Home of Wedderburn to William Spears, fisherman of Eyemouth (Edinburgh, June 1862)

Reply of William Spears to the Pamphlet Letter of David Milne-Home (Berwick, 1862)

Letter of David Milne-Home of Wedderburn to Robert Dougal, chairman of the Fishermen's Committee in Eyemouth (Edinburgh, 1862)

Pamphlet Letter to David Robertson MP from David Milne-Home of Wedderburn (Edinburgh, 1862)

Pamphlet Reply of the Fishermen's Committee of Eyemouth to the Letter of David Milne-Home Sent to David Robertson MP (Berwick, 1862)

4. OFFICIAL REPORTS

Committee appointed to inquire into the state of the British Fisheries, 1785, Reports from the House of Commons 1803, X

Extracts from Captain Washington's (unfinished) *report on the damage caused to fishing boats by the gale of 19 August 1848, 1849 LI*

Religious Worship and Education in Scotland, 1854, LIX

Report of the Commissioners of British Fisheries for 1855, 1856 XVII

Report of Select Committee appointed to inquire into the policy of making further grants of public money for the improvement and extension of harbours of refuge, 1857 XIV; 1857–8, XVII

Report of the Commissioners appointed to inquire into the sea fisheries of the United Kingdom, 1866 XVII-XVIII

Report on the Herring Fisheries of Scotland, 1878, XXI

Report of the Select Committee on Harbour Accommodation 1883 XIV; 1884 XII

Returns of Unexpended Funds to provide for dependants of Scottish Fishermen drowned at sea, 1896 LXXV

Amount of Public Money expended on harbours since 1860, 1896 LXXV

5. UNPUBLISHED THESES

Bussey, O 'The Religious Awakening of 1858–1860 in Great Britain and Ireland' (Edinburgh PhD Thesis, 1947)

Meikle, Maureen 'Lairds and Gentlemen: A study of the Landed Families of the eastern Anglo-Scottish borders 1540–1603' (Edinburgh PhD Thesis, 1989)

6. BOOKS AND ARTICLES

A list of Persons Concerned in the 1745 Rebellion (Edinburgh, 1890)

Aitchison, Peter 'The Eyemouth Fish Tithe Dispute: The State Church Promoting Voluntaryism', *Records of the Scottish Church History Society, 1987*

Aitchison, Peter 'By a Precarious Shore' *Scottish Local History Forum*, June 1989

Allan, Rev James 'The Storm of January at Eyemouth' *Scots Magazine,* 1767

Anonymous 'Eyemouth: By one who has been there' *Quarterly Maritime Magazine,* 1882

Anonymous 'The Storm at Eyemouth' *Life and Work,* 1882

Anson, Peter *Fishing Boats and Fisher Folk* (London, 1930)

Arnott, Hugo *Celebrated Criminal Trials in Scotland 1536–1784* (Edinburgh, 1785)

Ayton, R and Daniell W *A Voyage round Great Britain* (London, 1820)

Bain, Joseph (ed) *Calendar of Documents Relating to Scotland 1357–1509* (Edinburgh, 1888)

Bertram, James G *The Harvest of the Sea* (London, 1869)

Bertram, James G *The Unappreciated Fisher Folk* (London, 1883)

Bertram, James G *Fisher Life in Scotland* (London 1889)

Bertram, William 'Eyemouth and its fishing Industry', *Scots Magazine*, 1981

Binnie, G A C *The Churches and Graveyards of Berwickshire* (Berwick-upon-Tweed, 1995)

Black, G F *A Catalogue of Cases of Witchcraft in Scotland 1510–1727* (New York, 1938)

Black, G F *Some Unpublished Scottish Witchcraft Trials* (New York, 1941)

Black, William *What are Teinds* (Edinburgh, 1893)

Boyd, William K (ed) *Calendar of State Papers for Scotland 1547–1603* (Edinburgh, 1905)

Bradford, Thomas M *A Story of an Antient Lodge* (reprinted Berwick, 1981)

Bremner, David *The Industries of Scotland* (Edinburgh, 1869)

Briggs, Robin *Witches and their neighbours* (London, 1997)

Brims, John 'From reformers to Jacobins: The Scottish Association of the Friends of the People' In T M Devine (ed) *Conflict and Stability in Scottish Society 1700–1850* (Edinburgh, 1990)

Brown, Calum *The Social History of Religion in Scotland since 1730* (London, 1987)

Brown, P H *Early Travellers in Scotland* (Edinburgh, 1891)

Brown, P H *Scotland before 1700 from Contemporary Documents* (Edinburgh, 1893)

Burton, J H (ed) *Register of the Privy Council of Scotland* (Edinburgh, 1877)

Caldwell, David H *Scotland's Wars and Warriors: Winning against the odds* (Edinburgh, 1998)

Caldwell, David H 'The Battle of Pinkie' in N Macdougall (ed) *Scotland and War AD 79–1918*' (Edinburgh, 1991)

Canal Proposal to Link Kelso and Eyemouth, *Scots Magazine*, 1789

Carr, Alexander *Coldingham: Parish and Priory* (Edinburgh, 1836)

Campbell, R H *Scotland Since 1707: The rise of an industrial society* (Oxford, 1971)

Campbell, R H 'The landed classes' in T M Devine and R Mitchison (ed) *People and Society in Scotland: Volume One 1760–1830* (Edinburgh, 1988)

Chambers, R *The Domestic Annals of Scotland 1688–1743* (Edinburgh, 1861)

Checkland, Olive *Philanthropy in Victorian Scotland* (Edinburgh, 1980)

Claverhouse *Irregular Border Marriages* (Edinburgh, 1934)

Coupar, W J *Scottish Revivals* (Dundee, 1918)

Cullen, L M 'Smuggling in the north channel in the eighteenth century' in *Journal of Scottish Economic and Social History*, Volume 7, 1987

Coxe, William *Memoirs of the Duke of Marlborough* (London, 1848)

Crossman, Sarah M *In Memoriam William Nisbet* (London, 1881)

Deas, Christine 'The Boats', *The Border Magazine*, 1896

Defoe, Daniel *Tour of the whole islands of Great Britain* 1724–26

Devine, T M *Conflict and Stability in Scottish Society 1700–1850* (Edinburgh, 1990)

Devine, T M *The Transformation of Rural Scotland* (Edinburgh, 1994)

Devine, T M *The Scottish Nation* (Edinburgh, 2000)

Devine, T M and Mitchison, R (ed) *People and Society in Scotland: Volume I* (Edinburgh, 1988)

Dixon, Piers *Excavations in the Fishing Town of Eyemouth 1982–1984* (Edinburgh, 1986)

Dobson, David *Directory of Scots Banished to the American Plantations 1650–1775* (Baltimore, 1984)

Dobson, David *Scottish Emigration to Colonial America 1607–1785* (University of Georgia, 1988)

Dobson, David *Jacobites of the '15* (University of Georgia, 1993)

Donald, Jean *The British Fisheries Society 1786–1893* (Edinburgh, 1978)

Donaldson, G *Scotland: James V to James VII* (Edinburgh 1965)

Donaldson, William *The Jacobite Song: political myth and national identity* (Aberdeen, 1988)

Dorian, Nancy *The Tyranny of Tide* (Ann Arbor, 1985)

Drummond A and Bulloch J *The Church in Late Victorian Scotland* (Edinburgh, 1978)

Drummond A and Bulloch J *The Scottish Church 1688–1843: The Age of the Moderates* (Edinburgh, 1973)

Dunlop, Jean *The British Fisheries Society 1786–1893*

Dyer, Michael *Men of Property and Intelligence: The Scottish Electoral System Prior to 1884* (Aberdeen, 1996)

Dyer, Michael *Capable Citizens and Improvident Democrats: The Scottish Electoral System 1884–1929* (Aberdeen, 1996)

Escott, Harry *A History of Scottish Congregationalism* (Edinburgh, 1960)

Eyemouth Murder (Linthill murder of Lady Billie) *Scots Magazine*, 1751 and 1752

Ferguson, William *Scotland 1689 to the Present* (Edinburgh, 1978)

Gourlay, George *Fisher Life: or, the Memorials of Cellardyke* (Cupar, 1879)

Gray, Malcolm *The Fishing Industries of Scotland 1790–1914* (London, 1978)

Gray, Malcom *George Washington Wilson and the Scottish Fishing Industry* (Aberdeen, 1982)

Gray, Malcolm 'Organisation and growth in the east-coast herring fishing 1800–1885' in P L Payne (ed) *Studies in Scottish Business History* (London, 1967)

Green, David *The Churchills of Blenheim* (London, 1984)

H.M.S. 'The Eyemouth Disaster' in *Border Magazine*, 1898

Herbert, David (ed) *Fish and Fisheries: Selection of Essays from the International Fisheries Exhibition in 1882* (Edinburgh and London, 1883)

Historical Manuscripts Commission *Report on the Manuscripts of David Milne-Home* (1902)

Humes, Walter M and Paterson, Hamish (ed) *Scottish Culture and Scottish Education* (Glasgow, 1983)

Hutchison, I G C *A Political History o Scotland 1832–1934* (Edinburgh, 1986)

Imperial Gazetteer of Scotland (Edinburgh, 1855)

Landels, Thomas D *William Landels DD: A Memoir* (London, 1900)

Larner, C *Enemies of God: The Witchhunt in Scotland* (London, 1981)

Larner, C and Hyde Lee, C and Mclaulan, H *A Source Book of Scottish Witchcraft* (Glasgow, 1979)

Lawrie Alistair, Matthews Helen and Ritchie, Douglas (eds) *Glimmer of Cold Brine: A Scottish Sea Anthology* (Aberdeen, 1988)

Lenman, Bruce *The Jacobite Cause* (Edinburgh, 1986)

Lenman, Bruce *The Jacobite Risings in Britain 1689–1746* (Aberdeen, 1995)

Levi, Leoni *The Economic Condition of Fishermen* (London, 1883)

Lindsay, Jean *The Canals of Scotland* (Newton Abbot, 1968)

Lindsay, Maurice *The Discovery of Scotland* (London, 1964)

Lowe, Alexander *General View on the Agriculture of the County of Berwick* (London, 1794)

Lynch, Michael *A New History of Scotland* (Edinburgh, 1992)

Macdougall, N (ed) *Scotland and War AD 79–1918'* (Edinburgh, 1991)

McIvor, Rev Daniel *An Old Time Fishing Town: Eyemouth* (Greenock, 1906)

Maclean, Charles *The Fringe of Gold* (Edinburgh, 1985)

McNeill, P and Nicholson, R *An Historic Atlas of Scotland c. 400–c. 1600* (St Andrews, 1975)

Magnusson, Magnus *Scotland: The Story of a Nation* (London, 2000)

Maitment, J (ed) *Spottiswoode Miscellany* (Edinburgh 1844–45)

Marwick, D (ed) *Records of the Convention of Scottish Burghs* (Edinburgh, 1866–99)

Merriman, Marcus *The Rough Wooings* (East Linton, 2000)

Merriman, Marcus 'The Eyemouth Forts: Anvils of Union?' *Scottish Historical Review* LXXVII (1988)

Miller, James *A History of Dunbar* (Dunbar, 1859)

Mitchell, John *The Herring: its natural history and national importance* (Edinburgh, 1864)

Mitchison, R *A History of Scotland* (second edition, London, 1982)

Mitchison, R *The Old Poor Law in Scotland* (Edinburgh, 2000)

Morris, Ruth and Morris, Frank *Scottish Harbours* (Edinburgh, 1983)

Morrison's Dictionary of Decisions of the Court of Session

Mossner, E C and Ross, I S *The Correspondence of Adam Smith* (Oxford, 1977)

Myres, Douglas 'Scottish Schoolmasters in the nineteenth century: professionalism and politics' in Walter Humes and Paterson, Hamish (ed) *Scottish Culture and Scottish Education* (Glasgow, 1983)

New Statistical Account of Scotland, volume ii County of Berwick (1835)

Nicholson, R *Scotland: The Latter Middle Ages* (Edinburgh, 1974)

Nisbet, Robbie *Lest We Forget* (Berwick, 1983)

Paterson, William *Men on Fire* (London, 1911)

Phillipson N and Mitchison, R *Scotland in the Age of Improvement* (London, 1963)

Rankin, Eric *Cockburnspath: A Documentary History of a Border Parish* (Edinburgh, 1981)

Reid, Rev W (ed) *Authentic Records of the Revival* (London, 1860)

Report into the State of the Poor in Berwickshire (Edinburgh, 1841)

Ridpath, George *The Border History of England and Scotland* (reprinted, Edinburgh, 1979)

Ross, James *A History of Congregational Independancy in Scotland* (Glasgow, 1900)

Russell, J M 'Eyemouth Remembers', *Scots Magazine*, October 1981

Saunders, L J *Scottish Democracy 1815–1840* (Edinburgh, 1950)

Scott, Rev H *Fasti Ecclesiae Scoticanae, seven volumes* (Edinburgh 1917)

Sillett, Steve *The Whisky Smugglers* (Glasgow, 1990)

Smith, John and Stevenson, David (ed) *Fermfolk and Fisherfolk* (Aberdeen, 1989)

Stewart, J (ed) *Miscellany of the Spalding Club*, four volumes (Spalding Club, 1844)

Small, Rev Robert *History of the Congregations of the United Presbyterian Church 1733–1900* (Edinburgh, 1904)

Smout, T C *A History of the Scottish People 1560–1830* (London, 1969)

Smout, T C *A Century of the Scottish People 1830–1950* (London, 1986)

Smout, T C and Wood, Sydney *Scottish Voices 1745–1960* (London, 1990)

Somerville, A *The Autobiography of a Working Man* (London, 1848)

Spence, Alan 'Where the Merse meets the Sea', *Scots Magazine*, 1971

Spottiswoode Miscellany, Volume II (Edinburgh, 1945)

Statistical Account of Scotland, volume ii, county of Berwick (1791)

Stevenson, David *The Origins of Freemasonry* (Cambridge, 1988)

Stevenson, David *The First Freemasons* (Aberdeen, 1988)

Stevenson, Stephanie *Anstruther: A History* (Edinburgh, 1989)

Theta 'The Eyemouth Fish Tithe', *United Presbyterian Magazine*, Volume VI, 1862

Theta 'The State Church Promoting Voluntaryism', *United Presbyterian Magazine*, Volume VI, 1862

Thomas, John *A Regional History of the Railways of Great Britain': Volume VI Scotland, the lowlands and Borders* (London, 1971)

Thompson, Paul et al *Living the Fishing* (London, 1983)

Thomson, A *Coldingham: Parish and Priory* (Galashiels, 1908)

Thomson, James *The Value and Importance of Scottish Fisheries* (London, 1849)

Tranter, Nigel 'Coldinghamshire', *Scots Magazine*, 1961

Tucker, Thomas *Report by Thomas Tucker upon the settlement of the revenues of excise and customs in Scotland AD MDCLVI* (Bannantyne Club, Edinburgh, 1824)

Turnbull, George *Report into the Present State of the Poor in Berwickshire* (Edinburgh 1838)

Turnbull, Rev John 'Eyemouth, Berwickshire' in Rev William Reid *Authentic Records of the Revival* (London, 1860)

West, Richard *The Life and Strange Surprising Adventures of Daniel Defoe* (London, 1998)

Whatley, Christopher *Scottish Society 1707–1830* (Glasgow, 2000)

Whatley, Christopher 'How tame were the Scottish lowlands during the eighteenth century?' in T M Devine (ed) *Conflict and Stability in Scottish Society 1700–1850'* (Edinburgh, 1990)

Wilkie, T *The Representation of Scotland* (Paisley, 1895)

Wilson, Will *Ebb Tide* (Berwick, 1980)

Withrington, Donald J 'Scotland a half-educated nation in 1834? Reliable critique or Persuasive Polemic' in Walter M Humes and Hamish M Paterson, Hamish (eds) *Scottish Culture and Scottish Education* (Glasgow, 1983)

Wood, Lawson *Eyemouth in Old Picture Postcards Volume One* (Zaltbommel, 1991)

Wood, Lawson *Eyemouth in Old Picture Postcards Volume Two* (Zaltbommel, 1991)

Wood, Lawson *The Berwickshire Coast* (Ochiltree, 1998)

Wormald, Jenny, *Court, Kirk and Community: Scotland 1470–1625* (London, 1981)

Yeoman, Louise *Reportage Scotland* (Glasgow, 2000)

Young, Archibald 'Harbour Accommodation for fishing ports on the east and North coasts of Scotland' in David Herbert (ed) *Fish and Fisheries: Selection of Essays from the International Fisheries Exhibition in 1882* (Edinburgh and London, 1883)

Index